Big Business and the Crisis of German Democracy

Through the colorful world of Berlin's grand hotels, this book charts a new history of German liberalism and explores the changing relationships among big business, society, and politics. Behind imposing facades, managers and workers were often the picture of orderly and harmonious service, despite living in sometimes uncomfortable proximity. Then, during World War I, class tensions rose to the surface and failed to resolve in the following years. Doubting the ability of the Weimar Republic to contain these conflicts, a group of hotel owners, some of the most prominent Jewish industrialists and financiers in the country, chose to let Adolf Hitler use their hotel, the Kaiserhof, as his Berlin headquarters in 1932. From a splendid suite opposite the chancellery, Hitler and his henchmen engineered the assumption of power, the death of the Weimar Republic, and the ruin of their hosts, the Kaiserhof's owners: Jewish liberals now fleeing for their lives. *Big Business and the Crisis of German Democracy* asks how this came about and explores the decision-making processes that produced such catastrophic consequences. This title is also available as open access on Cambridge Core.

Adam Bisno is a historian of modern Germany. This book is based on his dissertation, which won the Fritz Stern Prize from the Friends of the German Historical Institute in 2018.

Publications of the German Historical Institute

Edited by
Simone Lässig
with the assistance of Kelly McCullough

The German Historical Institute (GHI) is a center for advanced study and research whose purpose is to facilitate dialogue and collaboration among historians across national and disciplinary boundaries. The GHI conducts, promotes, and supports research in three core fields: German/European and Jewish history, the history of the Americas and transatlantic history, and global and transregional history. The GHI works closely with partner institutions and organizations to provide scholars from around the world with opportunities to extend their professional networks and build relationships across borders.

A full list of titles in the series can be found at:
www.cambridge.org/pghi

Big Business and the Crisis of German Democracy

Liberalism and the Grand Hotels of Berlin, 1875–1933

ADAM BISNO

ghi German
Historical Institute
Washington

and

CAMBRIDGE
UNIVERSITY PRESS

CAMBRIDGE
UNIVERSITY PRESS

Shaftesbury Road, Cambridge CB2 8EA, United Kingdom

One Liberty Plaza, 20th Floor, New York, NY 10006, USA

477 Williamstown Road, Port Melbourne, VIC 3207, Australia

314–321, 3rd Floor, Plot 3, Splendor Forum, Jasola District Centre,
New Delhi – 110025, India

103 Penang Road, #05–06/07, Visioncrest Commercial, Singapore 238467

Cambridge University Press is part of Cambridge University Press & Assessment,
a department of the University of Cambridge.

We share the University's mission to contribute to society through the pursuit of education, learning
and research at the highest international levels of excellence.

www.cambridge.org
Information on this title: www.cambridge.org/9781316515631

DOI: 10.1017/9781009026154

First published 2024

A catalogue record for this publication is available from the British Library

Library of Congress Cataloging-in-Publication Data
NAMES: Bisno, Adam, author.
TITLE: Big business and the crisis of German democracy : liberalism and the grand
hotels of Berlin, 1875–1933 / Adam Bisno.
DESCRIPTION: Cambridge ; New York, NY : Cambridge University Press, 2023. |
Series: Publication of the German Historical Institute | Includes bibliographical references.
IDENTIFIERS: LCCN 2023016421 | ISBN 9781316515631 (hardback) |
ISBN 9781009026154 (ebook)
SUBJECTS: LCSH: Hospitality industry – Political aspects – Germany – Berlin. |
Hotelkeepers – Political activity – Germany – Berlin. | Business and politics –
Germany – Berlin – History – 20th century. | Berlin (Germany) – History – 1918–1945. |
Germany – Economic conditions – 1918–1945. | Germany – Politics and government – 1871–1933.
CLASSIFICATION: LCC TX910.G4 B57 2024 | DDC 647.940943–dc23/eng/20230602
LC record available at https://lccn.loc.gov/2023016421

ISBN 978-1-316-51563-1 Hardback

Contents

Figures

Acknowledgments

Thank you to my parents, Alison Peck and Edward Bisno, and my sister Amy Bisno and brother-in-law Jaimie Grant. They made this possible. Thank you to my friends: Elisabeth Boulos, who got me into this business; Susan Corbesero and Brooke McLane Higginson, who listened to my arguments and helped free me from the sticky parts; Nicholas Phillips, who helped me turn a better, clearer phrase; Dominic Sefton and Carla Heelan, who believe in me; Roland Justen, Kathryn Justen, Brigid von Preussen, and Angelika Hoelger, who made Germany such a nice place for me to be; Lekha Shupeck and Nandini Pandey for sticking around and giving me confidence; and Alex Bush, for the years of laughs and last-minute advice on translations.

I thank the organizations and people at those organizations who have supported me. The German Historical Institute, Washington, DC, has been my home a block away from home. My editor there, Kelly McCullough, gave crucial words of encouragement and secured me a nice place to finish the typescript. Axel Jansen and Atiba Pertilla helped make that happen, too, as we all tried to figure out access to scholarly literature and workspace during a pandemic. In the library, Anna Maria Boss sourced the hard-to-find volumes. Bénédicte Pillot-Bechtold made me feel welcome. The fellows and other guest scholars accompanied me through the lonely stages of revision. Simone Lässig shared valuable materials with me from her research into some of the Jewish businessmen at the center of this book's story. David Lazar read that story early on and assured me that it was a good one. Liz Friend-Smith at Cambridge University Press shepherded the typescript through review, editing, production, and publication. Elizabeth Tucker helped me polish the prose.

Before all that, at Johns Hopkins University, where the project started, my advisor Peter Jelavich, the *Doktorvater* who wants only the best for you and always takes you seriously, extended me care and guidance, backing my work in its more awkward phases. My dissertation committee, Katie Hindmarch-Watson, Douglas Mao, Katrin Pahl, and Ronald Walters offered insights and suggestions during my defense that helped me refine the arguments below. Graduate student colleagues Will Brown, Jessica Clark, Christopher Consolino, Katie Hemphill, and Ren Pepitone provided ideas and moral support. Outside Hopkins, I relied on the generosity of the Berlin Program for Advanced German and European Studies.

Finally, I thank Henryetta and Sam Peck, my great-grandparents. (I carry Sam's name as my middle name.) From the 1930s to the 1970s, they owned and operated a hotel in Little Rock, Arkansas, where my grandfather, my mother, and her siblings grew up. Their stories about "the hotel" fascinate me and must have had something to do with my choice of topic. I cannot claim to understand hoteliers any better for having them as my ancestors, but I see now that this book is part of their legacy.

I knew my great-grandmother, Henryetta, personally. Like everyone else, I called her by her nickname, Ana, the German pronunciation of Anne. Her parents had descended from Berliners who came to this country in the first wave of German-Jewish immigration to the United States, just after the Revolutions of 1848. Henryetta was elegant, charming, funny, eccentric, and organized – everything a hotelier is supposed to be. This book is about a different sort of hotelier, a different kind of hotel, and a different time and place. It's about businessmen, big business, and the collapse of German urban society in the first part of the twentieth century.

And yet this book offers a tale that might just have resonated with my great-grandmother and her heir, my grandfather: How do you make sense of your hotel's final days? It is the 1970s in Little Rock, downtown is in decline, speculators are buying up what has yet to collapse, and the hotel can't do business as usual. You sell it. Decades pass as the building changes hands several times and finally settles into disuse. In the end, all that remains of the family business, the Hotel Sam Peck, our legacy, are matchbooks, postcards, a few photographs, and a little correspondence. What are we supposed to do now? My answer has been this book.

Introduction

Before taking the chancellery in January 1933, Adolf Hitler had no formal headquarters in the German capital. On earlier campaign trips, he had opted for the Hotel Sanssouci, a middling concession near Potsdamer Platz. But in February 1931, electoral successes mounting, he transferred to a suite at a grand hotel, the Kaiserhof, that overlooked the chancellery – his goal – across the square. The hotel became Hitler's Berlin home. It swarmed with his hangers-on, who changed the face of the clientele almost overnight. The Jewish custom evaporated; business suffered. By the fall of 1932, the board of the Kaiserhof's parent company would need to decide whom to favor: Hitler and his men or Jews and other anti-Nazis.

A member of the hotel's managerial staff raised this issue in person with the corporate board of directors on September 15, 1932: "Hitler has been in residence at the Kaiserhof for some time," he said, and "the Stahlhelm have commandeered the house for use as a headquarters." As a result, "too much of the clientele has been lost," because "the whole Jewish clientele has stayed away." Profits, and the Kaiserhof itself, would have to be "won back" – and soon, he warned.

The board pushed discussion of the problem to the meeting's end, when, finally, the chairman, William Meinhardt, a leading industrialist, weighed in: "As a hotel company, we must remain neutral on matters of religion and politics. Our houses must remain open to all. Surely the situation as it has developed is no fun for any of the interested parties, but we, the directors, cannot do anything about it."[1] Next spoke Wilhelm

---

[1] Minutes of the meeting of the board of directors of the Hotel Management Corporation (Hotelbetriebs-Aktiengesellschaft), September 15, 1932, in Landesarchiv Berlin (hereafter LAB) A Rep. 225-01, Nr. 39.

Kleemann, member of the parent company's board, managing director of Dresdner Bank, and head of the Jewish Community of Berlin.[2] "I know for certain," he said, "that Jewish guests no longer stay at the Kaiserhof and no longer visit the restaurant, either." In response, Meinhardt conceded, "I know how hard it is for the house's restaurant manager to exercise the requisite tact in face of these difficult questions."[3] Most remarkable about this preemptive capitulation to the Nazis is that Meinhardt himself was Jewish, and so were most of the board members in attendance. Here was a group of Jews in 1932 grappling with whether to evict Hitler.

These men were also industrialists, financiers, and liberals – National Liberals before World War I and members of the Weimar coalition parties thereafter. Meinhardt, a member of the German Democratic Party (Deutsche Demokratische Partei), had been born to Jewish parents in Schwedt, a small city on the Oder River, in 1872.[4] In 1914, he became managing director of one of the world's great manufacturers of metal filaments for incandescent lamps, a concern he transformed, in 1919, into the new conglomerate OSRAM, which dominated the German market in light bulbs. As chairman of OSRAM's board and architect of the legal maneuvers that allowed his monopoly to form and flourish, Meinhardt, through speeches and the publication of two books, became a "recognized authority on the subject of the electrical industry," according to a study published in Britain in 1935.[5] Yet it would be in his capacity as chairman of the board of the Kaiserhof's parent company, the Hotel Management Corporation (Hotelbetriebs-Aktiengesellschaft), that Meinhardt came face-to-face with the Nazi menace.

Meinhardt's interlocutor at the September 15 meeting, Kleemann, was himself one of Germany's most prominent financiers. Other Jewish board members present included Eugen Landau, a diplomat and board member of the Schultheiß-Patzenhofer brewing concern as well as of two banks,

---

[2] Christoph Kreutzmüller, "An den Bruchlinien der Volkswirtschaft: Jüdische Gewerbebetriebe in Berlin, 1918 bis 1933," in *Was war deutsches Judentum, 1870–1933*, ed. Christina von Braun (Berlin: De Gruyter Oldenbourg, 2015), 245.

[3] Minutes of the meeting of the board of directors of the Hotel Management Corporation, September 15, 1932.

[4] Brigitte Heidenhain, *Juden in Schwedt: Ihr Leben in der Stadt von 1672 bis 1942 und ihr Friedhof* (Potsdam: Universitätsverlag Potsdam, 2010), 153.

[5] William Meinhardt, *Kartellfragen: Gesammelte Reden und Aufsätze* (Berlin: OSRAM, 1929); *Entwicklung und Aufbau der Glühlampenindustrie* (Berlin: C. Heymann, 1932); Hermann Levy, *Industrial Germany: A Study of Its Monopoly Organizations and Their Control by the State* (Cambridge: Cambridge University Press, 1935), 77.

and Walter Sobernheim, Landau's stepson, also a diplomat and director of Schultheiß-Patzenhofer.[6] Sobernheim, Landau, Kleemann, and Meinhardt were industrial and financial elites first, and hoteliers second, with liberal-democratic affiliations and tendencies.[7]

The term "liberal" here connotes three political orientations at once. The first is party-political and places these hoteliers as businessmen in the National Liberal tradition. Still intent on lowering taxes, freeing trade, and defanging labor unions, they had come around to a more democratic liberalism by the 1920s.[8] Second, with their manifold forays into civic altruism, these hoteliers expounded a liberal urbanism characteristic of European bourgeoisies.[9] Third, like their British counterparts,

[6] Minutes of the meeting of the board of directors of the Hotel Management Corporation, September 15, 1932.

[7] See Arndt Kremer, *Deutsche Juden – deutsche Sprache: Jüdische und judenfeindliche Sprachkonzepte und -konflikte, 1893–1933* (Berlin: De Gruyter, 2012), 164.

[8] On German liberalism and its relationship to the democratic impulse, see Margaret Lavinia Anderson, *Practicing Democracy: Elections and Political Culture in Imperial Germany* (Princeton: Princeton University Press, 2000), 141; Robert Arsenschek, *Der Kampf um die Wahlfreiheit im Kaiserreich: Zur parlamentarischen Wahlprüfung und politischen Realität der Reichstagswahlen, 1871–1914* (Düsseldorf: Droste, 2003), 256; Hartwin Spenkuch, *Das Preußische Herrenhaus: Adel und Bürgertum in der Ersten Kammer des Landtages, 1854–1918* (Düsseldorf: Droste, 1998); Michael B. Gross, *The War against Catholicism: Liberalism and the Anti-Catholic Imagination in Nineteenth-Century Germany* (Ann Arbor: University of Michigan Press, 2004), 173; Rudy Koshar, *German Travel Cultures* (Oxford: Berg, 2000), 204. On interwar liberalism in Germany, see Jens Hacke, *Liberale Demokratie in schwierigen Zeiten: Weimar und die Gegenwart* (Hamburg: Europäische Verlagsanstalt, 2021); *Existenzkrise der Demokratie: Zur politischen Theorie des Liberalismus in der Zwischenkriegszeit* (Berlin: Suhrkamp, 2018).

[9] Hartmut Pogge von Strandmann, "The Liberal Power Monopoly in the Cities of Imperial Germany," in *Elections, Mass Politics, and Social Change in Modern Germany: New Perspectives*, eds. Larry Eugene Jones and James Retallack (Cambridge: Cambridge University Press, 1993), 93–118; Despina Stratigakos, *A Women's Berlin: Building the Modern City* (New Haven: Yale University Press, 2008), 137–67; Brian Ladd, *Urban Planning and Civic Order in Germany, 1860–1914* (Cambridge, MA: Harvard University Press, 1990), 139; Friedrich Lenger, "Bürgertum, Stadt und Gemeinde zwischen Frühneuzeit und Moderne," *Neue Politische Literatur* 40 (1995), 14; Sylvia Schraut, "Burghers and Other Townspeople: Social Inequality, Civic Welfare and Municipal Tasks during Nineteenth-Century Urbanization," in *Towards an Urban Nation: Germany since 1780*, ed. Friedrich Lenger (Oxford: Berg, 2002), 164; Andrew Lees, *Cities, Sin, and Social Reform in Imperial Germany* (Ann Arbor: University of Michigan Press, 2002), 49–50; Andrew Lees and Lynn Hollen Lees, *Cities and the Making of Modern Europe, 1750–1914* (Cambridge: Cambridge University Press, 2007), 131; Andrew Lees, "Between Anxiety and Admiration: Views of British Cities in Germany, 1835–1914," *Urban History* 36 (2009), 42–44; Jan Palmowski, *Urban Liberalism in Imperial Germany: Frankfurt am Main, 1866–1914* (Oxford: Oxford University Press, 1999),

Berlin's grand hoteliers used regulation, infrastructure, and technologies of surveillance to maintain a balance between freedom and order in the metropolis.[10] In Germany, none of these liberalisms survived the Weimar period. The economic chaos of 1919–23 instilled in their adherents an incorrigible pessimism which, at the advent of the next crisis, in 1929, became a precondition for conservative elites to sabotage the economy and dismantle liberal republican institutions from within. This they did with impunity as the liberals looked on.

From the vantage of grand hotels, this book reveals the decision-making processes behind the failure of German liberalism in the 1920s and early 1930s and explains why businessmen, industrialists, and financiers let the institutions of Weimar culture, society, and politics collapse around them. As early as the winter of 1930/31, a fatalism seized the very liberals who would have resisted the forces arrayed against the Weimar Republic.[11] On September 15, 1932, the liberal board members of Berlin's principal hotel corporation chose, to the detriment of their business, to let Hitler stay. The ultimate task of this book will be to connect this decision to the experience

36, 254; Claus Bernet, "The 'Hobrecht Plan' (1862) and Berlin's Urban Structure," *Urban History* 31 (2004), 419; Jürgen Kocka, "The European Pattern and the German Case," in *Bourgeois Society in Nineteenth-Century Europe*, eds. Jürgen Kocka and Allan Mitchell (Oxford: Berg, 1993), 17–19; Thomas Adam, *Philanthropy, Civil Society, and the State in German History, 1815–1989* (Rochester, NY: Camden House, 2016), 124ff; Simone Lässig, "Bürgerlichkeit, Patronage, and Communal Liberalism in Germany, 1871–1914," in *Philanthropy, Patronage, and Civil Society: Experiences from Germany, Great Britain, and North America*, ed. Thomas Adam (Bloomington, IN: Indiana University Press, 2004), 198–218.

[10] Chris Otter, "Making Liberalism Durable: Vision and Civility in the Late Victorian City," *Social History* 27 (2002), 1; Patrick Joyce, *The Rule of Freedom: Liberalism and the Modern City* (London: Verso, 2003), 3, 121; Mary Poovey, *Making a Social Body: British Cultural Formation, 1830–1864* (Cambridge, MA: Harvard University Press, 1991); Elaine Hadley, *Living Liberalism: Practical Citizenship in Mid-Victorian Britain* (Chicago: University of Chicago Press, 2010), 23; Katie Hindmarch-Watson, *Serving a Wired World: London's Telecommunications Workers and the Making of an Information Capital* (Berkeley: University of California Press, 2020), 3–4; Asa Briggs, "The Language of 'Class' in Early Nineteenth-Century England," in *Literature and Western Civilization: The Modern World*, vol. 2, *Realities*, eds. David Daiches and Anthony Thorlby (London: Aldus, 1972), 11; Leif Jerram, "Bureaucratic Passions and the Colonies of Modernity: An Urban Elite, City Frontiers, and the Rural Other in Germany, 1890–1920," *Urban History* 34 (2007), 390–92; Reuben Rose-Redwood and Anton Tantner, "Introduction: Governmentality, House Numbering, and the Spatial History of the Modern City," *Urban History* 39 (2012), 607.

[11] See Peter Jelavich, *Berlin Alexanderplatz: Radio, Film, and the Death of Weimar Culture* (Berkeley: University of California Press, 2006), xii.

of dislocation in the interwar period. What was the logic that made acquiescence seem like the best option by 1932?

To answer this question, historians of Weimar Germany generally focus on the beginning and end of the republic. If it had not been doomed from the very start, then it was done in by the Great Depression. This book offers a different emphasis. The economic chaos of 1919–23 so discredited the republic that a representative sample of industrial and financial elites – in this case, the grand hoteliers of Berlin – made arguments in private and public that moved ever closer to the language and perspectives of the anti-republican right. The hoteliers' pessimism regarding the republic reached a crescendo in the hyperinflation of 1923 and reverberated down to Hitler's transfer, on January 30, 1933, from the Kaiserhof to the chancellery.

This history explains in material terms the increasing rightward list of German politics before 1933, by matching the ebb and flow of these hoteliers' pessimism to certain quotidian difficulties in the management of Berlin's grand hotels. Instead of pinning down these quotidian difficulties, I let them issue and recede in the text of this book, just as they do in the sources, just as they did for the hoteliers. In the prewar period, managers and owners worried most about hierarchies, trying to keep workers in place and control guests' experiences according to distinctions of gender, class, and nationality. At other intervals, such as 1918–22, labor relations took priority. In 1924–29, the focus shifted to taxes. Each of these areas of concern helped shape hoteliers' conception of the political – that is, what the state should do to stabilize the social and economic order. But complaints about policy quickly turned into indictments of the republic itself.[12] After 1923, Berlin's grand hoteliers heaped scorn on Germany's new democracy, blaming it for every threat to profitability.

This book uses traditional sources in business history to answer questions about politics, society, and culture.[13] What do ways of running

---

[12] Cf. Eric D. Weitz, *Weimar Germany: Promise and Tragedy* (Princeton: Princeton University Press, 2007), 365–68.

[13] This approach draws on Michel Crozier and Eberhard Friedberg, *L'acteur et le système: Les contraintes de l'action collective* (Paris: Seuil, 1977); Gary Bruce, *Through the Lion Gate: A History of the Berlin Zoo* (New York: Oxford University Press, 2017); Pamela E. Swett, S. Jonathan Wiesen, and Jonathan R. Zatlin, eds. *Selling Modernity: Advertising in Twentieth-Century Germany* (Durham, NC: Duke University Press, 2007); Timothy Alborn, *Regulated Lives: Life Insurance and British Society, 1800–1914* (Toronto: University of Toronto Press, 2009), especially chapter 3; Robert Proctor, "Constructing the Retail Monument: The Parisian Department Store and Its Property, 1855–1914," *Urban History* 33 (2006), 393–410.

a business tell us about shifting relationships of power? Where in the accounts, reports, minutes, and correspondence do we see signs of political and cultural continuity and change? For answers, I read some of the sources against the grain to extrapolate the leadership's strategies of social control. I also look for more explicit indications of political leanings. Berlin's grand hoteliers in the interwar period tended, in spite of the evidence, to blame most of their difficulties on workers and taxes. In doing so, owners and managers deflected attention from the sum of their mistakes: the failure to helm such large, complex enterprises over the choppy waters of an increasingly competitive and increasingly global economy. They thereby also obfuscated their record of disadvantageous borrowing and poor accounting.[14] While this sorry tableau reaches a vanishing point on September 15, 1932, it spans seven decades of German history, starting in the 1870s, when the Kaiserhof opened as Berlin's first grand hotel.[15]

The book's five chapters offer several overlapping episodes in chronological order: equipoise, exploitation, and heterogeneity in the imperial period (Chapters 1 and 2), the shortages and violent confrontations of World War I and its aftermath (Chapters 3 and 4), and finally the tumults of the 1920s and early 1930s (Chapters 4 and 5). Throughout, building on Habbo Knoch's cultural history of grand hotels in New York, London, and Berlin, I foreground the business model and its dependence on modes of economic domination.[16]

The dark view of affairs that led Meinhardt to accommodate Hitler had taken form in years of difficulties resulting from weaknesses in the grand hotel business model and hotel workers' newfound power to challenge it. World War I, defeat, and revolution exposed social and cultural cleavages that hoteliers had succeeded in concealing and managing during the old regime. After the war, Berlin's grand hotels became crucibles of conflict.[17] Hundreds of workers, their exploitation crucial to the

---

[14] See Jeffrey R. Fear, *Organizing Control: August Thyssen and the Construction of German Corporate Management* (Cambridge, MA: Harvard University Press, 2005), 591.

[15] On the "vanishing point" concept, see Helmut Walser Smith, *The Continuities of German History: Nation, Religion, and Race across the Long Nineteenth Century* (Cambridge: Cambridge University Press, 2008), 13–17.

[16] Habbo Knoch, *Grandhotels: Luxusräume und Gesellschaftswandel in New York, London und Berlin um 1900* (Göttingen: Wallstein, 2016), chapter 4, especially 233–46; cf. A. K. Sandoval-Strausz, *Hotel: An American History* (New Haven: Yale University Press, 2007).

[17] Cf. Paul Lerner, *The Consuming Temple: Jews, Department Stores, and the Consumer Revolution in Germany, 1880–1940* (Ithaca, NY: Cornell University Press, 2015), 18.

survival of the enterprise, refused to submit. As international hostilities continued past the peace treaties of 1919, guests, too, became restive. They seethed with resentments and, in some cases, even assaulted one another in dining rooms. With animosities out in the open, hoteliers saw no way back to the prewar state of equipoise.[18]

They were initially ambivalent about the republic and its capacity to reconcile Germans with each other and with the rest of the world. After the hyperinflation of 1923, however, that ambivalence tipped into antipathy, and Berlin's many hoteliers finally turned against the republic for good. Many of them branded the republic a failing, dangerous experiment and did not waver in their judgment, not even in the relatively stable period from 1924 to 1929. After the onset of the Great Depression in 1929, pessimism about the republic slipped into fatalism – the sense that the republic might or even should fail hardened into the certainty that it was a lost cause, indefensible at the very best. Recall Meinhardt's words on September 15, 1932: "Surely the situation, as it has developed, is no fun for any of the interested parties, but we, the directors, cannot do anything about it."

Rather than a comprehensive history, this book is a case study in the failure of liberalism and its institutions in pre-Nazi Germany. Responding to the economic chaos of 1919–23, the grand hoteliers of Berlin – a representative sample of economic elites – subscribed to, and even made, arguments in the public sphere that moved ever closer to the language and perspectives of the anti-republican right. In 1932 this case study and the grander historical narrative converge. Some of the infamous "backroom negotiations" that brought Hitler to power took place not only in back rooms but also in a corner suite at the Hotel Kaiserhof. Its owners, Meinhardt especially, kept that suite available all the way to Hitler's assumption of power on January 30, 1933. No match for the fascists, these businessmen failed themselves, their industry, and the republic.

---

[18] On "equipoise," in the historiography of Victorian Britain, see Martin Hewitt, ed. *An Age of Equipoise? Reassessing Mid-Victorian Britain* (London: Routledge, 2000); W. L. Burn, *The Age of Equipoise: A Study of the Mid-Victorian Generation* (New York: W. W. Norton, 1964).

I

Hospitality Incorporated

Berlin's grand hoteliers of 1932 had not created the business model they were using. They inherited it, the culmination of more than a century of experience in Europe and the United States. There, the world's first grand hotels emerged in the first half of the nineteenth century as part of the transportation revolution underway since the eighteenth century, when technological and infrastructural improvements increased travel and tourism in Europe. Hotels first emerged to answer the demand from a new traveling public for new standards. Largely middle class, this roving customer base insisted on greater privacy and cleanliness than older hostelries had provided. Hoteliers responded by modernizing and standardizing commercial hospitality across vast distances. Contributing to the ascendancy of the burgeoning middle classes, hotels as sites of bourgeois sociability and business became reflections of bourgeois values.[1]

The extension of rail networks in the mid-nineteenth century concentrated this traffic in cities, especially those at the nexus of regional, national, and international lines, such as Berlin. There, as in London, Paris, and Vienna, grand hotels arose to accommodate the influx. The urban grand hotels of the later nineteenth century shared six features.[2] First, an urban grand hotel had to have rooms numbering in the hundreds so that an economy of scale could, at least theoretically, pay for public spaces on ground floors. Second, these varied, large, and sumptuous public spaces had to outshine competitor hotels and even the finest

---

[1] Habbo Knoch, *Grandhotels: Luxusräume und Gesellschaftswandel in New York, London und Berlin um 1900* (Göttingen: Wallstein, 2016), 15, 23, 281ff.
[2] For the fullest definition of the grand hotel, see Knoch, *Grandhotels*, 15–19.

houses to the extent that locals and travelers would opt to meet there rather than in private spaces. Third, rates had to be higher than at most hostelries to ensure an elite clientele. Fourth, advanced technologies such as elevators, gas lighting, and radiator heating had to be available. Fifth, service must be thick on the ground so that elite guests missed none of the comforts of home. Sixth and finally, fine food, wine, spirits, and other beverages needed to be provided in-house to ensure self-sufficiency and to increase revenue. In short, the grand hotel had to be able to fulfill a guest's every need and at a cost that still promised profits. That meant establishing economies of scale, putting a price on all services and products, and finding opportunities for vertical integration – for example, buying and running wine import and export businesses to control prices and capture extra profits.

Although the Prussian capital waited longer than Paris and London for such a hotel, the rapid industrialization and expansion of Berlin prepared the way for the sudden emergence of grand hotels after 1871. From the early nineteenth century, Berlin's urban area reached farther and farther north, toward a new district of factories and workers' housing, and west and southwest, toward inland port facilities and new rail depots. Amid the thoroughfares between the new infrastructure in the southwest and the old city center in the northeast, Berlin's first grand hotel, the Kaiserhof, went up in 1875. Its home, the intermediate district of Friedrichstadt, now supplanted the old city as the center for commerce, entertainment, and administration, especially after the unification of Germany and the elevation of Berlin to the status of imperial capital in 1871.

An influx of indemnity payments from France after its defeat in the Franco-Prussian War (1870–71) and the liberalization of the laws of incorporation resulted in the foundation of thousands of limited liability joint-stock companies, including the Berlin Hotel Corporation (Berliner Hôtel-Gesellschaft). Its board, through the sale of shares, was able to raise enough capital to build the Kaiserhof. Still under construction, it became a model of modern hotel organization when Eduard Guyer, Europe's foremost expert on commercial hospitality, included an exegesis on the blueprints in his 1874 *Hotelwesen der Gegenwart* (Hotel Industry of Today), an instant classic in business literature.[3]

Guyer's study of the building, especially its cellars, and his further prescriptions on staffing and management, indicates the Kaiserhof and other

---

[3] Eduard Guyer, *Das Hotelwesen der Gegenwart* (Zurich: Orell Füssli, 1874).

grand hotels' status as liberal institutions par excellence. The Kaiserhof system – that is, the hotel's infrastructure and technologies, its organizational hierarchies, and the established models of guest-staff relations – mirrored the liberal order of the day and reflected its central irony:[4] The free movement and association of the minority upstairs depended on the economic domination and political subjugation of the majority downstairs.

With the emergence of a dozen or so additional grand hotels in Berlin, a professionalized upper class of corporate officers and on-site supervisors dominated the field of hotel management. From on high, and with huge, poorly remunerated workforces in their thrall, these professional hoteliers still struggled to turn a profit. In turn, the hotels' corporate boards of directors established a pattern of blaming the state and the workers for the shortfalls, rather than any inherent weaknesses in a business model that stipulated two or even three staff members per customer. The labor requirement hobbled grand hotels from the start and became their core weakness. Even a modest increase in wages would bring the enterprise to its knees. In all its fragility, the grand hotel as a liberal institution, much like the era's liberal constitutions, disenfranchised the majority for the material benefit and prestige of the minority.

EARLY GRAND HOTELS

In the eighteenth century, *hôtel* meant an aristocratic residence within the walls of the city of Paris. Such a townhouse served as a nobleman and noblewoman's home away from home, with room for guests and all the luxuries of a principal seat in the country.[5] Nineteenth-century usage of the word *hôtel* retained associations with elite, urban hospitality but added a commercial tinge and went beyond the French context. By the mid-nineteenth century, the word "hôtel," retaining its circumflex accent even outside France into the twentieth century, meant a commercial establishment that rented individual guest rooms for a price and provided most

---

[4] Cf. Heinrich Hartmann, *Organisation und Geschäft: Unternehmensorganisation in Frankreich und Deutschland, 1890–1914* (Göttingen: Vandenhoeck & Ruprecht, 2010), 256–70; Marcel Stoetzler, *The State, the Nation, and the Jews: Liberalism and the Antisemitism Dispute in Bismarck's Germany* (Lincoln: University of Nebraska Press, 2008), 9. On the central "emptiness" of National Liberalism in Germany, see James J. Sheehan, *German Liberalism in the Nineteenth Century* (Chicago: University of Chicago Press, 1978), 272–73.

[5] Norbert Elias, *The Court Society*, trans. Edmund Jephcott (Oxford: Blackwell, 1983), 78.

of the services of a middling-to-elite household.[6] These modern hotels distinguished themselves from the inns and taverns (*Gaststätten*) of the eighteenth century by selling a higher standard of service and privacy.[7] Some of the earliest new hotels catered only to people of rank, as was the case in England, but an increasing number of establishments welcomed people regardless of status at birth.[8] The advent of a sizable bourgeoisie with money to spend, the overcoming of barriers to geographic mobility, and an increasing internationalization of commercial and social life contributed in the 1820s and 1830s to the formation of this new institution, the hotel, that could accommodate the new traveling public.[9]

The first hotels to appear were at spas and in cities in the United States, Britain, France, Switzerland, the Low Countries, and German lands. Early examples included Nerot's Hotel in London, Corre's Hotel in New York City, the Royal Hotel in Plymouth, and the Hotel Badischer Hof (opened 1809) in Baden-Baden, where hospitality entrepreneurs had transformed a Capetian monastery into a resort complex of ballrooms, game rooms, dining rooms, baths, gardens, and galleries. More spa hotels cropped up in the ensuing decades in Baden-Baden, Wiesbaden, and other German and Swiss watering places. Meanwhile, in the cities, hoteliers began to build or adapt extant buildings into luxury hotels. By 1850, moneyed visitors to Geneva and Zurich could choose among several up-to-date hostelries behind imposing facades. Inside, they could expect public parlors, partitioned for quiet conversation, and private, well-appointed guest rooms on the upper floors.[10]

---

[6] Max Wöhler, *Gasthäuser und Hotels: Die Bestandteile und die Einrichtung des Gasthauses* (Leipzig: J. G. Göschen, 1911), 2:57. Bettina Matthias, *The Hotel as Setting in Early Twentieth-Century German and Austrian Literature* (Rochester, NY: Camden House, 2006), 30; and Carol Berens, *Hotel Bars and Lobbies* (New York: McGraw Hill, 1997), 26.

[7] J. H. Siddons, *Norton's Handbook to Europe, or, How to Travel in the Old World* (New York: Charles B. Norton, 1860), 246–52; John Murray, *A Hand-Book for Travellers on the Continent: Being a Guide through Holland, Belgium, Prussia, and Northern Germany, and along the Rhine from Holland to Switzerland*, 5th ed. (London: A. & W. Galignani, 1845); Maria Wenzel, *Palasthotels in Deutschland: Untersuchungen zu einer Bauaufgabe im 19. und frühen 20. Jahrhundert* (Hildesheim: Olms, 1991).

[8] Elaine Denby, *Grand Hotels: Reality and Illusion – An Architectural and Social History* (London: Reaktion, 1998), 25.

[9] Klaus Beyrer, "The Mail-Coach Revolution: Landmarks in Travel in Germany between the Seventeenth and Nineteenth Centuries," *German History* 24 (2006), 375–86; Wolfgang Kaschuba, *Die Überwindung der Distanz: Zeit und Raum in der europäischen Moderne* (Frankfurt am Main: Fischer, 2004); Tim Blanning, *The Pursuit of Glory: Europe, 1648–1789* (London: Allen Lane, 2007), part 1.

[10] Denby, *Grand Hotels*, 96; Wenzel, *Palasthotels*, 297–98; Michael Schmitt, *Palast-Hotels: Architektur und Anspruch eines Bautyps, 1870–1920* (Berlin: Gebr. Mann, 1982), 42, 112.

An increasing number of Europe's hotels catered to all functions of daily life. For a fee, a stranger could sleep, dine, socialize, entertain, and, if necessary, recover from an illness – all under one roof and as if at home. The hotels also became sites of class formation, the development of bourgeois-specific outlooks, attitudes, and behaviors – places where the bourgeoisie from all over Europe and the United States convened, conversed, and passed judgment.[11] Hotels even facilitated the accumulation of wealth and connections by offering spaces for free association at the intersection of multiple lines of communication, transportation, and capital. The economic-integrative function of early hotels was most pronounced in American cities. As early as the 1830s, for example, Barnum's Hotel in Baltimore designated rooms for business meetings and commodities trading. Similar establishments in New York, Philadelphia, Boston, and New Orleans even contributed to the social, political, and economic integration of the republic, as A. K. Sandoval-Strausz has shown. Beyond these locations, hotels proliferated in port cities, on major north–south roads, and on east–west canals.[12]

The first hotels depended on older modes of transportation, but as the newest conveyance, trains, extended across Europe and the United States in the mid-nineteenth century, hotel industries came to rely on the railroads for customers, supplies, and opportunities for growth. Railroads also shifted hotel development to those cities at the intersections of multiple lines. In some cases, new junctions created new towns, while in other cases the junctions concentrated streams of people and goods on established settlements. As travel times and expenses diminished, more people took to the rails. In expanding the market, the railroads also enabled the creation of ever larger hotels.[13] At mid-century, there were several such properties with rooms in excess of 100. The term "grand hotel" came into use specifically to distinguish the bigger hotels of the 1850s–70s from the smaller hotels of the 1800s–40s.[14] The first such urban grand

[11] On the composition of this class, see David Blackbourn, introduction to *The German Bourgeoisie: Essays on the Social History of the German Middle Class from the Late Eighteenth to the Early Twentieth Century*, eds. David Blackbourn and Richard J. Evans (London: Routledge, 1993), 8–10.

[12] Sandoval-Strausz, *Hotel*, 31–43, 50–52, 69. See also Wenzel, *Palasthotels*, 205–6, 330; Denby, *Grand Hotels*, 35; and Paul Groth, *Living Downtown: The History of Residential Hotels in the United States*, 2nd ed. (Berkeley: University of California Press, 1999).

[13] Wolfgang Schivelbusch, *The Railway Journey: The Industrialization of Time and Space* (Berkeley: University of California Press, 1986), 188.

[14] Cf. Matthias, *Hotel as Setting*, 17; Moritz Hoffmann, *Geschichte des deutschen Hotels: Vom Mittelalter bis zur Gegenwart* (Heidelberg: A. Hüttig, 1961), 226.

hotels in Europe were the railroad hotels of Great Britain, where rail networks spread earliest and fastest.[15]

Small and makeshift, the Prussian capital's luxury hostelries still occupied structures first built for residential use, a distinct disadvantage: Quirky layouts meant that a single traveler might be asked to share a room with a total stranger even at some of the better establishments. Landing one's own room did not necessarily guarantee privacy, either, because some rooms were accessible only by passing through another. Public space downstairs, however pretty, did not suffice, either. The best houses offered just two parlors – one for men and one for women – and a cramped ballroom or banquet hall. But even visitors willing to put up with all these deficiencies had trouble finding accommodation, since Berlin had too few hotels.[16]

BERLIN'S FIRST GRAND HOTEL

In Berlin, grand hotels became possible only with the unification of Germany in 1871 and as a result of changes to the laws governing how corporations could form. These changes made it feasible to raise enormous amounts of capital for industrial and commercial enterprises while limiting the liability of shareholders – hence the contemporary name for the period 1871–73: *Gründerzeit*. "The era of founders" referred not to the founding of the empire as such but rather to the establishment of thousands of limited liability joint-stock corporations.[17] These formations enabled hoteliers to raise the fabulous sums necessary for their capital-intensive enterprises.

Meanwhile, the influx of people and goods to the city center fueled a speculative boom in the real estate market west of the old medieval core, in the city's future hotel district. Friedrichstadt and Dorotheenstadt, long the preserve of Berlin's titled and well-to-do, thus emerged

[15] Schivelbusch, *Railway Journey*, 42–43.

[16] Architekten-Verein zu Berlin and Vereinigung Berliner Architekten, eds. *Berlin und seine Bauten* (Berlin: Wilhelm Ernst & Sohn, 1896), 1:29; Architekten-Verein zu Berlin and Verband Deutscher Architekten- und Ingenieur-Vereine, eds. *Berlin und seine Bauten* (Berlin: Architekten- und Ingenieur-Verein, 1877), 1:350; Wenzel, *Palasthotels*, 93–98; "Verzeichnis sämtlicher Gasthäuser der Residenz-Stadt Berlin," Royal Prussian Police report, n.d., ca. 1810, in LAB A Pr. Br. Rep. 030, Nr. 1569, f. 29.

[17] Laurenz Demps, *Geschichte Berlins von den Anfängen bis 1945* (Berlin: Dietz, 1987), 415–17; David Blackbourn, *The Long Nineteenth Century: A History of Germany, 1780–1918* (Oxford: Oxford University Press, 1997), 307; Herbert Schwenk, *Lexikon der Berliner Stadtentwicklung* (Berlin: Haude & Spencer, 2002), 162.

in the later nineteenth century as an intensified zone of commercial activity and became the meeting grounds for Berliners of all districts. Workers, white-collar employees, shoppers, and tourists arrived at newly constructed intra- and interurban railroad stops, which connected to the streetcar lines already in use. The elevated Friedrichstraße station went up in 1878 at the northern frontier of Dorotheenstadt, along the River Spree, in view of Feuerland (Fire Land, the unofficial name of the city's metalworking district) and the Mietskasernengürtel (Tenement Belt) to the north. In the west, Leipziger Platz pulled together myriad horse and then electric tram lines, which discharged passengers near Potsdamer Platz, one of the busiest squares in the empire, and the Potsdam and Anhalt rail stations. Farther southwest sat the enormous freight depot and one of the busiest ports of the Landwehr Canal. Most waterways, rails, and roads led to Friedrich- and Dorotheenstadt, which together formed the undisputed center of the new Berlin and the site of its first grand hotel.

Berlin's first hotel corporation, the Berlin Hotel Corporation, was amalgamated in 1872 by its first chairman, the liberal wheeler-dealer Adelbert Delbrück. Through the 1860s, Delbrück had taken an active role in the German National Union (Deutscher Nationalverein), a liberal organization composed of the middle strata of German society – manufacturers, professionals, small business owners, and master artisans – which was committed to obtaining liberal reforms from above, by means of a unified Germany under Prussian leadership. The German Progressive Party (Deutsche Fortschrittspartei, DFP), the liberals' umbrella party of the 1860s, also counted Delbrück as one of its leaders.[18] According to Friedrich Albert Lange, the philosopher and former DFP member, Delbrück and the other party bosses constituted "a small but influential Berlin clique," liberal in outlook but "distinguished by a Junker-like" aloofness and arrogance.[19]

Delbrück's confidence derived from success. He was becoming a titan of finance and industry, especially after the liberalization of the laws governing the formation of corporations. He founded or helped found several conglomerates: the German Construction Corporation of Berlin (Deutsche Baugesellschaft zu Berlin), the Corporation for Construction Works

[18] Hans-Henning Zabel, "Gottlieb Adelbert Delbrück," *Neue Deutsche Biographie*, ed. Historische Kommission bei der Bayerischen Akademie der Wissenschaften (Berlin: Duncker & Humblot, 1956), 3:576–77.
[19] Quoted in Todd H. Weir, *Secularism and Religion in Nineteenth-Century Germany: The Rise of the Fourth Confession* (Cambridge: Cambridge University Press, 2014), 145.

in Berlin (Actien-Gesellschaft für Bau-Ausführungen in Berlin); the Berlin Construction Consortium (Berliner Bauverein); Hinsberg, Fischer & Co. Banking Consortium of Barmen (Barmer Bank-Verein Hinsberg, Fischer & Co.); Donnersmarck Iron Works (Donnersmarckhütte); the Upper Lusatian Railroad Corporation (Ober-Lausitzer Eisenbahngesellschaft); and, finally, Deutsche Bank. Delbrück was its first chairman.[20]

Delbrück's board members at the Berlin Hotel Corporation also came from Germany's industrial and financial elite. Georg Siemens presided with Delbrück and others over Deutsche Bank. Siemens also had an interest in a financial services firm with another of the Berlin Hotel Corporation's board members, Eduard von der Heydt. The son of former Prussian finance minister August von der Heydt, Eduard sat on several boards in addition to that of the Berlin Hotel Corporation, including a real estate and construction corporation and two insurance companies, one of them incorporated in the United States. His partner in the American venture, Gustav Kutter, resident of New York City, also sat on the board of the Berlin Hotel Corporation, as well as the boards of companies involved in coal mining, import-export services, and shipping by rail and steamship. The other board members of the Berlin Hotel Corporation held similar positions and assets. All liberals, most of these men played roles in the financial and economic reforms of 1848, the failed revolution that nonetheless had lasting, liberalizing effects on the Prussian and then German economy. Julius Kieschke, for example, had entered the civil service in 1848 and then the Prussian Ministry of Trade (Preußisches Handelsministerium) and the executive office of Königsberg. He was mayor of that city when he joined the first board of the Berlin Hotel Corporation.[21]

The Berlin Hotel Corporation quickly raised the money for its debut venture, an establishment to rival the grand hotels recently opened in Vienna for the World's Fair of 1873. By the end of that year, the corporation had purchased twelve lots on or adjacent to Berlin's Ziethenplatz,

[20] *Die Berliner Emissionshäuser und ihre Emissionen in den Jahren 1871 und 1872: Ein Commentar zu dem Berliner Courszettel* (Berlin: Fr. Lobeck's Verlag, 1873), 21, 24, 54–55.
[21] State of New York, *Ninth Annual Report of the Superintendent of the Insurance Department: Life Insurance* (Albany: Charles van Benthuysen & Sons, 1868), 812; *Deutsche Versicherungs-Zeitung: Organ für das gesamte Versicherungswesen* 39 (May 14, 1871), 312; State of New York, *Laws of the State of New York, Passed at the Eighty-Fourth Session of the Legislature, Begun January First, and Ended April Sixteenth, 1861, in the City of Albany* (Albany: Munsell & Rowland, 1861), 493; Loyal National League, *The Great Questions of the Times* (New York: C. S. Westcott & Co., 1863), 38.

a major crossroads in the government district.[22] The board persuaded
the city to create a new street directly to the south to ensure that the
new hotel would be the first in Berlin to occupy a freestanding structure.[23] They called the property *Kaiserhof* (Emperor's Court), signaling
the arrival of a hostelry in line with Berlin's newly achieved status as an
imperial capital.

For the first time, private citizens of the Prussian capital succeeded
at changing the direction and style of development in the city center.[24]
Corporate capitalism had allowed them to do it – to raise the funds, to
acquire the land, to command the resources to lobby the government,
which had stakes in the neighborhood. New government ministries,
departments, and offices sprang up after unification, and many of them
occupied buildings around the future Kaiserhof. The project would go on
to supplant important buildings on Ziethenplatz, which had once housed
the Prussian capital's French and Italian embassies as well as several
notable eighteenth- and nineteenth-century residences.[25]

The transformation of Friedrichstraße, especially the intensification of
activity there, was already underway before the foundation of the empire,
but the pace of development increased in the 1870s. Berthold Kempinski
opened his first restaurant on Friedrichstraße in 1872. His was among
many large new establishments, including the Kaiser-Galerie shopping
and amusement arcade (1873), the Admiral's Palace baths (1874), and
the Café Bauer (1878). Before these arrivals, owners of the city's fine
hotels had chosen sites away from commercial activity, typically farther north, on or near Unter den Linden, the representative boulevard
connecting the royal palace to the Brandenburg Gate.[26] The Kaiserhof
changed that pattern by opening in the center of a booming commercial
district and thus acted not only as a hostelry but also as a place of respite
for well-heeled Berliners, including bureaucrats and businessmen.

The Kaiserhof dominated the neighborhood, attesting to the financial power of Berlin's new limited-liability corporations (Figure 1.1).[27]

---

[22] Laurenz Demps, *Berlin-Wilhelmstraße: Eine Topographie preußisch-deutscher Macht* (Berlin: Ch. Links, 2000), 124.
[23] Wenzel, *Palasthotels*, 134–35.
[24] See Bernet, "Hobrecht Plan," 404–8, 412.
[25] Architekten-Verein zu Berlin, *Berlin und seine Bauten* (1877), 1:352.
[26] Karl Baedeker, ed. *Baedeker's Berlin, Potsdam und Umgebung* (Leipzig: Karl Baedeker, 1878), 3.
[27] See Dolores L. Augustine, "Arriving in the Upper Class: The Wealthy Business Elite of Wilhelmine Germany," in Blackbourn and Evans, *German Bourgeoisie*, 51–52, 73.

FIGURE 1.1 The Hotel Kaiserhof, 1877
Image credit: Atlas zur Zeitschrift für Bauwesen/*Staatsbibliothek zu Berlin*

The rectangular facade had a perimeter of 310 meters and rose five floors above the pavement. A balustrade over the cornice lent additional height. A gigantic palazzo, the building featured a piano nobile over the mezzanine and an arched colonnade, in relief, of mock rusticated stone on the ground floor. The design also resembled Vienna's colossal apartment houses of recent years, particularly the Ringstraße's Heinrichshof.[28] A local referent was the German emperor's palace, the Stadtschloss (City Palace), distinguished by its occupation of an entire city block.

This first establishment of the Berlin Hotel Corporation was indeed a monumental intervention in the capital's built environment, and critics took note. Before the hotel even opened, the *Deutsche Bauzeitung* disparaged the undertaking: "Obviously, the architecture ... can never quite be interesting," since it had to accede to the demands of the business model – in this case, the need to house "rooms of nearly the same size" in rows ad nauseum.[29] The critic's misgivings reflected a more general

---

[28] Wenzel, *Palasthotels*, 136–37.
[29] "Die Berliner Bau-Ausstellung, 1874," *Deutsche Bauzeitung* 8 (1874), 357, cited in Wenzel, *Palasthotels*, 135–36.

response to the new large-scale commercial architecture. The utilitarian core of the Kaiserhof project was incompatible not just with precepts of beauty but also with any kind of architectural integrity. The facade in this case was an effort to mask what was un-beautiful – *utilitarian* – about the building's interior, a result of the architects' attention to function over form.[30] But when the hotel opened on October 1, 1875, the reviews turned laudatory. With Emperor Wilhelm I in attendance, the public had the chance to tour the sumptuous interiors. Ten days later, however, a fire broke out in the building, spread through the upper floors, and destroyed most of the guest rooms as well as the areas behind the front entrance (Figure 1.2).[31] No one was injured, and the blaze, in its way, generated spectacular publicity.

Socialists were quick to react. A contributor to the *Neuer Social-Demokrat*, a press organ of the Socialist Workers' Party of Germany, announced the irony to readers: "Another creation of the Kaiserzeit, the splendid hotel on the Wilhelms- and Ziethenplatz, which carries the proud name 'Kaiserhof,' has suffered damage in the first days of its existence."[32] The article identified the culprits as "bankers and large-scale industrialists," as well as a few "princes" or nobles given to financial speculation. Creating enormous and mighty monuments to the German Empire and their own vanity, these men, according to the journalist, forgot to do their homework. They built bells too big to be rung (Cologne Cathedral) and towers too awkward to be admired (the Victory Column in Berlin, which people had taken to calling the "Victory Asparagus" instead); the latest was a hotel too big to safeguard from fire. Implied was the charge that these men's obsession with gold, glitter, and grandeur had caused them to neglect the more mundane aspect of fire safety and thereby endanger the populace, putting money before people.[33] Correct or not about where to lay blame, the article's author became the first of many to use a Berlin grand hotel as the setting for a drama about the hypocrisies of the powerful and propertied classes.

In the end, successful insurance claims and the emperor's public support guaranteed reconstruction. The Kaiserhof reopened on the anniversary of

---

[30] On such critiques, see Maiken Umbach, *German Cities and Bourgeois Modernism, 1890–1924* (Oxford: Oxford University Press, 2009), 80–82.

[31] Architekten-Verein zu Berlin, *Berlin und seine Bauten* (1877), 1:353.

[32] Kurt Koszyk, *Geschichte der deutschen Presse*, vol. 2, *Deutsche Presse im 19. Jahrhundert* (West Berlin: Colloquium, 1966), 195.

[33] "Politische Uebersicht," *Neuer Social-Demokrat: Organ der Socialistischen Arbeiter-Partei Deutschlands* (October 18, 1875).

FIGURE 1.2 Contemporary illustration of the fire at the Kaiserhof
on October 11, 1875
Image credit: Karl Röhling/Illustrirte Zeitung (Leipzig)/Staatsbibliothek zu Berlin

its inauguration, on October 1, 1876. Baedeker described the property as "the largest and most elegant of Berlin's hotels ... comfortably outfitted in the style of the greatest Parisian and London hotels."[34] Newspapers, too, emphasized the Kaiserhof's many luxuries and its comparability to Viennese establishments.[35] The yearbook of the Berlin Association of Architects (Architekten-Verein zu Berlin) dwelled on the property's opulence while quietly bemoaning the destruction of a few "residential buildings of value" – the embassies, especially.[36] But in 1878, the Kaiserhof proved itself even more useful to diplomats than the chanceries and palaces. That year the property served as the hotel of choice for statesmen who were in town to participate in the Congress of Berlin, which took place across an adjacent square.[37] With all its gas lamps aglow, the Kaiserhof amplified Bismarck's message to the delegates about Germany's place in the new world order. This palace hotel showcased imperial ambitions even as it reassured foreigners with offers of peace and civility. To keep that peace, managers, owners, and their architects had to keep the classes apart and unequal.

Grand hotel buildings employed an architecture of extreme inequality, affording space, privacy, and safety, according to station.[38] Meanwhile, a system of regulations controlled the dress and comportment of workers, as well as their interactions with the guests. This was a managerial vision of a hierarchy undergirded by architecture, elaborated by regulation, and relegated to the basement, hidden from view.[39]

The Kaiserhof's cellar became the standard for the cellars of other grand hotels in Berlin. It provided workspace for the hotel's hundreds of workers who kept the hospitality machine running. In effect, they were confined to the lowest grade amid the heat, fumes, and din of service on an industrial scale. And yet, the cellar was not quite a factory. It lacked any expanse of shop floor. Instead, dozens and dozens of walls and doors

---

[34] Baedeker, *Baedeker's Berlin* (1878), 1.
[35] Demps, *Berlin-Wilhelmstraße*, 124.
[36] Architekten-Verein zu Berlin, *Berlin und seine Bauten* (1877), 1:352–53.
[37] Demps, *Berlin-Wilhelmstraße*, 124.
[38] Unless otherwise noted, the sources for the architectural specifications of the Kaiserhof are the architects' own figures, including floor plans, site plans, elevations, cross sections, and detail drawings. Although the originals do not survive, high-quality facsimiles are available in the *Atlas zur Zeitschrift für Bauwesen*, an official publication of the Royal Technical Buildings Deputation (Königliche Technische Bau-Deputation) and the Berlin Association of Architects (Architekten-Verein zu Berlin), vol. 27 (1877), 16–24.
[39] See Umbach, *German Cities*, especially chapter 6.

separated workers from each other, from white-collar employees, from managers, and from the guests. Where workers did interact with guests – and only a minority did – workers' uniforms and manners rendered them only marginally visible. They were supposed to be extensions of the system – unavailable personalities, of the hotel more than in it.

The cellar was the hotel's principal site of production, the attic its tenement. In this way, the allocation of space mirrored that of bourgeois and aristocratic houses of the nineteenth century, but the Kaiserhof was of a different order.[40] Here lay servants' quarters to sleep hundreds, kitchens to feed thousands, and laundries to boil bedlinens by the ton. At this scale, the work became more specialized, more monotonous, and more dangerous than in a manor house or urban palace. The pressures on workers were different, too, and perhaps greater. Hotel workers, unlike their domestic counterparts, were obliged not only to feed the elite but to do it at a profit.

The architects and owners of the Kaiserhof made the building plans, including cellar floor plans, available well before the opening of the hotel itself, using many of the projections as advertisements. More than architectural renderings, these floor plans and relief sketches were promises, visions, and prescriptions, as the hotel expert Eduard Guyer understood when he included them as exhibits in *Das Hotelwesen der Gegenwart*.[41] Guyer's book quickly became the standard for how to build and operate a grand hotel.[42]

With guest experience in mind, Guyer advised architects to design cellars that would trap as much noise and as many smells as possible.[43] Four decades later, in 1910, another expert, Paul Damm-Etienne, wrote more plainly. His principal concern was body odor. Sweating workers might

---

[40] Herbert Lachmayer, Christian Gargerle, and Géza Hajós, "The Grand Hotel," *AA Files* 22 (1991), 34.

[41] Cf. Sharon Marcus, *Apartment Stories: City and Home in Nineteenth-Century Paris and London* (Berkeley: University of California Press, 1990), 17–32.

[42] United States Centennial Commission, *International Exhibition, 1876: Reports and Rewards*, vol. 7, *Groups XXI–XXVII* (Washington, DC: Government Printing Office, 1880), 39; advertisement for *Das Hotelwesen der Gegenwart*, in Eduard Guyer-Freuler, ed. *Kritische Betrachtungen über Staats- und Gemeindehaushalt* 33 (1903), 41; notice of second printing, *Allgemeine Illustrirte Zeitung* (Stuttgart) 18, no. 2 (1875), 245; positive review by E. Tallichet, "Les hôtels modernes," *Bibliothèque universelle et Revue suisse* 51 (1874), 519–38; positive review by Eduard Reich, *Blätter für literarische Unterhaltung*, no. 44 (November 4, 1886), 698; Otto Henne-am-Rhyn, *Kulturgeschichte der jüngsten Zeit: Von der Errichtung des Deutschen Reiches bis auf die Gegenwart* (Leipzig: Otto Wigand, 1897), 582.

[43] Guyer, *Hotelwesen*, 98.

produce a miasma that threatened to contaminate the food, he reasoned. The solution was not to install mechanical ventilation systems to cool the cellars. Instead, Damm-Etienne told hoteliers to provide more sinks and more soap.[44]

Managers did in fact struggle to contain the smells and sounds of the cellars. The boilers, heaters, and pumps ran all day and night with only chimneys, transom windows, and air shafts for ventilation. What air was left to breathe contained coal dust, residue from the fuel that kept the machines running. This dust, along with soot, smoke, and water vapor, emanated from the cellar's smoldering core, where men stoked furnaces and operated other heavy machinery and where steam, heat, dust, and fumes spewed from open fires and filterless grates. In the surrounding warrens, still more workers sorted, lifted, carried, and distributed goods and raw materials by hand or by cart. Around the periphery, in the kitchens, bakers finished bread and pastries in gigantic ovens. Dishwashers – people, not machines – pumped in scalding water so they could clean china by hand. From the laundries, wastewater flowed in torrents as women transferred bedsheets, towels, and table linens from cauldrons to mangles. The Kaiserhof's cellar was a sweltering dungeon of the industrial age (Figure 1.3).

The sharp delineation of space, as well as the order in which the architects, Hermann von der Hude and Julius Hennicke, arrayed rooms and facilities, showed an abundant concern for the productive division of labor and for the qualitative distinctions between guest and staff space – distinctions which reflected the architects' and owners' profit motive, as well as their view of class relations. Plans for the cellar would result in an environment that limited workers' access to light, air, mobility, and privacy, the very privileges being sold to guests upstairs. This regime measured social class by the extent to which a subject could maintain health, freedom of movement, and privacy. In the service of productivity but also of the maintenance of class power, Hude and Hennicke's cellar did nothing to spare workers a state of undignified living and unending toil.

Conditions aside, the building code made it impossible for hoteliers to house all of their workers in cellars. The attics, on the other hand, were suitable so long as their ceilings were high enough.[45] The Kaiserhof's attic, like any other, would have been frigid in winter and sweltering by

---

[44] Paul Damm-Etienne, *Das Hotelwesen* (Leipzig: B. G. Teubner, 1910), 76.
[45] Statement of regulations of the Building Authority of the Berlin Police Presidium (Abteilung III), n.d., ca. 1880–1900, in LAB A Pr. Br. Rep. 030, Nr. 1884, f. 9.

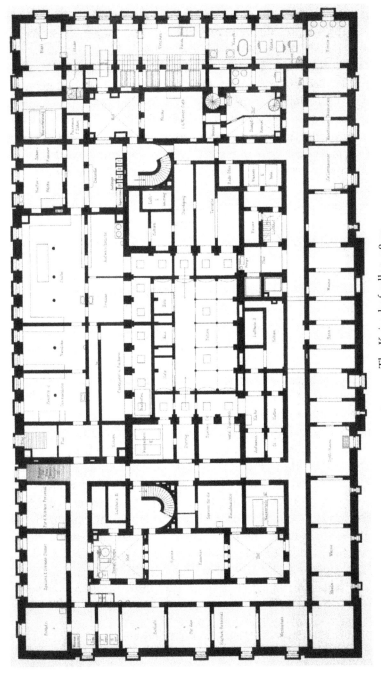

FIGURE 1.3 The Kaiserhof cellar, 1877

Image credit: Atlas zur Zeitschrift für Bauwesen/Staatsbibliothek zu Berlin

June. Technically on the sixth floor of the building, Kaiserhof workers' sleeping quarters lay right under the eaves. (Small windows were hidden from view by a high balustrade over the cornice.) Large, sex-segregated rooms slept multiple people under low, raked ceilings. Staircases connected the attic to the guest floors directly so that workers could be roused and called to duty in the middle of the night. As in bourgeois and aristocratic households of the period, privacy and peace were luxuries only for the employers; servants had neither.[46]

But attic sleepers might have had it better than their coworkers unlucky enough to have their beds in the cellar. Together with a workshop and chambers for the water and gas meters, basement bedrooms for hotel and kitchen workers spanned the building's eastern side; these had smaller windows below street level. Away from the street lay rooms without windows or with only one window opening onto a lightless airshaft that had been given over to a steam pump. One such machine stood directly in front of the only window, wedged into a corner, of the men's dining room, where hundreds would have taken meals in shifts, since it occupied less than thirty square meters. Across the hall and toward the center of the building was the women's dining room, smaller than the men's and windowless, surrounded by water heaters, air heaters, and food stores.[47] The swelter, noise, and crush were functions of the building's design.

Among the loudest and hottest spaces were the kitchens, which sat underneath the guests' dining room and covered more than 600 square meters (exclusive of storage, a prep kitchen, and kitchens for the café concession and staff meals). Some ninety people labored here elbow-to-elbow over open flames and scalding water. To the heat, noise, and danger of the kitchens, meanwhile, the front cellar provided a striking contrast. In an area larger than all the gastronomy spaces combined, thousands of bottles of wine rested under controlled and quiet conditions, with whites on the eastern, cooler, darker side and reds on the western, warmer, lighter side. The cellar manager and technician, who sat atop the cellar hierarchy, had their offices down here. The plans had spared these managers, and the wines, the full asperity of the rest of the cellar.

Directly upstairs, the Kaiserhof's ground floor of public rooms for guests was something else (Figure 1.4). In its scale and layout, it

---

[46] On servants and privacy, see Jürgen Kocka, *Arbeitsverhältnisse und Arbeiterexistenzen: Grundlagen der Klassenbildung im 19. Jahrhundert* (Bonn: J. H. W. Dietz, 1990), 125–30.

[47] Architekten-Verein zu Berlin, *Berlin und Seine Bauten* (1877), 1:354.

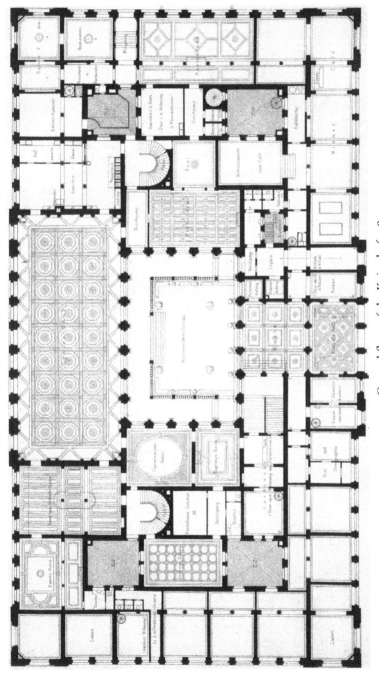

FIGURE 1.4 Ground floor of the Kaiserhof, 1877

Image credit: Atlas zur Zeitschrift für Bauwesen/Staatsbibliothek zu Berlin

resembled a department store, another site of conspicuous consumption in the metropolis.[48] Architects of department stores and grand hotels had envisioned the same optics, after all – upon entry, a guest's gaze took in the glowing expanse. She might cast her eyes from one rich detail to another, one option for respite and pleasure to another, before settling on exactly what she wanted.[49] And from the outside, the main entrance of the Kaiserhof, like that of a department store, was easily recognizable, with the house's name affixed over the arches of a generous portico. Coming through this entrance, guests would have witnessed what made the Kaiserhof a hotel on par with the best of larger, more established capitals: the hotel's public interior.

Never in Berlin had the public rooms of a hotel been granted so much space and expenditure. The allocation of areas for shops evoked the arcades of Parisian, Viennese, and London hotels, while the provision of smaller social rooms for intimate conversation owed much to the Swiss example and lent a domestic scale to these parts of the ground floor. Finally, through its organization around a central axis, the ground floor facilitated motion. The axis drew guests from the entry to the hotel's grandest spaces, thereby making evident the ground floor's spectacular dimensions. Then, having passed through the public, commercial spaces, guests were encouraged to move to the semi-private, domestic spaces nearby.[50]

The least domestic feature of earlier grand hotels in Berlin and elsewhere, particularly the Kaiserhof, was the courtyard (Figure 1.5). The Kaiserhof's building plans labeled the courtyard an anteroom (*Vorsaal*), emphasizing its function as the meeting place before passage to the adjoining dining room, breakfast room, or parlors. A glass roof shielded the 330 square meters below from rain and cold. Terraces on three sides provided access to the principal public rooms, making the court a pass-through, a way station, and public piazza in one, the social and spatial

[48] On conspicuous consumption, see Knoch, *Grandhotels*, 15ff.; Warren G. Breckman, "Disciplining Consumption: The Debate about Luxury in Wilhelmine Germany," *Journal of Social History* 24 (1991), 485–505; Thorstein Veblen, *The Theory of the Leisure Class* (New York: Macmillan, 1899), 91ff.

[49] Michael B. Miller, *The Bon Marché: Bourgeois Culture and the Department Store, 1869–1920* (Princeton: Princeton University Press, 1981), 5, 177; Erika Diane Rappaport, *Shopping for Pleasure: Women in the Making of London's West End* (Princeton: Princeton University Press, 2000), 143ff.

[50] Habbo Knoch, "Das Grandhotel," in *Orte der Moderne: Erfahrungswelten des 19. und 20. Jahrhunderts*, eds. Habbo Knoch and Alexa Geisthövel (Frankfurt am Main: Campus, 2005), 132; Wenzel, *Palasthotels*, 140.

FIGURE 1.5 The Kaiserhof courtyard, 1877
Image credit: Atlas zur Zeitschrift für Bauwesen/*Staatsbibliothek zu Berlin*

center of the Kaiserhof.[51] Its decor was nationalist, monarchist, and magnificent, appropriate to the room's public function as a showcase for status and a space for public heterosociability.[52]

The architecture signaled this heterosocial functionality by supplying both masculine and feminine ornamentation. The Doric (severe, masculine) order balanced the Ionic (soft, feminine), while the seven full-length portraits of Emperor Wilhelm I, in various military uniforms, complemented some dozen female caryatids in soft, flowing drape.[53] These features framed interior windows that opened into public rooms on the ground floor and guest rooms above, so that the courtyard's associations with masculinity and femininity were further complicated along the lines of public and private. Even the scale of the space was softened by its protectiveness. Gilt surfaces and underfloor heating likewise mitigated the outdoor aspect, an effect achieved by natural light and wrought-iron lampposts, and helped classify the court as an area of indoor-outdoor, public-private, masculine-feminine hybridity.

---

[51] Architekten-Verein zu Berlin, *Berlin und seine Bauten* (1877), 1:354.

[52] Knoch, *Grandhotels*, 53–58.

[53] Architekten-Verein zu Berlin, *Berlin und seine Bauten* (1877), 1:355. On orders, gender, and balance, see Adrian Forty, *Words and Buildings: A Vocabulary of Modern Architecture* (London: Thames & Hudson, 2004), 44–50; Joseph Rykwert, *The Dancing Column: On Order in Architecture* (Cambridge, MA: MIT Press, 1998), 237.

In general, however, male-female interactions were kept to a minimum in the Kaiserhof's public rooms. Rules and design conventions placed the female patron somewhere between guest and worker in the hotel hierarchy, which dispensed space, luxury, and comforts according to class. A woman could enter the banquet hall, for example, only if in the company of a male chaperone. (This was also the case if she wanted to book a guest room.) Indeed, the hotel barred single women from most spaces, relegating them to a remote, rear-facing ladies' parlor (*Damensaal*). The women's lavatory (note: singular), tucked behind the ladies' parlor on the ground floor, had one sink and one toilet. Conversely, the men enjoyed large lavatories (note: plural), each with space for several sinks and toilets. These inequalities reflected and reinforced the privileged status of certain guests over others – in this case, men over women.[54]

What female guests lacked in access to amenities, space, and mobility, they made up for, somewhat, in their rights to make demands of staff, consume luxury goods and services, and sleep and dine as well as money could afford. This was hospitality at a price, after all, and the architects, Hude and Hennicke, designed the upper floors, with guest rooms, to reflect and reproduce divisions even among guests. First- and second-floor ceilings were the highest, and these levels contained the largest and most richly decorated guest rooms, as well as six parlors. Most of these parlors offered privileged views, either of Wilhelmplatz or Ziethenplatz, and could be connected to adjacent rooms via communicating doors, allowing the transformation of rows of guest rooms and parlors into apartments. This was ideal either for visiting families or long-term residents. Even if most of its guests were not traveling with children, the Kaiserhof earned the moniker "family hotel" (*Familienhotel*) through its provision of such suites on the lower floors.[55]

A further innovation came with the rooms off corner parlors, the Kaiserhof's finest bedrooms. A small private hall connected each chamber to the public corridor and adjacent parlor and thus acted as a sound and light lock, minimizing the disturbances associated with such a large hotel and ensuring privacy and peace. By contrast, the smaller, cheaper rooms in the rear of the first two floors had no such provisions for sound mitigation. Several opened onto narrow light wells with machinery at the

---

[54] "Ein heikles Thema," a series about women's difficulties navigating public spaces in 1880s Berlin, especially when it came to finding lavatories, *Berliner Tageblatt*, September 10 and 16, 1884.

[55] See Knoch, *Grandhotels*, 43–48.

bottom. The most modest of all these backrooms lay on the building's third and fourth floors. Here, compact rooms best suited such single travelers as businessmen and couriers. Their rooms had lower ceilings and simpler furnishings and fittings than the rooms on lower levels.

Nonetheless, a few common factors united all four upper floors, with a total number of guest rooms at around 240, for as many as 400 people.[56] On each floor, dozens of rooms shared eight toilets and one bath, and no rooms were en suite, a luxury on offer nowhere in Berlin at the time. Most bathing could be accomplished with washstands in each of the rooms, and servants were always on hand to fetch hot water and remove wastewater. Chamber pots and workers to service them likewise made up for the paucity of water closets. These practices – the use of labor in lieu of plumbing – were common among the rich, who had yet to adopt the faucet and drain for the maintenance of their hygiene, even in Berlin's newest apartment houses.

For the Kaiserhof, Hude and Hennicke had borrowed the European apartment house convention that placed the finest rooms on the second floor, the middling rooms above that, and workers' and servants rooms higher still, with one added distinction: The Kaiserhof plan meant to segregate guests not only on the basis of class or income but also on the basis of gender, with the least dense areas reserved for women with their husbands and children and the most tightly packed for single male travelers. Although all guests could enjoy the amenities of the ground floor, the guestroom levels above incorporated material and architectural distinctions of income and social position and ensured that the lower guestroom floors would be populated more by married couples and families, the upper by single men.[57]

As much as the grand hotel brought people together, its design kept them separated along lines of gender and class.[58] On the public, ground floor, female guests would find their movements prescribed by gendered conventions that required a chaperone in any of the spaces except the diminutive ladies' parlor at the back corner of the building. Workers would labor under surveillance in dank, dangerous, dirty, toxic environments. The extent to which these visions of a segregated society became reality, after the fulfilment of Hude and Hennicke's plans, is hard to

[56] Architekten-Verein zu Berlin, *Berlin und seine Bauten* (1877), 1:354.
[57] Wenzel, *Palasthotels*, 140; Knoch, "Grandhotel," 132.
[58] See Emma Short, *Mobility and the Hotel in Modern Literature: Passing Through* (Cham, Switzerland: Palgrave Macmillan, 2019), 103–4.

measure, since worker testimony for the period before 1914 does not survive, nor does the architecture itself. Nevertheless, the plans and prescriptions afforded workers and women limited room for maneuver at the Kaiserhof.

BERLIN'S NEXT GRAND HOTELS

The Kaiserhof was Berlin's only grand hotel for just a few years. The city's second such property, the Central-Hotel, opened in 1880 and integrated seamlessly into the capital's intra- and interurban train lines.[59] Nine thousand square meters of land across from Friedrichstraße station had been acquired by its parent company, the Railroad Hotel Corporation (Eisenbahn-Hotel-Gesellschaft), which was itself owned by the Hotel Management Corporation, one of the principal hospitality companies in the city. The lots fronted Friedrichstraße, Berlin's premier commercial thoroughfare and one of the longest streets in the city. It housed cafés, shops, arcades, hotels, theaters, and other amusements. The Central dominated this activity and fed it with customers, much as the Kaiserhof did several streets to the south. What made the Central different from the Kaiserhof was its position directly across the street from a station entrance. This unparalleled proximity to the railroad helped classify the Central as a "through-traveler's hotel" (*Passantenhotel*). The target guest was someone in town for a short period to conduct business or rest for the night before connecting to other trains.[60] Capitalizing on the concentration of industry to the north and commerce and government to the south and southeast, the Central-Hotel was more American in style and function than the Kaiserhof, which was farther from the train stations.[61]

Nevertheless, the Railroad Hotel Corporation had engaged the same architects, Hude and Hennicke, who devised for the Central-Hotel project a long building of four floors divided into three horizontal zones (Figure 1.6). With few vertical elements to draw the eye upward, lateral embellishments accentuated the building's horizontal expanse. Rounded

---

[59] Advertisement for the Central-Hotel in Berlin, *Die Gegenwart: Wochenschrift für Litteratur, Kunst und öffentliches Leben* 18 (September 11, 1880), 176.

[60] Wenzel, *Palasthotels*, 131.

[61] Habbo Knoch, "Geselligkeitsräume und Societyträume: Grandhotels im wilhelminischen Berlin," in *Berliner Villenleben: Die Inszenierung bürgerlicher Wohnwelten am grünen Rand der Stadt um 1900*, ed. Heinz Reif (Berlin: Gebr. Mann, 2008), 332; Sandoval-Strausz, *Hotel*, 242.

FIGURE I.6 The Central-Hotel, 1879
Image credit: Illustrirte Zeitung *(Leipzig)/Staatsbibliothek zu Berlin*

towers, each emblazoned with the name of the hotel, stood at the corners marking the longest side, which featured rich ornamentation, wrought-iron balustrades, and state-of-the-art plate glass windows. The transparency they afforded made the Central look more penetrable than the Kaiserhof, whose high ground-floor windows alternated with a heavy layer of rusticated mock-stone. On the upper floors of the Central, balconies and large windows helped integrate the building into the city outside, also in contrast to the Kaiserhof, which was set back on one side in the manner of a palace. The Central, conversely, presented itself as the northern gateway to the city's premier commercial thoroughfare. Using its frontages to display the building's overwhelming volume, the new hotel changed the visual profile of the surrounding neighborhood.

The Central also brought the outside in, with the hotel's Wintergarten concert house and adjacent banquet hall, restaurant, and café. The combination of luxury accommodation, fine dining, and nightly entertainment had never been tried in Berlin. The designation of so much space to show business and gastronomy, at the expense of intimate parlors and conversation spaces, added to the hotel's profile as a place for short visits and quick pleasures, despite the availability of apartments upstairs. Movable screens and windows could integrate the Wintergarten, dining rooms, restaurant, and café into a visual whole. If the Kaiserhof had been a place for the bourgeois traveler to find privacy and peace, the Central provided stimulation and diversion.[62]

Entertainments and technologies at the Central attracted attention from critics and journalists. The Central's promise of steam heat (newsworthy in a city where people relied on coal ovens to warm individual rooms), advanced ventilation systems, generous numbers of toilets and baths, and such in-room amenities as sleeping nooks and built-in closets all signaled the capacity of the Central to provide the latest comforts. Critics touted it as "a hotel in the English and American style," equal "in scale, splendor, and comfort" to the grand hotels of "London, New York, and Paris." The "magnificent Wintergarten," moreover, made the Central "one of a kind," casting its "shadow over all things similar now in existence."[63] Publicists interpreted the Central as a promising entry in the imaginary contest of whose capital had the best grand hotels.

Berlin welcomed six more grand hotels before 1900, all in the city center. Most of those properties not founded by corporations were acquired by them in short order. Each hotel struck its own balance between models: the Central, the archetypal *Passantenhotel*, oriented to business travelers, and the Kaiserhof, the urban *Familienhotel*, oriented to the leisured class. The second such *Familienhotel* to arrive was the Hotel Continental (1885), with its "noble, peaceful, and comfortable accommodations in the immediate vicinity of the Central Station," wrote one reviewer.[64] When the hotel opened, the suites – full-fledged apartments, many with their own bathrooms and toilets – were the finest in Berlin. In private hands for its first five years, the Continental transferred to the Berlin Hotel Corporation, the Kaiserhof's parent company, in 1890. In 1891, the Lindenhof (Unter den Linden Real Estate Corporation) presented a different approach, with a greater area devoted to public space at the expense of rooms, by incorporating a variety theater and 1,000-seat café. Next came the Bristol, opened the same year by the competing Hotel Management Corporation, owner of the Central. The Bristol would appeal to worldly travelers and local elites, who flocked to the hotel's so-called American Bar. Two years later, in 1893, the Savoy distinguished itself with a sumptuously outfitted "conversation area" (*Unterhaltungsbereich*) intended

---

[62] Wenzel, *Palasthotels*, 156.

[63] "Central-Hôtel," *Illustrirte Zeitung* (Leipzig) 107 (1879), 480, quoted in Wenzel, *Palasthotels*, 160.

[64] "Berliner Neubauten: Das Hôtel Continental zu Berlin," *Deutsche Bauzeitung* 20 (1886), 37.

for Berlin's rich and powerful.[65] By the mid-1890s, a variegated, robust grand hotel scene had coalesced in the city center, offering fertile ground for the bourgeoisie's pursuit of luxury.[66]

The next wave of hotel building, in the early 1900s, occurred to the southwest of previous developments, around the Potsdam and Anhalt stations, in the direction of a new city center some three miles farther west. From the southeastern corner of the Tiergarten (Berlin's central park), where Potsdamer Platz joined major east–west and north–south thoroughfares, there was easy access to the fashionable west, the city's largest railroad stations, and its central districts. Finally, the area bordered Berlin's most elite residences between the southern frontier of the Tiergarten and the northern bank of the Landwehr Canal. New grand hotels bridged the gap between this leafy quarter and the raucous economy of pleasure and leisure nearby: the myriad theaters, beer halls, restaurants, and shops of Potsdamer Platz and Leipziger Straße.[67] A cruising ground and sexual marketplace, this was also a zone of illicit pleasures.[68]

Between 1898 and 1913, four grand hotels replaced many of the smaller hostelries in the neighborhood. Most of these new grand hotels followed the Kaiserhof model: rarified, quiet, and somewhat smaller than *Passantenhotels* such as the Central. The exception to this rule was the Excelsior, the largest hotel in Berlin to date, built across the street from Anhalt station between 1906 and 1908. Even bigger after a 1913 expansion, the property contained 550 guest rooms, cavernous public spaces, multiple restaurants, generous anterooms, and a sweeping ballroom.[69] Here was a *Passantenhotel* at its grandest, twice the size of the Central. Until 1945 the Excelsior remained the largest hotel in Germany, and possibly the largest on the European continent.[70]

---

[65] Savoy Hotel promotional book, n.p., n.d., ca. 1893, in Historisches Archiv für Tourismus (hereafter HAT) D060/11/01/900/SAV.

[66] Knoch, *Grandhotels*, 281–301.

[67] Dieter Radicke, "Verkehrsentwicklung und Suburbanisierung durch Villenvororte: Berlin, 1871–1914," in Reif, *Berliner Villenleben*, 50–52.

[68] On pleasure/danger, see Miles Ogborn, *Spaces of Modernity: London's Geographies, 1860–1780* (New York: Guilford, 1998); Joachim Schlör, *Nights in the Big City: Paris, London, Berlin, 1840–1930*, trans. Pierre Gottfried Imhof and Dafydd Rees Roberts (Chicago: University of Chicago Press, 1998); Rappaport, *Shopping for Pleasure*, 4ff.; Judith R. Walkowitz, "The 'Vision of Salome': Cosmopolitanism and Erotic Dancing in Central London, 1908–1918," *American Historical Review* 108 (2003), 340–41.

[69] Wenzel, *Palasthotels*, 307.

[70] Land register entry for the Hotel Excelsior, Königgrätzer Straße 112–113, Anhaltstraße 6–7, in LAB A Pr. Br. Rep. 030-07, Nr. 626; *Katalog der Bibliothek des Hotel Excelsior* (Berlin: Hotel Excelsior, 1926), in the archival collection of the Preußischer

In contrast stood the Palast-Hotel, which had opened in 1893 with 100 rooms, 15 baths, a wine distributor, a banquet hall, a smoking room, and a restaurant. This intimacy was belied by the bombast of the facade, however, which faced two of Berlin's most trafficked squares. As viewed from the apex of the V-shaped structure, the Palast-Hotel appeared in its promotional postcards to offer immediate access to the rush of Potsdamer Platz as it emptied into Budapester Straße. The Brandenburg Gate and Reichstag stood in the background, and off to the right peeked a corner of the octagonal expanse of Leipziger Platz.[71] Advertisements emphasized bustle and calm, centrality and retreat, conspicuousness and exclusivity – the best of all worlds.

Next came the Fürstenhof, facing the Palast at the bottleneck separating Potsdamer and Leipziger Platz and built in 1905–6 as an elaborate extension to an extant hostelry. The balconied facade, a baroque and Jugendstil pastiche, was the longest of all the city's hotels so far (Figure 1.7). The ground floor contained several shops, two full-service restaurants, an automat diner, a café, and a cake shop, as well as the requisite common spaces: the ladies' common area, smoking and writing rooms, and a garden court. Upstairs, the placement of closets on the hallway side of each of the hotel's 300 guest rooms reduced sound, offered ample storage space for the personal possessions of longer-term residents, and provided a barrier between the private and public lives of hotel guests. Finally, and perhaps most appealingly, the Fürstenhof boasted the highly favorable guestroom-to-bathroom ratio of 3:1, boosting the hotel's popularity among American tourists.[72] Yet Aschinger's Incorporated (Aschinger's Aktien-Gesellschaft), the corporation that built and owned the Fürstenhof as well as dozens of fast-food cafés for working-class Berliners, did not see a profit from this venture into elite commercial hospitality for at least a decade.

Aschinger's annual reports provide uncommonly detailed accounts of how the corporation financed the construction of its first grand hotel, and

Kulturbesitz – Staatsbibliothek zu Berlin, Unter den Linden Ao 5710/10; front page of the *Excelsior-Zeitung* of November 1, 1929, a publication produced by the hotel, in LAB A Rep. 225, Nr. 908; and frequent advertisements in the 1920s in foreign papers, such as *Le Matin* (Paris) and the *Daily Mail* (London), clipped and collated in LAB A Rep. 225, Nr. 643.

[71] Guest brochure produced for the Palast-Hotel, n.d, ca. 1911, and a promotional postcard, postmarked 1911, in LAB A Rep. 225, Nr. 345.

[72] Tax estimates for 1909, prepared by accountants for Aschinger's Incorporated, in LAB A Rep. 225, Nr. 1175; Otto Sarrazin and Friedrich Schulze, "Hotel Adlon in Berlin," *Zentralblatt der Bauverwaltung* 28 (1908), 416.

„Der Fürstenhof"
Aschinger's Act.-Ges.
Potsdamer Platz

FIGURE 1.7 Promotional postcard for the Hotel Fürstenhof, ca. 1910
Image credit: author's collection

it is in the details that the pitfalls of capital-intensive, speculative investment in early-twentieth-century Berlin become most clear.[73] Although the board blamed conservative trade policies and the burdens of a series of fiscal reforms, which fell heavily on the commercial sector, the corporation's weakness was mostly a product of its foolhardy forays into the securities and real estate markets.[74]

When Aschinger's incorporated in 1900, its board used the influx of capital to raise even more capital through speculation on the stock exchanges. Scarcely a year later, in 1901, stock prices collapsed, and Aschinger's lay exposed to serious risk.[75] The corporation now found itself having leveraged assets – stocks that had now lost much of their value – to make large investments in Berlin real estate for use as workers' cafés, some of which took years to open. Moreover, revenues at existing

[73] Annual reports of Aschinger's Incorporated for the years 1901–10, in LAB A Rep. 225, Nr. 634, and 1911–14, in LAB A Rep. 225, Nr. 139.

[74] On resentments, policies, and reforms, see Sheehan, *German Liberalism*, 121; Niek Koning, *The Failure of Agrarian Capitalism: Agrarian Politics in the United Kingdom, Germany, the Netherlands and the USA, 1846–1919* (London: Routledge, 1994), 101, 108, 142–44; Caroline Fohlin, *Finance Capitalism and Germany's Rise to Power* (Cambridge: Cambridge University Press, 2006), 23–43.

[75] "Germany (from Our Own Correspondent)," *The Economist* 60 (April 5, 1902), 534.

cafés began to slip as early as 1901, when national rates of unemployment among industrial workers more than tripled and the purchasing
power of that class diminished. Although joblessness declined in 1902,
the rate of unemployment remained higher than it had been in 1900.[76]
Still, Aschinger's charged ahead in 1905 with plans to purchase the
Leipziger Hof hotel and transform it into the city's most luxurious hostelry to date.

The Fürstenhof hotel project nearly bankrupted the corporation.
According to the board, "the multiple and incessant stoppages among
the construction workers" at the site of the nascent hotel were to blame
and had accounted for the eight-month delay in opening the premises to
customers. The cost of stoppages notwithstanding, it is extraordinary
that developers such as Aschinger's, in an era of stormy labor relations,
would be caught unawares by the objections of labor unions to having
so many men work for so little pay on what was shaping up to be a ver-
itable pleasure palace for the world's elites. Even more extraordinary is
that Aschinger's fashioned a construction budget so tight that an eight-
month delay could result in a 60 percent drop in profits when, in fact,
the corporation's main areas of revenue were not supposed to be the new
hotel but rather, café concessions and rents on retail spaces throughout
the city.[77] The managing directors had in effect robbed the corporation's
profitable enterprises in order to pay for their own imprudent speculation
and real estate acquisitions dating back to 1901. They deflected criticism
by shifting the blame to political adversaries, in this case the socialists
and workers, a move some of the very same men would repeat after
World War I. A longer-term problem for Aschinger's was the competition, which intensified mere months into the Fürstenhof's first year. The
Adlon and Esplanade – on a per-bed basis, two of the most expensive
hotels ever built – were ready for business almost as soon as the Fürstenhof welcomed its first guests.

The Adlon owed much of its resounding success to its location at the
corner of Unter den Linden and Pariser Platz, next to the Academy of Art
and steps from the British and French embassies, the Brandenburg Gate,
and the Reichstag. For decades, the site had accommodated the Palais
Redern, whose facade had been redesigned by Karl Friedrich Schinkel.
When plans emerged for the destruction of the palace and its replacement

---

[76] Table 18 in Volker R. Berghahn, *Modern Germany: Society, Economy and Politics in
the Twentieth Century*, 2nd ed. (Cambridge: Cambridge University Press, 1987), 284.
[77] Annual report of Aschinger's Incorporated for the years 1907 and 1906.

with yet another grand hotel, a debate broke out in the city's dailies. Eventually, however, the weight of opinion tipped in favor of the project, particularly after the emperor gave it public support.[78]

So, a new building, largely financed on the credit of restaurateur and hotelier Lorenz Adlon himself, went up at this desirable address. (The property also incorporated the Hotel Reichshof, on a rear lot facing Wilhelmstraße.) Most of the building was five stories high, and it extended south and east from fronts on Pariser Platz and Unter den Linden respectively. The ground level sported rusticated stone around large arched bays. Above, half columns, generous windows, balconies of stone and iron, and relief sculptures graced the first through fourth stories. At the top, a sloping roof loomed behind an iron balustrade. The whole was sober and understated, in keeping with the clean lines of the Brandenburg Gate across the square and a classic, older Prusso-Hohenzollern commitment to austerity and restraint.[79]

In degree and kind, the Adlon distinguished itself from all other grand hotels. It was indeed magnificent. A tamed rendition of the Louis XVI idiom reigned throughout, each element of interior design personally overseen by the famed furniture designers and interior decorators Wilhelm Kimbel and Anton Pössenbacher.[80] The interior palm garden, open all winter, balanced the ostentation of mosaic floors and a giant skylight with informal, low-slung wooden chairs. In the reception hall, simple furnishings and a white coffered ceiling mitigated the impact of a splendid staircase clad in bold carpet and colorful marble. In the American Bar, a heavy, dark ceiling presided over the simple, clean lines of wood panels and light parquet. And the Beethoven Parlor, with its ebony columns and heavy ornamentation, welcomed light by way of oversized French doors (Figure 1.8). The effect there and throughout was a harmonious, balanced whole.[81]

For privacy and quiet, rooms incorporated sleeping alcoves, a double set of doors, and concrete walls.[82] For hygiene and convenience, most

[78] "Das Hotel Adlon am Pariser Platz," *Deutsche Bauzeitung* 41 (1907), 693–94.

[79] "Ein amerikanischer Kunstkritiker über Berlin und New-York" *Deutsche Bauzeitung* 21 (1886), 2; Max Landsberg, "Eine interessante Anregung für eine Umgestaltung des Leipziger Platzes in Berlin," *Berliner Illustrirte Zeitung* 22 (1913), 288. See also Walther Rathenau, "Die schönste Stadt der Welt," *Die Zukunft* 26 (1899), 39.

[80] See Afra Schick, *Möbel für den Märchenkönig: Ludwig II. und die Münchener Hofschreinerei Anton Pössenbacher* (Stuttgart: Arnold, 2003); Felix Becker, *Allgemeines Lexikon der bildenden Künstler von der Antike bis zur Gegenwart* (Leipzig: Seemann, 1927), s.v. "Wilhelm Kimbel," 20:309.

[81] Wilhelm Michel, "Das Hotel Adlon in Berlin," *Innen-Dekoration* 19 (1908), 6.

[82] "Hotel Adlon in Berlin," *Zentralblatt der Bauverwaltung* 28 (1908), 417.

FIGURE 1.8 The Beethoven Parlor at the Adlon, 1908
Image credit: Innen-Dekoration/*Staatsbibliothek zu Berlin*

rooms connected to private bathrooms of marble tile, porcelain amenities, and nickel fixtures (Figure 1.9).[83] For space and in the service of domesticity, apartments were available along the Unter den Linden front. With its well-appointed rooms, tasteful yet luxurious spaces, and prime location, the Adlon soon became the favorite of diplomats, royals, aristocrats, and American society mavens. The emperor himself frequented the establishment and chose to house his personal and state guests there. (The court paid a yearly fee for privileged access, which even His Majesty could not expect to enjoy for free.)[84] Louis Adlon capitalized on this association with the court by letting it be known that he had instructed his chef de reception to rent rooms to Germans only if they were of noble or royal blood.[85] It is doubtful he meant for that instruction to be heeded; the point was to advertise the Adlon's exclusivity, which served to increase its popularity among titled and nontitled alike.

---

[83] Michel, "Das Hotel Adlon in Berlin," 51.

[84] Wenzel, *Palasthotels*, 213.

[85] Cf. Hedda Adlon, *Hotel Adlon: Das Berliner Hotel, in dem die große Welt zu Gast war* (Munich: Barrie, 1958), 8.

FIGURE 1.9 En suite bathroom at the Hotel Adlon, 1908
Image credit: Innen-Dekoration/*Staatsbibliothek zu Berlin*

Yet even if the origins, ethos, and clientele of the grand hotels remained predominantly bourgeois, aristocrats had participated in the scene as guests, diners, and socializers since the beginning. And then in the twentieth century, aristocrats began to invest in hotels of their own.

Shares in the German Hotel Corporation (Deutsche Hotel-Gesellschaft), which built the Esplanade between 1907 and 1908, were owned largely by members of such family lines as Hohenlohe, Fürstenberg, and Henckel-Donnersmarck.

The German Hotel Corporation conceived of, outfitted, and priced the Esplanade to appeal to the aristocracy and upper reaches of the commercial bourgeoisie, making it the city's most exclusive hotel. Innovations for Berlin included the availability of handsome conference rooms for business travelers and elite Berliners, the use of electric bells for summoning servants, and the provision of a separate building for accommodating hotel staff. The designation of sixty rooms for household servants accompanying guests, moreover, endeared the Esplanade to the very wealthy and the landed.[86] The building materials themselves signaled riches: marble floors extended to many of the guest rooms, exotic woods clad the high walls, and oriental rugs muffled the footfalls of hundreds.[87] Like the Fürstenhof, the Esplanade had cost too much, but unlike Aschinger's, the Esplanade's owner, the German Hotel Corporation, had few other sources of revenue to support its adventure in commercial hospitality. The corporation went into partial receivership in 1913 and then liquidation in 1919.[88]

HOTEL HIERARCHIES

The public spaces, guest rooms, and guest lists of the Esplanade, the Adlon, and the other grand hotels dazzled contemporaries and can dazzle us still – blinding us, in effect, to these businesses' important function as liberal institutions of class domination. Upstairs was a lavish and expensive show of free association among rational, well-behaved, well-dressed individuals of means. To stage it, architects, hotel owners, and managers directed that most of the stagehands, ropes, and winches be concealed in the wings, the loft, and under the stage itself. This is where the majority of people in the grand hotel could be found: in the dark, at their workstations. To keep these people in thrall, the managers forged

---

[86] Wenzel, *Palasthotels*, 226, 306.

[87] "Das Hotel Esplanade in Berlin," *Deutsche Bauzeitung* 47 (1913), 777, 780–81; Damm-Etienne, *Hotelwesen*, 61–62.

[88] Robert Liefmann, *Beteiligungs- und Finanzierungsgesellschaften: Eine Studie über den modernen Effektenkapitalismus in Deutschland, den Vereinigten Staaten, der Schweiz, England, Frankreich und Belgien*, 3rd ed. (Jena: Gustav Fischer, 1921), 175; Lothar Gall et al., *Die Deutsche Bank, 1870–1995* (Munich: C. H. Beck, 1995), 137.

and maintained elaborate hierarchies – interlocking chains of command that complemented the grand hotels' architectural delineations of space, class, and power.

Grand hotel hierarchies had three genealogies: older modes of aristocratic authority over household workers, newer bourgeois distinctions between public and private, and the social relations of modern industrial techniques of exploitation. Hotel managers assembled these traditions into a model of efficiency and equilibrium that might counter the dangers of social heterogeneity in the hotels and the district surrounding them. As a project, the grand hotel illuminates another side of urban modernity. Behind the great new commercial enterprise stood a managerial class that by turns attempted to reproduce, refigure, and even concretize the power relations and distinctions among the classes.[89] In microcosm, Berlin's grand hotels reveal nothing less than the architectural and managerial mechanisms of bourgeois power in urban, Imperial Germany.[90]

Among managers and architects, the managerial class of Berlin's grand hotels, certain tendencies emerged. First, managers and architects had a conciliatory relationship to the aristocracy. They sought and received honorary titles from royalty.[91] And like royalty, managers were transnational. They did stints all over Europe and beyond. These foreign sojourns, and the language skills they afforded, became necessary ingredients of a successful career.[92] Architects, too, traveled throughout Europe as part of their training. Both architects and managers read widely in foreign and international trade publications. Yet, managers and architects differed in their educational paths and in the social positions that those educations helped determine. Managers attended vocational high schools before accepting apprenticeships or internships. Their instruction was practical, practicality being a central value of the commercial bourgeoisie, the subclass to which managers belonged.[93] Architects, on the other hand, were members of the educated bourgeoisie (*Bildungsbürgertum*), and usually attended a classical high school (*Gymnasium*) before going on to earn

---

[89] On such authorities (*Obrigkeit*) in German political culture, see James Retallack, *The German Right, 1860–1920: Political Limits of the Authoritarian Imagination* (Toronto: University of Toronto Press, 2006), 13–14.

[90] On the grand hotel as a microcosm, see Justin Kaplan, *When the Astors Owned New York: Blue Bloods and Grand Hotels in the Gilded Age* (New York: Viking, 2006), 17.

[91] Police files on the hoteliers Hubert Schaurté and Leopold Schwarz, in LAB A Pr. Br. Rep. 030, Nr. 13390 and 13495.

[92] Job applications for the position of hotel manager at the Fürstenhof, n.d., ca. 1919, LAB A Rep. 225, Nr. 1143.

[93] Blackbourn and Evans, *German Bourgeoisie*, 6–7.

certifications from such prestigious state architecture schools as the Berlin Bauakademie (Academy of Architecture).[94] The architects of Berlin's first two grand hotels, Hude and Hennicke, attended the Bauakademie in the 1850s before co-founding their own firm in 1860.[95] To realize their creations, they regularly partnered with members of the commercial bourgeoisie. The fruits of such partnerships, grand hotels were a field in which the commercial and educated bourgeoisies collaborated. Inside these hotels, a general pattern, based on the fusion of operating principles of factories, armies, and great households, existed by the 1870s.

In his 1874 textbook for "hoteliers, architects, managers, and hotel company shareholders," Guyer supplied a chart specifying ideal hierarchies for three different types of hotels: the "seasonal," such as a seaside property, usually in "private" hands; the "year-round" hotel, such as the Kaiserhof, usually in the hands of a joint-stock company (*Actienhotel*); and the spa resort (*Curetablissement*), also corporate. Italicized letters in the chart connoted a particular office's rank (*Rangstufe*), a term that harked to the organization of the military or the palace. A further level of distinction was that between "inner" and "outer" departments (*départements*). The outer comprised employees who dealt directly with outsiders (*Fremden*) – that is, guests and vendors. Hence, members of the outer department included porters, concierges, and waiters. The inner department contained everybody else: maids and maintenance workers, laundresses, cellar workers, and kitchen staff. On the management and maintenance of the hierarchies within each department, Guyer advised that regulations and distinctions of rank and role (*Reglement* and *Dienstordnung*) be "binding."[96]

The 1874 original and the revised, expanded edition of 1885 evinced the same understanding of hierarchy as fixed and nonnegotiable. The goal was a closed universe in which distinctions of rank, class, and gender were more solid than the outside world could achieve.[97] Labor agitation

---

[94] On architects' place in the educated bourgeoisie, see Vincent Clark, "A Struggle for Existence: The Professionalization of German Architects," in *German Professions, 1800–1950*, eds. Geoffrey Cocks and Konrad H. Jarausch (New York: Oxford University Press, 1990), 143–62; Anna Guagnini, "Technology," in *A History of the University in Europe*, ed. Walter Rüegg (Cambridge: Cambridge University Press, 2004), 603.

[95] Eva Börsch-Supan, *Berliner Baukunst nach Schinkel, 1840–1870* (Munich: Prestel, 1977), 582, 597.

[96] Guyer, *Hotelwesen*, vi, ix, 171–72, 217–31.

[97] On women and factory work, see Mary Nolan, "Economic Crisis, State Policy, and Working-Class Formation in Germany, 1870–1900," in *Working-Class Formation: Nineteenth-Century Patterns in Western Europe and the United States*, eds. Ira

and intraclass animosities that so cleaved European societies outside should have little meaning in the hotel, where owners, architects, and managers had built the system and created the patterns by which it had to run. This hierarchy, based on the application of the productive division of labor to the enterprise of commercial hospitality, in theory was supposed to be unshakable.

The hierarchy depended upon the ability of hotel managers to oversee the actions and interactions of hotel workers. Indeed, Guyer went so far as to claim that the main role of the manager was to maintain "a total overview" of the business. His gaze should easily capture disciplinary infractions, according to a sample list of rules that encoded sharp distinctions of rank in dress, comportment, access to space, and rights. The rules circumscribed workers' physical appearance ("Every employee should always be dressed neatly and appropriately to his station"), access to spaces ("Loitering in the staircases, corridors, in front of the hotel entrance, and particularly in the kitchen and cellar ... is forbidden"), and personal liberty most generally ("Going out without special permission is prohibited").[98] Guyer's proscriptions distilled a familiar formula for social stratification by assembling men, women, and youths of all social levels under one roof, in one self-contained enterprise.

At the apex of the hotel hierarchy sat the owners (usually on a corporate board), the managing directors appointed by that board, and the individual hotel managers hired by those managing directors. Owners and managing directors were entrepreneurial men of property such as Lorenz Adlon or skilled businessmen such as Hans Lohnert (the managing director of Aschinger's Incorporated). Managing directors at this corporate level oversaw managers of particular hotels. These on-site managers, in turn, oversaw the day-to-day operation of the business. The on-site manager served as the public face of the property, his name often gracing letterheads, brochures, and hotel menus.[99] Many of these

Katznelson and Aristide R. Zolberg (Princeton: Princeton University Press, 1986), 360–62; Karin Hausen, "Family and Role-Division: The Polarisation of Sexual Stereotypes in the Nineteenth Century – An Aspect of the Dissociation of Work and Family Life," in *The German Family: Essays on the Social History of the Family in Nineteenth- and Twentieth-Century Germany*, eds. Richard J. Evans and W. Robert Lee (London: Routledge, 1981), 51–83; Kathleen Canning, "Social Policy, Body Politics: Recasting the Social Question in Germany," in *Gender and Class in Modern Europe*, eds. Sonya Rose and Laura Frader (Ithaca, NY: Cornell University Press, 1996), 219–29.

[98] Guyer, *Hotelwesen*, 140, 175–76.

[99] Brochure and menu for the Palast-Hotel, n.d., ca. 1911, in LAB A Rep. 225, Nr. 345; letterhead of the Monopol-Hotel dated May 15, 1897, in LAB A Pr. Br. Rep. 030, Nr.

managers received honors from the emperor, sharing them with the hotel itself in the form of the moniker *Hoflieferant* (purveyor to the court). Titles from other royal houses extended managers' prestige still further. Moritz Matthäi of the Kaiserhof accepted from the King of Saxony the Knight's Cross Second Class of the Order of Albrecht in 1899. Leopold Schwarz of the smaller Reichshof got the Order of the Siamese Crown from Prince Chakrabongse in 1906 for service to this personal guest of the German emperor.[100] Royal honors as a confirmation of status contributed to the health of a hotel's business.[101] More effective than these honors, however, was a publicized personal friendship with the emperor himself. Only Lorenz Adlon enjoyed this distinction, and his hotel benefitted accordingly.

Distinctions mattered to individual hotel managers, many of whom before 1900 had risen from the ranks of the petty bourgeoisie, working class, or even peasantry. Emil Vollborth, for example, born in 1854, started as a waiter. He learned several languages, became a regular contributor to the trade publication *Gasthofs-Gehilfen-Kalender* (Hospitality Employees' Digest), and published several booklets on gastronomy. He worked his way from waiter to headwaiter at hotels in Stettin and Pichelsdorf (near Berlin) before acquiring a building at Wilhelmstraße 44. There, Vollborth opened a hotel with thirty rooms and an apartment for himself, where he spent the rest of what appears to have been a comfortable, middle-class life.[102]

Eduard Gutscher, one of the last to climb to the top, spent time at several intermediary rungs on the ladder before he could be master of the business. Stints as a waiter in London and Paris solidified his command of English and French. Once in Berlin, Gutscher persuaded the Hotel Bristol to take him on as a secretary in the manager's office. In 1899, he moved up and over to the Palast-Hotel to be its chef de reception, one of the

13390, f. 11; newspaper advertisement for the Hotel Schaurté-Westminster, *Berliner Lokal-Anzeiger*, August 13, 1910, in LAB A Pr. Br. Rep. 030, Nr. 13390, f. 47; bill form from the Hotel Schaurté-Westminster, n.d., ca. 1910, in LAB A Pr. Br. Rep. 030, Nr. 13390, f. 53.

[100] Leopold Schwarz to the Berlin Police Presidium, November 7, 1906, in LAB A Pr. Br. Rep. 030, Nr. 13495.

[101] On commodifying the monarchy in this way, see Eva Giloi, *Monarchy, Myth, and Material Culture in Germany, 1750–1950* (Cambridge: Cambridge University Press, 2011), 326; Frank Lorenz Müller, *Our Fritz: Emperor Frederick III and the Political Culture of Imperial Germany* (Cambridge, MA: Harvard University Press, 2011), 270.

[102] Berlin Police Presidium to the Office of the High Marshal of the Court (Oberhofmarschall-Amt), December 20, 1901, in LAB A Pr. Br. Rep. 030, Nr. 13979, f. 20.

highest-ranking posts. Two years later, he stepped in as the hotel's new manager and lessee. An erstwhile waiter from Graz, Gutscher now presided over 130 employees and enjoyed an annual income of 26,000 marks.[103]

Those managers born after Gutscher, however, and coming of age in the early twentieth century, tended to come from the commercial bourgeoisie and thus started their careers with white-collar work. Max Dörhöfer, for example, was born to a hotelier and wine merchant in Rüdesheim am Rhein in 1883, attended vocational high school, completed a certificate program in hotel management, worked in white-collar positions across Europe and in Cairo, ran the family hotel business, and then assumed the position of manager for a world-famous hotel.[104] Dörhöfer's trajectory is representative of this second generation of hotel managers who were born into the commercial middle class and were fitted for the work through formal, costly training.[105] Evidence of class mobility among hotel managers disappears for the period after 1900.

At the next level down stood restaurant managers. These men tended to rise from the rank of waiter to that of headwaiter. Andreas Nett's career is typical. Born in the 1870s in Fürth, he traveled to London in 1895 to work as a waiter at the Langham Hotel, a position he held for two years.[106] Nett then assumed posts as sommelier in Paris and Switzerland.[107] He returned to service as a waiter shortly thereafter, this time in Bad Kreuznach and then Zurich.[108] Finally, in the 1900s, he attained the position of manager at the Café-Restaurant Bristol of the Hôtel de l'Europe in Munich.[109] A move to Berlin in the early 1910s resulted in a

---

[103] Berlin Police Presidium to the Marshal of the Court of Saxony (Großherzerzogliches Sächsisches Hofmarschallamt), April 7, 1905, in LAB A Pr. Br. Rep. 030, Nr. 10359.

[104] Max Dorhöfer to Aschinger's Incorporated, letter including a curriculum vitae, n.d., ca. 1919, in LAB A Rep. 225, Nr. 1143.

[105] On apprenticeship and the bourgeois family, see Jürgen Kocka, "The Entrepreneur, the Family and Capitalism: Some Examples from the Early Phase of Industrialisation in Germany," in *German Yearbook on Business History 1981*, eds. Wolfram Engels et al., (West Berlin: Springer, 1981), 59.

[106] Reference from Walter Gosden, manager of the Langham Hotel, London, March 15, 1897, in LAB A Rep. 225, Nr. 797.

[107] Reference from the manager of the Hôtel d'Iéna, Paris, June 30, 1898, in LAB A Rep. 225, Nr. 797; reference from the manager of the Hôtel Bonivard, Veytaux-Chillon, Switzerland, May 10, 1899, in LAB A Rep. 225, Nr. 797.

[108] Reference from W. Reichardt, manager of the Hotel & Badehaus Kauzenberg, Bad Kreuznach, September 28, 1899, in LAB A Rep 225, Nr. 797; reference from F. A. Pohl, manager of the Grand Hôtel-Pension Bellevue au Lac, Zurich, March 28, 1900, in LAB A Rep. 225, Nr. 797.

[109] Reference from Elise Schmöller, owner of the Hôtel de l'Europe, Munich, April 17, 1901, in LAB A Rep. 225, Nr. 797.

slight demotion: There, Nett worked for larger, more prestigious establishments but again as a waiter and headwaiter.[110] At two points, though,
Nett managed to secure white-collar hotel work, first as a secretary at the
Hôtel de la Ville de Paris in Strasbourg and then as an accountant at the
Grand Nouvel Hôtel in Lyon.[111] Neither of these stints as a supervisor
kept Nett from service for long, however, nor did they win him promotion to the higher managerial levels of the hotel hierarchy. Those posts
were now reserved for Nett's social betters, men who had never been
waiters.

Waiters, nonetheless, occupied pride of place as the highest-ranked
members of a hotel-restaurant's service apparatus. While their earnings
were on a par, waiters maintained strict hierarchical distinctions among
themselves. At the top stood the headwaiters (*Oberkellner*). These were
always men, normally without children. Their pay and their hours discouraged the establishment of a family, and employers avoided hiring
and retaining family men. Job advertisements requested that a prospective headwaiter be single, as well as "presentable, solvent, experienced,
and conscientious."[112]

Below these masters of service and next in the chain of command were
the staff waiters. Like the headwaiter, staff waiters had to have a command of European languages. "Perfect" French and English were a must.
And only well-turned-out men needed apply. Next came the sommeliers,
and then the floor waiters (*Etagenkellner*), who assisted the headwaiter.
Floor waiters and sommeliers were not necessarily novices. Job advertisements stressed that they should have had experience in one of the
"bigger houses" before taking on work at one of Berlin's grand hotels.[113]
Another category of server, room waiters (*Zimmerkellner*), fell under the
supervision of the floor waiters and provided what we now call room
service. With some experience, room waiters tended to be younger than
their bosses, the floor waiters, and strived for promotion.

---

[110] Reference from M. Kempinski & Co., Berlin, March 20, 1907, in LAB A Rep. 225, Nr.
797; reference from the Weinhaus "Zum Rüdesheimer," Berlin, December 1, 1910, in
LAB A Rep. 225, Nr. 797.

[111] Reference from the Hôtel de la Ville de Paris, Strasbourg, August 1, 1903, in LAB A
Rep. 225, Nr. 797; reference from the Grand Nouvel Hôtel, Lyon, September 16, 1903,
in LAB A Rep. 225, Nr. 797.

[112] From a supplement to the *Wochenschrift des Internationalen Hotelbesitzer-Vereins*,
April 20, 1907, in the Schweizerisches Wirtschaftsarchiv, Basel (hereafter SWA), B Verb.
E10. The terms and gradations for waiters varied slightly across the German-speaking
world.

[113] Ibid.

Neophytes crowded the lowest level of the wait staff. These were the apprentices, teenage boys, often unpaid, who rendered their unskilled services for anywhere from six months to two years. These boys did most of the manual work, delivering and clearing china and glassware, disposing of detritus, assembling trays, and performing any and all other services that headwaiters, staff waiters, floor waiters, and sommeliers required. For these boys especially, but for almost everyone working for the gastronomy concessions, hotel service was physically demanding and poorly remunerated, yet it was also a career that held many advantages over factory work and domestic service. For one thing, it allowed some chance of advancement, which factory work and domestic service often precluded.

Hotel service could also pay better than factory and domestic work. At the finest establishments, such as a restaurant specializing in fine wines (*Weinhaus*) in Friedrichstadt around 1910, a waiter could expect to earn 15 marks per month. Tips augmented this income at rates of 10 percent of the bill for exceptional service and petty change in most other cases.[114] (A waiter thus earned between 1 percent and 3 percent of the salary of a corporate managing director, who took home 50,000 marks per year in the years around 1910.[115]) Waiters used their tips to cover regular deductions: a monthly 10 pfennigs for the dishwasher, 30 pfennigs for the cloakroom staff. There were also punitive deductions – one-half of 1 percent of a month's wages for each broken glass, for example – and further financial penalties for lateness or other minor infractions.[116] Yet, becoming a waiter represented an improvement for many career hopefuls, usually born into the peasant or working classes. Fritz Haas, for example, born in Linz around 1860, son of a stonemason, began as a waiter's apprentice and moved up to the position of waiter, a post he held for the rest of his working life.[117]

For white-collar workers, upward mobility was swifter and easier.[118] Their tier in the hierarchy offered several managerial positions into which

---

[114] Ibid.; see also Patricia Van den Eeckhout, "Waiters, Waitresses, and Their Tips in Western Europe before World War I," *International Review of Social History* 60 (2015), 349–78.

[115] Employment contract between Hans Lohnert and the board of directors of Aschinger's Incorporated, March 2, 1911, in LAB A Rep. 225, Nr. 396.

[116] "Kellner-Misere: Die Zustände in den Berliner Restaurants," *Berliner Zeitung*, March 16, 1905.

[117] Managing directors of the Hotel Management Corporation to Fritz Haas, April 14, 1923, in LAB A Rep. 225-01, Nr. 150.

[118] On the upward social mobility of white-collar workers, see Geoff Eley, *From Unification to Nazism: Reinterpreting the German Past* (London: Allen & Unwin, 1986),

a hard-working and lucky secretary could infiltrate. The highest position under the hotel manager was the chef de reception. In many cases, this post was preparation for the assumption of the post of manager. The chef de reception oversaw bookings and enjoyed direct contact with the hotel's most distinguished guests. He was a master of customer service, enabled by a command of European languages, and carried his responsibilities with an easy dignity that signaled a grand hotel's uprightness and elegance.[119] Chefs de reception could earn a good deal of money. The Bristol's Robert Gonné took home 4,200 marks per year in the early twentieth century.[120] Clerks, other accountants and bookkeepers, and lower-level managers of the kitchens and cellars came next. Finally, there were female office workers and female members of the lower managerial staff, who earned little more than waiters and occupied the lowest level of the white-collar hierarchy.

But many people working *in* the hotel were not *of* the hotel. Corporations leased several of their concessions to sole proprietors (*Pachtträger*). These were the ticket, flower, and cigar sellers, barbers and hairdressers, barkeeps, café owners, automat supervisors, porters, and cloakroom managers. Cloakrooms were typically leased to women. Martha Windisch held the cloakroom concession at the Fürstenhof at a monthly cost of about 830 marks in 1913. With it, she earned enough money to pay for an apartment in the fashionable west, on Lützowstraße. Windisch's lease required that her cloakroom attendants, girls visible behind a window in the vestibule, be representatives of the hotel, even if they were not its employees. "Politeness" and "courtesy" were essential. "Only personnel of handsome and clean appearance" would do. Moreover, these hirelings had to be women, wear a uniform, respond to guests' wishes, demand no tips, and above all, respect their "social betters," as the lease put it.[121] In such terms, the Fürstenhof and its parent company, Aschinger's Incorporated, maintained control over the cloakroom personnel. Yet at the same time, the corporation could

237–38; Richard J. Evans, "Liberalism and Society: The Feminist Movement and Social Change," in *Society and Politics in Wilhelmine Germany*, ed. Richard J. Evans (London: Routledge, 1976), 197; Peter Bailey, "White Collars, Gray Lives? The Lower Middle Class Revisited," *Journal of British Studies* 38 (1999), 273–90.

[119] Guyer, *Hotelwesen*, 44–46; Damm-Etienne, *Hotelwesen*, 102–3.

[120] Minutes of a meeting of the board of the Hotel Management Corporation, June 10, 1912, in LAB A Rep. 225-01, Nr. 1.

[121] Contract between Martha Windisch and Aschinger's Incorporated, December 21, 1912, in LAB A Rep. 225, Nr. 1162.

claim a steady income from the cloakroom while outsourcing the risks and responsibilities of daily operation.

Like cloakroom girls, porters and pages often worked for a sole pro-prietor lessee, usually the head porter, who employed more than a dozen boys to do the heavy lifting. They wore uniforms and were bound to the house rules of politeness and deference. Boys as young as twelve, and in rare cases younger than that, donned militaristic garb and took orders. While guests were checking in at reception, these boys ticketed the lug-gage and loaded it onto a hydraulic lift that went down, not up. In the cellar, more porters sorted the cases and waited for instructions from the reception desk. Page boys delivered these instructions on tickets that included guests' room numbers and a code or color that matched that of the guest's luggage tag (Figure 1.10). On finding a match, a porter would take the cases in hand and haul them onto a service elevator. At the right floor, another porter would be waiting to take the luggage and rush it to the room of its owner. All this was supposed to happen ahead of the owner's arrival upstairs. Tips were de rigueur but collected in full by the head porter, who first covered his own costs and then distributed the surplus to his staff.

Next came the servants, who acted as personal butlers to several mas-ters at once. Responsible for packing, unpacking, and connecting guests to other concessions in the hotel, servants often delegated tasks to more specialized providers such as floor waiters, messengers, shoe shiners, hairdressers, barbers, seamstresses, and laundresses.[122] Servants tended to be men, and many had been porters or pages first. Most were still young. Only a few women served in this capacity, normally as hired ladies' maids.

Toward the bottom of the hierarchy were the parlor maids, all women. In their late teens and twenties, they worked directly under female house-keepers, the lowest managerial level. These housekeepers earned as much as 60 marks per month, whereas parlor maids could expect 12 to 15 marks and the rare tip.[123] They cleaned rooms, hallways, public spaces, and the servants' areas in the cellar and attic. Like most lower

---

[122] Guyer, *Hotelwesen*, 185–99. On the hair trades, see Svenja Kornher, "Hairdressing around 1900 in Germany: Traditional Male versus Illicit Female Work?" in *Shadow Economies and Irregular Work in Urban Europe: 16th to Early 20th Centuries*, eds. Thomas Buchner and Philip R. Hoffmann-Rehnitz (Berlin: Lit, 2011), 183–96.

[123] Guidelines in a supplement to the *Wochenschrift des Internationalen Hotelbesitzer-Vereins*, April 20, 1907, in SWA, B Verb. E10.

FIGURE 1.10 Page boys at the Elite Hotel, a midsize luxury hostelry in Berlin,
ca. 1910
Image credit: Landesarchiv Berlin

hotel workers, parlor maids slept and ate on the premises and got a half day off every other week.[124] In this way, the life of a parlor maid in one of Berlin's grand hotels resembled that of a parlor maid in a bourgeois household.[125]

Still more women and girls found employ below stairs alongside skilled and unskilled male counterparts (Figures 1.11, 1.12, 1.13, and 1.14). Women cleaned dishes, polished silver, and did laundry with the aid of machinery that increased the speed of work. Slated for the most menial tasks, still more women served as kitchen maids and maids of all work. They labored among better paid men such as engineers, carpenters, furnace stokers (Figure 1.14), and haulers.[126]

Whatever their gender, hotel workers were not as organized as their counterparts in industry, yet a few labor organizations did attend to employment, working conditions, and rights. One such group was the Union of German Hotel Workers (Verband Deutscher Gasthofsgehilfen), founded in Geneva in 1877. A branch operating in Dresden extended to hotel workers in Berlin.[127] The farther-reaching Union of Hospitality and Gastronomy Workers (Verband der Gastwirtsgehilfen), with offices in Berlin, Paris, London, and Antwerp, was another option. Finally, the Ganymede Union Waiters League (Kellner-Bund Union Ganymed), founded in Leipzig in 1878, represented waiters into the twentieth century.[128] These organizations made little progress in the fight for safer working conditions, higher pay, and increased awareness of hotel workers' plight. A replaceable and increasingly mobile workforce, divided by strict distinctions of rank, could not be particularly amenable to arguments for solidarity. Moreover, working conditions varied dramatically from place to place. For every worker in a grand hotel there were many more at lower establishments. These less fortunate men and women, boys and girls, lived in misery. Some slept under staircases or adjacent to coal stores.[129] Their best hope was

---

[124] Damm-Etienne, *Hotelwesen*, 111.
[125] Simon Morgan, "Between Public and Private: Gender, Domesticity, and Authority in the Long Nineteenth Century," *Historical Journal* 54 (2011), 1197–1210; cf. Carolyn Steedman, *Labours Lost: Domestic Service and the Making of Modern England* (Cambridge: Cambridge University Press, 2009), 15.
[126] Guyer, *Hotelwesen*, 172, 217–18, Damm-Etienne, *Hotelwesen*, 76.
[127] "Statut des Verband Deutscher Gasthofsgehilfen," pamphlet of 1901, in LAB A Pr. Br. Rep. 030, Nr. 1723.
[128] Newsletter of the Ganymede Union Waiters League, Leipzig and Berlin, February 1903, in LAB A Pr. Br. Rep. 030, Nr. 1723.
[129] Ibid.

FIGURE 1.11 Women and men at work in the cellar of the Hotel Esplanade, ca. 1915
Image credit: Landesarchiv Berlin

FIGURE 1.12 Cooks in the main kitchen of the Esplanade, one of the first cellar kitchens in a Berlin hotel to feature mechanical ventilation, ca. 1915
Image credit: Landesarchiv Berlin

FIGURE 1.13 Pastry cooks and a sugar sculptor in the Esplanade patisserie, ca. 1915

Image credit: Landesarchiv Berlin

FIGURE 1.14 Furnace stoker at the Esplanade, ca. 1915

Image credit: Landesarchiv Berlin

to find a job at one of the better hotels, where there would at least be a bed, a bath, and enough to eat.

For most hotel workers, finding or keeping a job trumped all other concerns, and it did not necessarily matter whether an employment agency belonged to a labor union or to the employers. An organization in the hands of hotel owners themselves did more to place workers than all the unions combined. The International Association of Hotel Owners (Internationaler Hotelbesitzer-Verein) found hundreds of positions for workers in the early twentieth century. The association's placement rates were favorable: 10 percent of male applicants and 40 percent of female applicants received work in 1906–7.[130] The higher figure for women reflects the difficulty hotel managers had in retaining female workers. In their roles as silver polishers, laundresses, kitchen assistants, and maids, women and girls were exposed to physical dangers at every waking hour, whether from harsh chemicals, poor ventilation, open flames, boiling liquids, or lecherous male guests and staff. Their rates of attrition were high.

Why in all the years between 1875 and 1918 did hotel workers never quite come together to change their situation? The question is misplaced. Because many workers tended to live in the hotel itself and spend almost all their time in workrooms there, managers could enact programs of surveillance through their agents down the hierarchy's chains of command that left workers little privacy, independence, or recourse. Meanwhile, strict divisions among workers themselves – particularly spatial ones – impeded the development even of a common standpoint from which to build a sense of class consciousness and common purpose.[131]

In this system designed and imposed by a managerial cadre, there was no space and no time for resistance.[132] The grand hotel had none of the infrastructures and establishments of working-class community

---

[130] "Stellenvermittlung vom 1. April 1906–31. März 1907," Department of Placement Services (Abtheilung der Stellenvermittlung), International Association of Hotel Owners, n.d., in SWA B Verb. E10.

[131] On the "new microgeography of labor" in hotels, see Sandoval-Strausz, *Hotel*, 269; cf. Michel Foucault, *The History of Sexuality*, vol. 1: *An Introduction*, trans. Robert Hurley (New York: Pantheon, 1978), 95, 103–6; "Governmentality," in *The Foucault Effect: Studies in Governmentality*, eds. Graham Burchell et al., (London: Harvester, 1991), 87–104.

[132] On space and resistance, see Henri Lefebvre, *The Production of Space*, trans. Donald Nicholson-Smith (Oxford: Blackwell, 1992), 17–18; Michel de Certeau, *The Practice of Everyday Life*, trans. Steven Rendall (Berkeley: University of California Press, 1984),

building. There were no taverns where people might spread news and make plans, no apartment block courtyards or working-class boulevards, no communal kitchens or public parks, no street corners for soapboxes.[133] Moreover, when workers in the outside world were fired, they were still living in a community of their former co-workers, who might help them find a new job or even, out of sympathy, engage in everyday forms of resistance.[134] In contrast to fired factory workers, fired hotel workers dropped from existence, disappeared from the universe of the hotel. Perhaps they joined workers' movements wherever they landed, but whatever their style of agitation or resistance, little news of it would come to light in the hotel cellars where they formerly spent their days.

CONCLUSION

Berlin's grand hotel scene developed fast. In 1875, there had been no purpose-built grand hotels in the city. By 1900, there were several. Although smaller and specialty hostelries continued to turn profits and multiply, the grand hotels commanded ever larger market shares at the high end of the social scale. Four factors contributed to this expansion: First, the availability of credit and capital on a limited liability basis ensured that huge, expensive physical plants could be erected and maintained at a lower risk than before. Second, the technologies that such investment and innovation produced allowed grand hotels to offer more than their smaller counterparts ever could. Third, an increasingly mobile bourgeois society produced a growing demand for services and accommodations that only grand hotels could provide. And fourth, the maintenance of strict hierarchies, and hierarchies within hierarchies, kept these large businesses running.

48, 96; Alf Lüdtke, *Eigen-Sinn: Fabrikalltag, Arbeitererfahrung und Politik vom Kaiserreich bis in den Faschismus* (Münster: Westfälisches Dampfboot, 2015); Knoch, *Grandhotels*, 26.

[133] On space and labor organizing, see Thomas Welskopp, *Unternehmen Praxisgeschichte: Historische Perspektiven auf Kapitalismus, Arbeit und Klassengesellschaft* (Tübingen: Mohr Siebeck, 2014), 181–208; Cedric Bolz, "From 'Garden City Precursors' to 'Cemeteries for the Living': Contemporary Discourse on Krupp Housing and *Besucherpolitik* in Wilhelmine Germany," *Urban History* 37 (2010), 113.

[134] Alf Lüdtke, "Organizational Order or *Eigensinn*? Workers' Privacy and Workers' Politics in Imperial Germany," in *Rites of Power: Symbolism, Ritual, and Politics since the Middle Ages*, ed. Sean Wilentz (Philadelphia: Temple University Press, 1985), 303–10.

From an institution conceived to bring people together, bourgeois hotel owners, directors, managers, architects, and designers created a complex that mostly kept them apart. Inequities inside grand hotels mirrored in microcosm classed power relations outside, though with some distortion. The superior control enjoyed by grand hoteliers allowed the grand hotel to flourish as a social system, unimpeded by protest or resistance, well into the twentieth century. It was only in the decade after 1914 that the heterogeneity of grand hotel society became impossible to manage.

2

Managing Heterogeneity

Grand hoteliers in Berlin and elsewhere made it a pillar of their business model to exclude most people. Yet, such exclusivity depended upon the presence of hundreds of working-class people who toiled, ate, and slept in the hotel. Interclass equilibrium rested on the existence of a strict, intricate hierarchy for workers and unspoken norms of dress and comportment for guests, among whom interregional and international equilibria were prerequisite. How was it possible to bring together and sustain equilibrium among such vastly different social groupings, and what does the maintenance of that equilibrium tell us about the nature of bourgeois power in imperial Berlin?

In grand hotels, the classes and nations mixed in higher concentrations than anywhere else except the ocean liner. As on ocean liners, grand hotels offered spaces for the elite exercise of freedom under conditions of staff surveillance and mutual policing on the part of the guests. These practices, facets of the liberal order, continued until August 1914, when everyone – guests, white-collar employees, managers, workers, owners – went to war. Then, and all of a sudden, violence erupted in grand hotel lobbies under the impotent gaze of the chefs de reception. In one blow, World War I shattered the liberal ideal upon which Berlin's grand hotels were founded. That ideal, dependent upon an equilibrium supported by little more than architecture, regulation, and unspoken rules, had serious weaknesses, it turned out.

The tensions had always been there. A postcard from the Hotel Schaurté from around 1900 encapsulates the ironies and contradictions of grand hotel culture in the Wilhelmine era (Figure 2.1).[1] In the foreground, a

---

[1] A similar image appeared atop the hotel's bill forms: LAB A Pr. Br. Rep. 030, Nr. 13390, f. 53.

FIGURE 2.1 Promotional postcard from the Hotel Schaurté, ca. 1900
Image credit: author's collection

military parade traverses the frame, and in the background, a crowd of
spectators is assembled in front of the hotel. Festooned on the beaux-arts
facade (in the French style) are advertisements for a "restaurant français"
and English "grill room," while at the same time a parade of Prussian
and imperial might proceeds down the street. Nationalist and cosmopolitan references perch together here in a delicate balance.[2]

IN THE PLEASURE ZONE

The consumer economy of Friedrichstadt and its environs, Berlin's grand
hotel district, attracted ever larger, more heterogeneous crowds until the

---

[2] On the fragility of cosmopolitanism, see Margaret C. Jacob, *Strangers Nowhere in the
World: The Rise of Cosmopolitanism in Early Modern Europe* (Philadelphia: University
of Pennsylvania Press, 2006), 145.

outbreak of World War I.³ Food was a major draw. The 1904 edition of *Baedeker's* listed dozens of first-class restaurants, including those of the luxury hotels, as well as the wine houses Rheinische Winzerstuben, Eggebrecht, and Zum Rheingau. Down-market options also abounded, especially beer halls for men: Augustinerbräu, Pschorrbräu, Sedlmayr zum Spaten, Weihenstephan, Tucherbräu, Münchener Hofbräu, and Dortmunder Unionbräu. Women tended to frequent the cafés and cake shops (*Konditoreien*). At least one café, Buchholz, had the reputation of being "visited almost exclusively by women." The cafés Viktoria and Kranzler occupied the most prestigious intersection of Friedrichstraße, at the corner of Unter den Linden, while up and down that boulevard, Leipziger Straße, and the side streets lay plush concessions such as the cafés Klose, Reichshallen, and Kaiser.⁴ The neighborhood had been given over to shopping, dining, entertainment, and the sexual commerce attending those activities.⁵

At the northern end of Friedrichstraße, near the station and the Central-Hotel, loomed the grandest bathhouse in Berlin, a gargantuan spa and entertainment establishment. For dry amusement, there were several shopping arcades, including the Kaiser-Galerie, with its panorama, cabaret, and food and fashion concessions.⁶ "The best shops" were in an area comprising Friedrichstraße and Leipziger Straße. There were department stores and stores specializing in jewelry, books, antiques, engravings, furniture, furs, glassware, hats, lace, leather, fabric, perfume, porcelain, silk,

---

³ Peter Jelavich, *Berlin Cabaret* (Cambridge, MA: Harvard University Press, 1993), 93–94.
⁴ *Baedeker's Berlin und Umgebung* (Leipzig: Baedeker's, 1904), 8, 11, 12.
⁵ Licensing applications for bars, cafés, dance locales, and restaurants, 1870s–90s, in LAB A Pr. Br. Rep. 030, Nr. 1580–1584; newspaper clippings and pamphlets, booklet on the proliferation of prostitution in and around Friedrichstraße (n.d., ca. 1860s), an article in the *Staatsbürger Zeitung* of May 9, 1884, supplementary section to the *Real-Encyclopädie der gesammten Heilkunde*, a reference publication for doctors, in LAB A Pr. Br. Rep. 030, Nr. 16927. On Friedrichstadt as a pleasure zone, see Kathleen James, "From Messel to Mendelsohn: German Department Store Architecture in Defence of Urban and Economic Change," in *Cathedrals of Consumption: The European Department Store, 1850–1939*, eds. Geoffrey Crossick and Serge Jaumain (Aldershot: Ashgate, 1999), 256; Jelavich, *Berlin Cabaret*, 93. On prostitution, see Lynn Abrams, "Prostitutes in Imperial Germany, 1870–1918: Working Girls or Social Outcasts?" in *The German Underworld: Deviants and Outcasts in German History*, ed. Richard J. Evans (London: Routledge, 1988), 190–205; Jill Suzanne Smith, *Berlin Coquette: Prostitution and the New German Woman, 1890–1933* (Ithaca, NY: Cornell University Press, 2013), 16–18; On the pleasure zone as a concept, see Rappaport, *Shopping for Pleasure*, 5–7ff.
⁶ Angelika Hoelger, "The History of Popular Culture in Berlin, 1830–1918," (PhD dissertation, Johns Hopkins University, 2011), 171–72, 241; Johann Friedrich Geist, *Die Kaisergalerie: Biographie der Berliner Passage* (Munich: Prestel, 1997), 1.

and underwear. The "Mourning Warehouse" of Otto Weber catered on multiple floors to every stage of public grief.[7] Throughout the district, men, women, and children – consumers and clerks, foreigners and locals, sex workers and bourgeois ladies, aristocrats and thieves – circulated in proximity.[8]

This heterogeneity presented dangers and pleasures alike.[9] Hans Ostwald, editor of the *Großstadt-Dokumente* (Documents of the Metropolis), a massive, multivolume sociology of Berlin, titillated readers with copious description of an urban underworld in plain sight. Moralists complained about prostitutes "openly" plying their "horizontal wares" in ordinary cafés.[10] For their part, the police carefully collected information on the infractions of Friedrichstadt's demimonde.[11] They harassed women circulating through the city, as did barkeeps, café maîtres d', and restaurateurs.[12] Urban reportage and fiction published in both elite and popular serials represented Friedrichstadt as replete with vice and dangers – it was an area inhospitable to bourgeois women, even as it beckoned them to enter as consumers. In 1913, one department store went so far as to send engraved invitations to ladies of the finest households in town; the same store then ran afoul of the authorities by populating its window displays with lifelike mannequins in various stages of undress.[13]

---

[7] *Baedeker's Berlin and Its Environs* (Leipzig: Baedeker's, 1912), 32–34.

[8] Dorothy Rowe, *Representing Berlin: Sexuality and the City in Imperial and Weimar Germany* (Aldershot: Ashgate, 2003), 2ff.

[9] Paul Lerner, "Consuming Pathologies: Kleptomania, Magazinitis, and the Problem of Female Consumption in Wilhelmine and Weimar Germany," *WerkstattGeschichte* 42 (2006), 47; cf. Rappaport, *Shopping for Pleasure*, 5; Ogborn, *Spaces of Modernity*, 119.

[10] "Unsere Budiker," *Deutsche Hochwacht*, July 7, 1904, clipped and included in police files alongside articles and complaints about alcohol consumption in department stores, possible houses of assignation, and the harassment of women, in LAB A Pr. Br. Rep. 030, Nr. 1589. On the *Großstadt-Dokumente*, see Peter Fritzsche, "Vagabond in the Fugitive City: Hans Ostwald, Imperial Berlin, and the Grossstadt-Dokumente," *Journal of Contemporary History* 29 (1994), 385–402; Ralf Thies, *Ethnograph des dunklen Berlin: Hans Ostwald und die "Großstadt-Dokumente," 1904–1908* (Cologne: Böhlau, 2006).

[11] The police recognized the connections among theaters, hotels, cafés, dance venues, and prostitution. Investigators collected and collated books and articles on these subjects over the course of decades: LAB A Pr. Br. Rep. 030, Nr. 16927.

[12] Minna Cauer, Chairwoman of the Association for Women's Welfare (Verein Frauenwohl), to Georg von Borries, Berlin police president, August 13, 1904, in LAB A Pr. Br. Rep. 030, Nr. 1589, f. 233; cf. "Ohne Herrenbegleitung," *Die Frauenbewegung: Revue für die Interessen der Frauen* 10 (1904), 107–8.

[13] Sherwin Simmons, "Ernst Kirchner's Streetwalkers: Art, Luxury, and Immorality in Berlin, 1913–1916," *Art Bulletin* 82 (2000), 125.

The mix of dissolution and respectability, sex and commerce, danger and pleasure, was the neighborhood's defining feature.

These layers of ambivalence alienated many observers. "Ruthless progress" in the city had produced a "clumsy young giant with all the ungainliness that comes after too fast a growth spurt," a "world city in the constant state of becoming," "immoderate," and ready to "grab indiscriminately at the pleasures of life." Friedrichstadt was also a meeting point for the deracinated.[14] As Kurt Tucholsky famously quipped, "the sense of home has ... become transportable" and Berlin the capital of "the impersonal, the unconnected, the strange, and the ambivalent."[15]

Berlin's grand hoteliers responded by positing their establishments as the best mediators between the consumer and the pleasure zone. In answering questions and providing maps and recommendations, hotel staff made the city intelligible, navigable, and accessible. In-house theater and railroad booking agents, carriage and courier services, currency exchanges, and barber shops – these amenities helped a guest manage, interact with, and be ready for a metropolis that by the early 1900s was the fastest-growing capital city in Europe.

PARVENUS

Berlin was also one of Europe's newer national capitals. Locals and visitors alike identified it as the parvenu metropolis, comparable to Chicago in its heavy industry, flashy architecture, and central location in a continental railroad network.[16] The comparison was common enough that it appears in a turn-of-the-century book promoting the Savoy Hotel.[17]

---

[14] Arthur Eloesser, "Die Straße meiner Jugend" (1907), in *Die Straße meiner Jugend: Berliner Skizzen* (Berlin: Arsenal, 1987), 7.

[15] Tucholsky, quoted in Klaus Strohmeyer and Marianne Strohmeyer, eds., *Berlin in Bewegung: Literarischer Spaziergang* (Reinbek bei Hamburg: Rowohlt, 1987), 33; see also Georg Simmel, "The Metropolis and Mental Life," trans. Kurt Wolff, in *Georg Simmel: On Individuality and Social Forms – Selected Writings*, ed. Donald N. Levine (Chicago: University of Chicago Press, 1971), 324.

[16] Walther Rathenau, "Die schönste Stadt der Welt," *Die Zukunft* 26 (1899), 39; Mark Twain, "The Chicago of Europe," (1892), in *The Complete Essays of Mark Twain* (Garden City, NY: Doubleday, 1963), 87–89.

[17] Savoy Hotel promotional book, n.p., n.d., ca. 1893, in Historisches Archiv für Tourismus (hereafter: HAT) D060/11/01/900/SAV. On Berlin as "Chicago on the Spree," see Daniel Kiecol, *Selbstbild und Image zweier europäischer Metropolen: Paris und Berlin zwischen 1900 und 1930* (Frankfurt am Main: Peter Lang, 2001), 256.

As a large European capital, however, Berlin also invited comparison with Paris and London. Walther Rathenau saw Berlin, or "Parvenupolis," outpacing those cities, now old and tired.[18] Still others thought Berlin lacked the patina of West European capitals.[19] The city's architecture, a symphony of buildings and building styles that expanded in the 1860s and exploded after 1871, was cacophonous by 1900. To critics, the city lacked pedigree.[20] To its fans, that very lack appeared to open a range of new possibilities, especially for the thousands of moneyed Germans who arrived every day, some to stop and some to stay, all with needs that grand hotels stood ready to meet.

Berliners oscillated between seeing Berlin as a *Parvenupolis* and a *Weltstadt* (world city).[21] The *Zentralblatt der Bauverwaltung* (newsletter of Berlin's construction administration) reported in 1907 that this "youngest of world cities" did not have enough hotels near railroad stations, a problem that the Hotel Baltic, an establishment near Stettin station and one of the "more dignified constructions in the *Weltstadt* Berlin," was supposed to solve.[22] The understanding of Berlin as a *Weltstadt* redirected urban development toward grander projects, as historian Peter Fritzsche has observed.[23]

The grand hotel scene saw a flurry of new construction in the decade before World War I. In his description of the new Hotel Adlon in 1908 for the publication *Innen-Dekoration*, Anton Jaumann celebrated the building's potential: "It takes the competitive edge from those wonderful luxury hotels with which New York, Paris, and London once showed their superiority."[24] Jaumann and others presented the city's grand hotels as signs and symbols not just of the city's arrival on the world stage but also of its preeminence there.

---

[18] Walther Rathenau, "Schönste Stadt," 38.

[19] Wilhelm II, "Die wahre Kunst" (1901), in *Die Berliner Moderne, 1885–1914*, eds. Jürgen Schutte and Peter Sprengel (Stuttgart: Reclam, 1987), 571–74.

[20] Johannes Gaulke, *Führer durch Berlins Kunstschätze: Museen, Denkmäler, Bauwerke* (Berlin: Globus, 1908), 165.

[21] On commercial leisure and the *Weltstadt*, see the chapters by Tobias Becker ("Unterhaltungstheater") and Kerstin Lange ("Tanzvergnügen"), in *Weltstadtvergnügen: Berlin, 1880–1930*, eds. Daniel Morat et al., (Göttingen: Vandenhoeck & Ruprecht, 2016), 28–73, 74–108.

[22] "Hotel Adlon in Berlin," in *Zentralblatt der Bauverwaltung* 28, no. 61 (August 1, 1908), 415; description of the Hotel Baltic in Berlin by H. Suhrbier, January 17, 1925, in LAB A Rep. 225, Nr. 1077.

[23] Peter Fritzsche, *Reading Berlin 1900* (Cambridge, MA: Harvard University Press, 1996), 10.

[24] Jaumann, "Das Hotel Adlon in Berlin," *Innen-Dekoration* 19 (1908), 1.

This municipal jingoism reflected an inferiority complex pervasive among Berliners, celebrants and detractors alike. In an article on why Berlin did not need any more foreign visitors than it was already attracting, a contributor to the *Berliner Tageblatt* disparaged his city as unsophisticated, not "broad-minded enough to become a city of foreigners (*Fremdenstadt*) like Paris." In industry and growth, "of course," Berlin had "been overtaking Paris throughout the last generation," according to the Scottish town planner Patrick Geddes, but the German capital lacked status.[25] Disjointed and rough, Berlin was "missing a merging point" for the great and the good, a local journalist complained.[26] In the eyes of Julius Klinger, a graphic artist from Vienna, the city's *beau monde* lacked a *je ne sais quoi*: "In the [Hotel] Bristol at breakfast ... one can see the upstanding gentlemen and sophisticated socialites in the style of Ernst Deutsch [one of Berlin's most celebrated commercial illustrators] but in their live form, they do not come close to attaining the charm of the illustrated."[27]

The same seemed true at other hotels and other mealtimes. Hungry after the opera one night in 1912, the cultural critic and literary scholar Arthur Eloesser and his friend from the provinces decided on a late dinner in the grill room of a first-class hotel. (Grill rooms were informal dining concessions, where patrons ordered à la carte.) Eloesser's account inventories gilded mirrors, blue silk wallpaper, and "opulent" furnishings. Yet the luxury was missing "that last stamp": a sense of "peace," the "imperturbability of naturalness." The interiors had an aristocratic touch, to be sure, complemented by "waiters in the livery of court lackeys," but the evidence of an effort was too great. The grill room was trying too hard, and in the trying, it belied its authenticity as an informal space of noble repose.[28] This assessment of the grill room's ultimate failure, through excessive striving, to be truly elegant provided Eloesser a metaphor for Berlin itself.

---

[25] Patrick Geddes, *Cities in Evolution* (1915; New York: Oxford University Press, 1950), 22.

[26] "Hebung des Berliner Fremdenverkehrs: Generalversammlung der Berliner Zentralstelle," *Berliner Tageblatt*, May 9, 1914.

[27] Julius Klinger, "Ernst Deutsch," *Mitteilungen des Vereins Deutscher Reklamefachleute*, no. 38 (March 1913), 83; Anita Kühnel, ed. *Julius Klinger: Plakatkünstler und Zeichner* (Berlin: Gebr. Mann, 1997). On Ernst Deutsch, later known as Ernst Dryden in the United States, see Anthony Lipmann, *Divinely Elegant: The World of Ernst Dryden* (New York: Penguin, 1989), 40.

[28] Arthur Eloesser, "Gedanken in einem Grillroom" (1912), in Eloesser, *Straße meiner Jugend*, 74, 80.

Some of the failures were real. In the decade before World War I, Berlin's hoteliers faced a shortfall in foreign custom. Although tourism to the city had increased after 1900, the duration of a single stay in Berlin was short relative to Paris and London.[29] In June 1908, for example, Berlin's hotels seemed to be full of Americans, but most of them were using Berlin as a post on the routes to and from spas in southern Germany, Austria, and Switzerland. In other cases, Berlin became the last stop of a European tour, a place to change trains and rest a little before continuing to Hamburg and a steamer home. By 1913, according to *The New York Times*, Berlin had "degenerated into a mere way-station for American travelers," not a destination in its own right.[30] This fact alarmed hoteliers and piqued their envy. Why should Berlin not hold its own against Paris and London?

In 1911, when the World Congress of Hoteliers (founded only a few years earlier) held its meeting in Berlin, the Association of Berlin Hoteliers (Verein Berliner Hotelbesitzer) lobbied the city government for support.[31] In advance of the event, Ernst Reissig, president of the association, wrote to the lord mayor (*Oberbürgermeister*) and the magistrate to ask that they receive a delegation from the World Congress. After all, the mayor of Rome had done the same for the last congress, Reissig wrote.[32] Here was a chance to impress a large group of important foreigners who might go home and give favorable reviews of what they had seen in Berlin.

The program for the World Congress of 1911 aimed to impress. It included events at major hotels and tourist attractions, as well as a banquet and ball at the Zoologischer Garten (zoo). According to the participating institutions – the Universal Federation of Hoteliers' Associations (Fédération Universelle des Sociétés d'Hôteliers), the International Association of Hotel Owners, and the Association of Berlin Hoteliers – the

[29] "Hebung des Berliner Fremdenverkehrs"; "Berlin Seeking More Visitors," *The New York Times*, May 22, 1910.

[30] "Americans Fill Berlin," *The New York Times*, June 21, 1908; "Berlin's Banner Season," *The New York Times*, August 27, 1911; "Host of Tourists Invading Berlin," *The New York Times*, August 17, 1913; "Berlin Way-Station for Spa Visitors," *The New York Times*, June 22, 1913. On foreign correspondents at hotels, see John Maxwell Hamilton, *Journalism's Roving Eye: A History of American Foreign Reporting* (Baton Rouge: Louisiana State University Press, 2009), 70, 125, 139, 165–66, 225.

[31] In LAB A Rep. 001-02, Nr. 438: "Resoconto Ufficiale del I Congresso Internazionale degli Albergatori," Genoa, 1909; Ernst Reissig to the magistrate, May 26, 1911 (f. 8).

[32] Reissig to Martin Kirschner, lord mayor (Oberbürgermeister) of Berlin, April 18, 1911, in LAB A Rep. 001-02, Nr. 438, f. 3.

purpose was to provide an "international conference" that would "give testament to the sense of solidarity felt by all members of our profession," regardless of nationality. And this cosmopolitan pose would be modeled for prominent Berliners. Dozens attended, including the lord mayor, the mayor, the president of the Central Bureau of Tourism (Centralstelle für den Fremdenverkehr), and the editors of the city's largest newspapers.[33] Their presence reinforced Berlin hoteliers' commitment to a stance of openness toward the foreign, on the one hand, and the desire to compete, on the other.

NATIONALISTS

Berlin was brimming with sites of local, Prussian, and national-imperial pride that attracted domestic and foreign visitors alike. Hoteliers exploited the city's status as the capital of the German Empire by touting connections to royalty, even as the construction of new hotels and other buildings erased traces of Berlin's past as a principal *Residenzstadt* (royal seat) of the bygone German Confederation and, before that, the Holy Roman Empire. Near the palace, Mühlendamm, once the city's major commercial thoroughfare, had lost its calling to Friedrichstraße by the 1880s. By the end of the century, few Berliners would have remembered the old city hall, replaced in the 1860s with a gargantuan building of little relation to the original.[34] Wilhelm II had Schinkel's stately, small cathedral on Spree Island razed and replaced with something suited to the bombastic Protestantism of the last Hohenzollerns. Royal and noble residences were also torn down to make way for hotels like the Adlon. In these cases, hoteliers tended to preserve in advertisements the memory of what had come before. Having supplanted the site of the palace of Prince Louis Ferdinand, the Savoy Hotel distributed promotional books that traded on his reputation as "the hero of Saalfeld," a lost battle against Napoleon's forces in 1806.[35]

Alongside the Prussian tradition, Berlin's relatively new status as imperial capital generated extra revenue and opportunities for hoteliers.

---

[33] Representatives of the Universal Federation of Hoteliers' Societies (Fédération Universelle des Sociétés d'Hôteliers), the International Association of Hotel Owners (Internationaler Hotelbesitzer-Verein), and the Association of Berlin Hoteliers (Verein Berliner Hotelbesitzer) to members, invitation to the World Congress of Hoteliers (Weltkongress der Hotelbesitzer) of September 1, 1911, in LAB A Rep. 001-02, Nr. 438.

[34] Eloesser, "Straße meiner Jugend," 12.

[35] Promotional book for the Savoy Hotel, n.d. but likely the 1890s, in HAT D060/11/01/900/SAV. The book is in German, not French.

The Adlon became a focal point of informal state business, Prince Bülow having stayed there regularly after his retirement in 1909 and granted audience not only to admirers but also to the emperor's advisers.[36] To broadcast their hotel's pride of place in such official circles, the Adlon family made sure to fly the imperial flag as high and prominently as it could, at the corner of the building facing the Brandenburg Gate and thus along the route from the emperor's palaces at Potsdam to his residence at the other end of Unter den Linden.

The excess of imperial flags across the Adlon's frontages advertised the hotel's special relationship with Wilhelm II, as the Kaiserhof had done with Wilhelm I, though to a greater extent. In fact, the Adlon became something like the Court Hotel even before it opened. Jaumann wrote of "all Berlin" following the hotel's construction because the emperor himself had given the project and building plans his precious attention. To Jaumann, this meant the emperor's own "acknowledgment and support of the international implications of the undertaking." The Adlon "should show the excellence Germany is able to obtain in all respects: in luxury, in comfort, in hygiene."[37] Inside, the emperor's likenesses graced fireplaces and niches, with especial prominence in the banquet hall, where his bust complemented portraits and royal-imperial insignia. Many showed him in armor as the Supreme War Lord of Germany, one of his official titles, in an era of frequent, ominous, near-miss conflicts among the Great Powers.[38]

At other hotels, designers and owners avoided displays of militant nationalism or balanced them with cosmopolitan touches. At the Central-Hotel, guests passed through sumptuous public rooms outfitted in a pastiche of French, not German, styles to get to the restaurant Zum Heidelberger, a showcase of German regional decor but not Prussian or German-imperial militarism (Figure 2.2). Several themed rooms, borrowing from local traditions, comprised a grand tour of German beer hall design. For guests from elsewhere in Germany, Zum Heidelberger peddled an alternative nationalism to that of the Adlon. Where the Adlon and other hotels signaled Prussian hegemony, Zum Heidelberger assembled the riches of regional histories to conjure an earlier, idealized Germany

[36] "Kaiser Favors Buelow," *The New York Times*, October 24, 1909.
[37] Jaumann, "Hotel Adlon," 1.
[38] "Carnegie Reaches Berlin," *The New York Times*, June 15, 1913. On "Supreme War Lord" as one of the emperor's official titles, see John C. G. Röhl, *Kaiser Wilhelm II: A Concise Life* (Cambridge: Cambridge University Press, 2014), 36.

FIGURE 2.2 Promotional postcard for Zum Heidelberger,
the Central-Hotel's beer hall, ca. 1900
Image credit: author's collection

of loosely confederated principalities, united by a single language and
shared traditions, free from the political machinations of Berlin.[39] The
decor made sense at the Central, a magnet for business travelers from all
over the Reich.

At the same time, the Central broadcast mixed messages about its
roots and its purpose. Notwithstanding the Germanism of the sign
promoting Zum Heidelberger, the exterior of the building (1880) was
decidedly French, and the French fashion, after the Parisian example,
proliferated at Berlin's grand hotels well into the twentieth century. One
critic, writing for the *B.Z. am Mittag*, found the trend insupportable:
"It so happens that we in Germany have the greatest of strengths at our
disposal [for creating] buildings of the hotel and commercial variety,"

---

[39] See Abigail Green, *Fatherlands: State-Building and Nationhood in Nineteenth-
Century Germany* (Cambridge: Cambridge University Press, 2001), 340; Siegfried
Weichlein, "Regionalism, Federalism and Nationalism in the German Empire," in
*Region and State in Nineteenth-Century Europe: Nation-Building, Regional Iden-
tities, and Separatism*, eds. Joost Augusteijn and Eric Storm (Basingstoke: Palgrave
Macmillan, 2012), 93–110.

yet the use "of the French style" continued. The contributor saw this as an insult, as would the emperor, who believed that the use of French and other foreign motifs in the architecture of the capital undid the achievements of his dynasty.[40] For architects and designers, there was always the pressure to revert to the idioms of the *Volk* or the Prussian tradition.[41] And yet, these pressures counteracted the nationalist drive for Berlin to be the German *Weltstadt*, a showcase of cosmopolitanism, which would attract and retain the custom of foreign social, cultural, academic, and political elites.

COSMOPOLITANS

The cosmopolitanism of grand hotel guests manifested along several lines: the cosmopolitanism of the aristocracy and royalty who visited; the accentuation and celebration of difference among national groups within the grand hotels; cultural exchange among such groups; the phenomenon of intermarriage, particularly between American women and German men; and even sexual nonconformism. The early 1900s was a heyday of cosmopolitanism, which Judith Walkowitz has called the "privileged stance of openness toward abroad," exemplified by the tango craze, the success of the orientalism of the Ballets Russes, and the appeal of exotic dancing.[42] The cosmopolitanism of the grand hotels could be more mundane, too – utilitarian even, particularly among the staff, whose openness to abroad had to be a fact of everyday life.[43]

Berlin's grand hotels, especially the Adlon, Esplanade, and Continental, mimicked the private accommodations of royalty and the high aristocracy.[44] Services were modeled on the well-run households of the nobility, so that guests enjoyed "elegant breakfast[s] served on huge silver platter[s]," as journalist Marion Dönhoff remembered of her East Prussian childhood. At her family's Schloss Friedrichstein, as in a grand hotel, "formal dinners" featured "a constant stream" of guests

---

[40] "In klassischem französischen Stil," *B.Z. am Mittag*, March 5, 1914.

[41] Uwe Puschner, *Die völkische Bewegung im wilhelminischen Kaiserreich: Sprache, Rasse, Religion* (Darmstadt: Wissenschaftliche Buchgesellschaft, 2001), 25.

[42] Mica Nava, *Visceral Cosmopolitanism: Gender, Culture and the Normalisation of Difference* (Oxford: Berg, 2007), 26–35; Walkowitz, "Vision of Salome," 338.

[43] See Judith R. Walkowitz, *Nights Out: Life in Cosmopolitan London* (New Haven: Yale University Press, 2012), 10–11, 21–24, 43–44, 92–93, 140–42.

[44] On aristocratic cosmopolitanism in Central Europe, see Rita Krueger, *Czech, German, and Noble: Status and National Identity in Habsburg Bohemia* (Oxford: Oxford University Press, 2009), 19.

"from the world of diplomacy, the upper nobility, and the intellectual elite."[45] Berlin's finest grand hotels supported the urban version of this elite cosmopolitan sociability.[46] For the 1913 wedding of Princess Victoria Louise of Prussia to Ernest Augustus of Cumberland, descendants of George III of Great Britain, the court reserved "entire floors of fashionable hotels" for the accommodation of "so many different royal personages." *The New York Times* described the event as "an aristocratic cosmopolitan galaxy of ladies and gentlemen in waiting on the rulers of Russia, England, Italy, Denmark, and Austria."[47] Such spectacles involved a cast of characters who stood above nationality, whose connections and customs set them apart from national groupings altogether.

In addition to tending to such royals and aristocrats, Berlin's grand hoteliers had to accommodate commoners from all over Europe and the world. This group, the bulk of the clientele, identified more closely with their nationalities than did royalty and the high aristocracy. Thus, certain national groups gravitated toward certain hotels. The Baltic Hotel, for example, attracted Danes, Swedes, and Norwegians. Americans liked the Adlon, the Fürstenhof, and the Esplanade.[48] And then there were the occasional visitors from farther afield. *The New York Times* reported in 1912 that "a touch of color was lent to the exclusively Caucasian guest list at the Adlon this week by the arrival of the Indian nabob, Sir Rajenda Mockerjee [*sic*] and Lady Mockerjee [*sic*] of Calcutta," racializing its story and referring to the Bengali Indian industrialist-engineer Rajendra Nath Mookerjee and his wife. Mookerjee traveled extensively in Europe, delivering speeches on corporate management, labor relations, imperial rule, and political economy.[49]

---

[45] Marion Dönhoff, *Before the Storm: Memories of My Youth in Old Prussia*, trans. Jean Steinberg (New York: Knopf, 1990), 6.

[46] Habbo Knoch, "Simmels Hotel: Kommunikation im Zwischenraum der modernen Gesellschaft," in *Sehnsucht nach Nähe: Interpersonale Kommunikation in Deutschland seit dem 19. Jahrhundert*, ed. Moritz Föllmer (Stuttgart: Franz Steiner, 2004), 87–108; Armin Owzar, "'Schweigen ist Gold': Kommunikationsverhalten in der wilhelminischen Gesellschaft," in Föllmer, *Sehnsucht nach Nähe*, 65–86; Georg Simmel, "The Sociology of Sociability," trans. Everett Hughes, *American Journal of Sociology* 55 (1949), 254–61.

[47] "Guests of Kaiser Will Fill Hotels," *The New York Times*, April 27, 1913.

[48] Description of the Hotel Baltic in Berlin by H. Suhrbier, January 17, 1925, in LAB A Rep. 225, Nr. 1077.

[49] "Miss Farrar Again at Berlin Opera," *The New York Times*, September 13, 1908; "Americans in Berlin," *The New York Times*, June 24, 1910; "Tourists Shun Spas," *The New York Times*, July 18, 1909; "Berlin Is Popular Despite the Cold," *The New*

For distinguished guests of all nations, hotel staff had to create and maintain a pleasant, secure, and peaceful home away from home.

When it involved people of rank, guests themselves had to ensure that cultural exchange would happen along civilized, prescribed lines. One night in August 1911, General Nogi Maresuke of the Imperial Japanese Army was dining in the Adlon restaurant. As he rose to leave the table, he found himself being assailed by an American guest, who, in front of all the patrons, including a few dozen Americans, gave the general a slap on the back and exclaimed, "Good old Nogi! Hurrah for Japan!" Many of the Americans present became incensed and met immediately to discuss the incident and find a way to tell "their effervescent fellow countryman what they thought of such an exhibition."[50] Such breaches threatened to tarnish the reputation of Americans in Berlin, who policed each other accordingly.

No group made itself at home more insistently in Berlin's grand hotels than did the Americans. For a time in 1908, the US ambassador to Germany actually lived at the Adlon. Two years later, in May 1910, *The New York Times* reported on a wave of American tourists "now in full possession of Berlin hotels, shops, summer gardens, and all other establishments in the Kaiser's town that cater for foreign patronage." That same year, in the month of June alone, nearly 4,000 Americans had taken rooms in hotels and pensions, with the Adlon, Kaiserhof, Bristol, and Esplanade accepting the majority of the elite custom. Such was the critical mass at the Adlon, Bristol, and Esplanade in July that crowds gathered in the lobbies to wait for *The New York Times* to announce the latest news of a boxing match in Reno.[51] American visitors en masse made spectacles of themselves, and hoteliers were eager to accommodate them, given the depth of the American market and of individual Americans' pocketbooks.

Cultural exchange between Anglo-Americans and Germans ensued, especially in sports and entertainment. In the early twentieth century, a group of American and British men founded the city's only golf club and used hotel spaces for meetings. As late as 1912, the club "remain[ed] ...

York Times, August 25, 1912; Siddha Mohana Mitra, *Anglo-Indian Studies* (London: Longmans, 1913), 83.

[50] "American Slaps Nogi on the Back," *The New York Times*, August 21, 1911.
[51] "Ambassador Hill Selects a Home," *The New York Times*, May 10, 1908; "Berlin Seeking More Visitors," *The New York Times*, May 22, 1910. "Arrivals in Berlin Break All Records," *The New York Times*, July 10, 1910; "Greatest Interest in Berlin," *The New York Times*, July 4, 1910.

pretty much of a monopoly of the Anglo-American element." Two years later, however, the club had become "largely Teutonic." Meanwhile, in 1911, the Adlon became a nexus of transatlantic entertainment when James C. Duff and his wife arrived in pursuit of new acts for their lineup on Broadway. The hope, according to *The New York Times*, was that Max Reinhardt, among others, would be persuaded "to present some examples ... in the United States." Duff and others relied on institution-alized networking under the auspices of the Adlon, where the American Luncheon Club promised to connect American visitors and expatriates with prominent Berliners.[52]

The American Luncheon Club and its members facilitated a flurry of transatlantic academic and philanthropic exchange, too.[53] In 1908, Andrew Carnegie had the cast of a diplodocus skeleton delivered to Berlin. He sent a representative of the Carnegie Museum of Pittsburgh to be the special guest of honor at a celebratory dinner at the Adlon. Exchanges like these occurred until the outbreak of World War I. In 1913, a member of the board of the Christian Scientists' principal church, in Boston, gave a speech in German to a sizable crowd in the Adlon's Beethoven Parlor.[54]

This academic cosmopolitanism had diplomatic implications. Here was a model for how liberals across the world might use free trade and the exchange of ideas to avoid war. At the 1909 annual banquet of the American Association of Trade and Commerce, held at the Adlon, the US ambassador expressed hope that free trade might silence "the voice of the 'jingoes'" and cause "passions to be still." In 1911, the ambassador repeated this argument in his farewell dinner at the Adlon, confessing, "We in America have hopes for a more closely united world." States and governments should avail themselves of "the gift of mutual inter-pretation," the ambassador continued. If he did not go so far as to pro-pose a cosmopolitan vision of world citizenship, he did insist that "law, justice, and righteousness ... [were] things applicable internationally" – even as American and German foreign policy were becoming ever more aggressive. Under these conditions, Andrew Carnegie came to Berlin in June 1913 to present an address to the emperor on behalf of dozens of

[52] "Americans Leaving Berlin for Italy," *The New York Times*, March 8, 1914; "Duff Seeks German Plays," *The New York Times*, April 16, 1911; "Thanksgiving Day Fete Day [*sic*] in Berlin," *The New York Times*, November 13, 1914.

[53] See Sebastian Conrad, *Globalisation and the Nation in Imperial Germany*, trans. Sorcha O'Hagan (Cambridge: Cambridge University Press, 2010), 3.

[54] "Guests of Kaiser Will Fill Hotels," *The New York Times*, April 27, 1913.

American peace societies. Carnegie stayed, naturally, in the royal suite of the Adlon, where so much had already been said for a cosmopolitan worldview that favored international friendship and peace.[55]

The following year, some four months before the assassination of Archduke Franz Ferdinand and his wife in Sarajevo, Archibald Cary Coolidge of Harvard University and Paul Shorey of the University of Chicago, two visiting exchange professors, bid farewell to Germany at the Adlon's Kaisersaal. The dinner held in their honor, which attracted the "aristocracy of German intelligence," was one of the greatest ever "aggregation of brains gathered around a Berlin banquet board," including Max Planck, Adolf von Harnack, and the city's most eminent scholars of medicine, history, archaeology, and classics. Harnack gave a toast to the "quadruple intellectual alliance of Germany, America, England, and Austria-Hungary," whose succuss he believed sprang from a common Germanic heritage, an imaginary alliance founded on racist mythology and wishful thinking.[56]

The alliances that received by far the most press, however, were engagements and marriages between German men and American women. In 1909, the widow Elsie French Vanderbilt became engaged to Count Wilhelm von Bentinck, a member of the Potsdam guards, but the agreement fell through when his relatives dissuaded him from this union of unequals. In 1913 alone, a wealthy woman from Detroit, a widow from Philadelphia, and a granddaughter of a former ambassador to Berlin found advantageous matches among Germany's elites. Although the ceremonies themselves happened in churches, it was common to hold the ball, banquet, and wedding breakfast at the Adlon or other such establishment. The city's grand hotels also became places where American wives of German aristocrats could reunite with friends, display new status, help organize intermarriages for others, and find opportunities for charity work in the dense network of liberal women's urban interventionism.[57]

---

[55] "Commerce as Peacemaker," *The New York Times*, January 17, 1909; "Farewell Dinner to Hill," *The New York Times*, June 28, 1911; "Carnegie Reaches Berlin." On the emperor's increasingly aggressive foreign policy after 1900, see John C. G. Röhl, *Wilhelm II: Der Weg in den Abgrund, 1900–1941* (Munich: C. H. Beck, 2008), 50ff. For Carnegie's contribution to international peace movements, see Peter Brock, *Pacifism in the United States: From the Colonial Era to the First World War* (Princeton: Princeton University Press, 1968), 930. On the advent of a "transnational lobby" for peace after 1890, see Sandi E. Cooper, *Patriotic Pacifism: Waging War on War in Europe, 1815–1914* (New York: Oxford University Press, 1991), 60–90.

[56] "German Savants Honor Americans," *The New York Times*, February 22, 1914.

[57] "Hill to Entertain at Berlin Musicale," *The New York Times*, March 28, 1909; "Wedding the Event of Week in Berlin," *The New York Times*, May 11, 1913; "Host of

Grand hotels, particularly the Adlon, provided space for women to engage themselves in diplomatic circles, too. At the Adlon in 1908, the US ambassador's first Berlin reception had barred women's entry "in accordance with the strict rules of the Kaiser's capital." But unofficial events were open to women and even came to be their distinct purview. In the relative privacy of her apartment in the Adlon, Bertha Palmer of Chicago entertained the US ambassador and other prominent Americans and Europeans.[58] In 1913, two unmarried sisters from Washington, very much at home "in diplomatic circles on both sides of the Atlantic," had a dinner given in their honor by the French ambassador to Berlin.[59] The grand hotel was thus a place where women could entertain and be entertained by a diplomatic set otherwise off limits. These engagements played out in more public spaces such as sitting rooms, dining rooms, conference rooms, and ballrooms, not the private areas upstairs, where access still depended in most cases upon a male chaperone.

Berlin's grand hotels hosted well-to-do women even as vice persisted there and elsewhere in the city center. Here was the dark side of cosmopolitanism, its association with sex and even sexual danger.[60] Iwan Bloch, medical doctor and author of *Das Sexualleben unserer Zeit* (The Sexual Life of Our Time), attributed the increased publicity of vice to an expanding, accelerating circulation of people and information more generally. With the advent of mass media, sex played a "greater, more meaningful role" in public than it had before, he claimed.[61] Men were now taking out ads in newspapers to request the addresses of women they had seen on trains, trams, and omnibuses.[62] Prostitution, both male and female, flourished, particularly in hotels, as Oscar Commenge noted for Paris in 1897 and Ostwald observed

Tourists Invading Berlin," *The New York Times*, August 17, 1913; "Americans Leaving Berlin for Italy." On women's interventions in the metropolis, see Stratigakos, *Women's Berlin*, especially chapter 5.

58 See Barbara Peters Smith, "From White City to Green Acres: Bertha Palmer and the Gendering of Space in the Gilded Age" (MA thesis, University of South Florida, 2015), 26.

59 "Dr. Hill's First Reception: Monday Next in Honor of the Berlin Diplomatic Corps," *The New York Times*, June 25, 1908; "Berlin Is Popular Despite the Cold," *The New York Times*, August 25, 1912; "Americans Flit through Berlin," *The New York Times*, August 10, 1913.

60 Walkowitz, "Vision of Salome," 2.

61 Iwan Bloch, *Das Sexualleben unserer Zeit in seinen Beziehungen zur modernen Kultur* (Berlin: Louis Marcus, 1907), 778.

62 Tyler Carrington, *Love at Last Sight: Dating, Intimacy, and Risk in Turn-of-the-Century Berlin* (New York: Oxford University Press, 2019), 7ff.

for Berlin in his 1906 study of male sex work.[63] Two of the city's principal cruising grounds could be found in and around Friedrichstadt.
The Central-Hotel was located on one of them, Friedrichstraße itself.
The Bristol was located on another (Unter den Linden). Many of the
other grand hotels lay within walking distance of the Tiergarten, which
contained its own crowded cruising area.[64]

Grand hotels attracted gay men, especially powerful ones. Events at
the Bristol in 1902 precipitated the greatest homosexual sex scandal in
Germany to date. There, the great industrialist Friedrich Krupp (scion of
Alfred) was supposed regularly to have entertained a handful of Italian
pages. The hotel manager had hired them for Krupp's private gratification, the socialist publication *Vorwärts* reported. The editors, trying
to take down Krupp, implicated the Bristol and its management in an
international economy of exploitative pederasty. Such rumors piqued the
attention of the chief inspector (*Kriminalkommissar*) Hans von Tresc-
kow, who launched an investigation. In the glare of this publicity, Krupp
committed suicide.[65]

In their advertisements, of course, hoteliers presented the lighter side
of cosmopolitanism in the pleasure zone. They emphasized the international profile of their clientele and the concessions renting space on
their ground floors.[66] In 1912, the Adlon let the location of its grill
room to the steamship company North German Lloyd.[67] The Kaiserhof housed a branch of the Hamburg-based Havana Import Company,
where guests and visitors could buy exotic tobacco products.[68] The
Savoy boasted twenty French cooks, and the Palast-Hotel made sure to
print its menus in both French, prominently, and German, in smaller

[63] Oscar Commenge, *La prostitution clandestine à Paris* (Paris: Schleicher, 1897), 88–89;
   Hans Ostwald, *Männliche Prostitution im kaiserlichen Berlin* (Berlin: Janssen, 1991),
   58, 113–16, first published in 1906.
[64] Robert Beachy, *Gay Berlin: Birthplace of a Modern Identity* (New York: Knopf, 2014),
   65; Magnus Hirschfeld, *Die Homosexualität des Mannes und Weibes* (Berlin: Louis
   Marcus, 1912), 698.
[65] See Hendrik Bergers, *Der Fall Krupp: Ein Skandal der Homosexualität?* (Munich:
   GRIN, 2014); William Manchester, *The Arms of Krupp, 1587–1968* (Boston: Little,
   Brown, 1968), 259–60; Robert Aldrich, *The Seduction of the Mediterranean: Writing,
   Art and Homosexual Fantasy* (London: Routledge, 1993), 127.
[66] Front-page advertisement in the *Illustrirte Zeitung* (Leipzig), December 29, 1898.
[67] "Gets Fine Berlin Site: North German Lloyd Line Rents Part of the Adlon for Offices,"
   The New York Times, September 29, 1912.
[68] Addendum to a lease between the Hotel Management Corporation and the Havana
   Import Company (Havana-Import-Compagnie in Hamburg), April 8, 1919, in LAB A
   Rep. 225, Nr. 1052.

type. As if to temper this favoring of the foreign, the restaurant manager had the menu decorated with the heraldry of nine of Germany's princely houses.[69] Where hoteliers responded to cosmopolitan cultural imperatives, they liked to balance the effects with local, national, and German-imperial symbols.

While the early grand hotels such as the Kaiserhof and the Central in the 1870s and 1880s had balanced German art and symbols with French décor, Berlin's grand hotels of the 1890s and 1900s added American offerings to the mix as part of the imperative, first, to appear welcoming to new sorts of visitors from much farther away and, second, to appear open to the foreign after the cosmopolitan fashion of the day. In 1904, the Kaiser-Keller, a large gastronomy concern, opened an "American bar," which the management nonetheless decided to call the "Kaiser-Büffet."[70]

One hotelier came to the United States in 1911 chiefly for the purpose of learning the art of American bartending. He "made the rounds of the new hotels in all the leading cities of the country, with a view to finding out the new drinks which make Americans feel at home." The result, according to *The New York Times*: "Transatlantic wayfarers who happen to put up at [the Adlon] will find it hard to believe that they had left 'God's country.'"[71] The Esplanade soon created an American bar of its own, complete with a billiards table. The amenity was as much for the gratification of American visitors as it was a way of showing that the Esplanade was as up-to-date and cosmopolitan as the Adlon and other properties with American cocktail bars (Figure 2.3).

To draw American and British customers upstairs to the accommodations, hoteliers advertised the bathrooms. The Savoy promised facilities that were up to the standards of any expert "hygienist." As early as 1897, the architect Carl Gause, who would later design the Adlon, had called for using American and British hotels as a model for inclusion of extra bathing amenities. The increase in visitors from Great Britain and the United States, he contended, necessitated an increase in the number of en suite rooms and apartments.[72] And so, in the next decade, new hotels such as the Fürstenhof emerged "after the American pattern," with

69 Menu of the restaurant at the Palast-Hotel, June 7, 1912, in LAB A Rep. 225, Nr. 345.
70 Report on the Kaiser-Keller Corporation (Kaiser-Keller Aktiengesellschaft) by General Trust Incorporated (Allgemeine Treuhand-Aktien-Gesellschaft), July 9, 1928, in LAB A Rep. 225, Nr. 941.
71 "Berlin to Provide American Drinks," *The New York Times*, April 9, 1911.
72 "Mitteilungen aus Vereinen," *Deutsche Bauzeitung* 31 (March 2, 1898), 162–63.

FIGURE 2.3 The American Bar in the grill room of the Esplanade, 1915
Image credit: Landesarchiv Berlin

300 rooms and 100 private bathrooms, "practical, comfortable, and hygienic."[73] These measures contributed to the "commonplace" impression "that, from year to year, Berlin is becoming more American."[74] For hoteliers, one of whom even established a New York office for the purpose of capturing potential guests before they set sail for Europe, Americanization meant greater profitability.[75]

In the spring of 1909, Louis Adlon, son of Lorenz Adlon, founder of the eponymous hotel, traveled to the United States on a fact-finding mission. He recorded and broadcast his impressions in a long interview in *The New York Times* in May – an interview that outlined the complex relationship between the American and German hotel industries. In the article, he referred to American hotels as the "university in which

---

[73] Otto Sarrazin and Friedrich Schulze, "Hotel Adlon in Berlin," *Zentralblatt der Bauverwaltung* 28 (1908), 415; "5. ordentliche Versammlung des XVI. Vereinsjahres," *Brandenburgia: Monatsblatt der Gesellschaft für Heimatkunde der Provinz Brandenburg zu Berlin* 16 (1908), 449.

[74] "Der erste Berliner Wolkenkratzer," *National-Zeitung*, January 22, 1911, clipped and included in LAB A Rep. 010-02, Nr. 16596.

[75] "Berlin to Provide American Drinks."

European hotel keepers complete their education. Not all European hotel keepers ... but the best, the most progressive, the most up-to-date." He compared himself to "an American art student [traveling] to France to study art," but in reverse. Adlon even credited Americans for a "small revolution in Continental hotel fashions." Throughout the interview, Adlon praised the American hospitality industry even as he asserted Europe's competitive edge.[76]

If Louis Adlon went to Philadelphia, Washington, Chicago, and New York to understand what *The New York Times* referred to as the "fastidious American taste" in hotel design and amenities, he also did so to project his establishment's readiness to please American visitors. "We have our own engine room, running water, [and] laundry," Adlon boasted, plus "the American plan of bathrooms in individual rooms," while many of Berlin's hostelries "still lack[ed] some of these things." American visitors to Berlin demanded all manner of niceties, which Adlon also promised: he planned to have grapefruit and terrapin imported, he would build en suite rooms throughout the hotel, he would supply in good order the American "characteristics of quick service, comfort, [and] intelligence." The Adlon was "an up-to-date American hotel, even the café being modeled after the cafés in the best American hotels."[77]

In this rendering, the Adlon was at once German and not German, entrenched in Berlin society and politics, yet tethered to American culture and custom. Adlon took pains in the interview to distinguish European from American hotel culture. The Adlon and its European counterparts were more "homelike" than American hotels, which he saw as more spectacular and commercial. "When a man stops in an American hotel," Adlon contended, "he retains all the time the feeling that he is stopping, not at home, but in a hotel – that he is buying the comforts that are showered upon him." The Adlon family, on the other hand, tried harder to mask the exchange of money for hospitality: "We make friends of our patrons. That's it. Here [in the United States] ... you do not do that." Adlon attributed the difference to the scale of American hotels and that country's large hotel-dwelling population. Adlon was thus treading a fine line between presenting his establishment as

[76] "American Hotels Lead," *The New York Times*, May 9, 1909. On Europeans and American hegemony, see Victoria de Grazia, *Irresistible Empire: America's Advance through Twentieth-Century Europe* (Cambridge, MA: Belknap Press of Harvard University Press, 2005), 4–5.

[77] "German Bonifaces Eager for Tourists," *The New York Times*, April 11, 1909; "American Hotels Lead"; "Here to See Our Hotels," *The New York Times*, May 1, 1909.

Americanized and promising a good dose of old-world charm, care, and refinement. When he spoke of amenities, Adlon emphasized the American; when he spoke of hotel culture, he emphasized his staff's personal touch.

Staff at the Adlon and Berlin's other grand hotels were indeed impressive, especially for their command of foreign languages and customs, usually gained through work experience abroad.[78] Ludwig Müller, headwaiter at the Fürstenhof, had worked his way up the ranks as far away as Buenos Aires.[79] Andreas Nett (see Chapter 1) had served in four European countries before he applied to be a member of Müller's staff.[80] Higher up the chain of command, hotel manager Alfred Jensen listed, in addition to his native Denmark, three other countries where he had found employ before 1914.[81] Restaurant and hotel manager Hubert Lyon had a similar résumé. With some hyperbole, one hotel's promotional book described its head porter as being able to "speak Spanish like a Castilian, Italian like a Tuscan" and even a regional variety of French originating in Gascony, with its "friendly, whirring rrr." Indeed, he "might [even] be said to muster a bit of *Orientalia*" when the situation required.[82] There existed a staff cosmopolitanism, that, in maintaining openness toward foreign languages, manners, and customs, made the cosmopolitanism of the elites easier to practice.

REPUBLICANS

Sometimes Berlin's grand hotels brought people of different nationalities together, the better to show each other their differences. Hotels became key sites for Americans, especially, to make sense of their own ambivalence toward the German juggernaut, a foil for an imagined United States characterized by its lighter, brighter, more enlightened political culture and associational life. A superiority complex developed among Americans that sat uneasily with the mix of elite cosmopolitanism and German nationalisms on display at Berlin's grand hotels on the eve of World War I.

---

[78] "Internationales Hotel-Industrie-Vereinsblatt des Internat. Genfer Verbandes," pamphlet, October 20, 1910, in LAB A Pr. Br. Rep. 030, Nr. 1723. On language requirements for workers, see Guyer, *Hotelwesen*, 144.

[79] References for Ludwig Müller, 1905–1926, in LAB A Rep. 225, Nr. 1150.

[80] References for Andreas Nett, 1895–1910, in LAB A Rep. 225, Nr. 644.

[81] Curriculum vitae of Alfred Jensen, n.d. (likely 1930s), in LAB A Rep. 225, Nr. 1152.

[82] Savoy Hotel promotional book, n.p., n.d., ca. 1893, in HAT D060/11/01/900/SAV.

The spectacle of German orderliness provided opportunities for American journalists to reckon with the apparent accomplishments of German civilization. "Berlin's solid and orderly appearance" was impressive, "but isn't everything forbidden?" a journalist asked in 1912 – "even blades of grass grow according to police regulations." The theme of grass-cutting and authoritarianism returned in the summer of 1913, when the American critic James Huneker published a long piece on Berlin in *The New York Times* in which he served the city a series of backhanded compliments. Praise for the well-cropped grass in the median of Hardenbergstraße became a comment, again, on policing and the obedience characteristic of German subjects. Berlin's police had "argus" eyes whose gaze "no one escapes." The story's headline, "The Kaiser's Jubilee City," identified the city as belonging to the emperor himself.[83]

Yet, Berlin's authoritarian and imperial spectacles were part of what drew Americans to the city in the first place. Huneker observed that "one of the chief 'sights' in the Tiergarten is the daily return of the Kaiser from Potsdam," accompanied by a bugler who riffed on a Wagnerian theme. A review of the Guards Corps at Tempelhof field in September 1913, according to another *New York Times* correspondent, was "the great ... social event of the year," with Americans "as usual, much in evidence on the vast parade ground." When in May of the same year Berlin hosted the king and queen of England and the czar of Russia at the same time, "countless exclamations of delighted enthusiasm in unmistakable transatlantic English broke forth" at the sight of the royal procession down Unter den Linden, past the Adlon and the Bristol. *The Times* correspondent approached this incident with some sense of irony: "A little royalty," he conceded, might be "a dangerous thing for the patriotic sons and daughters of Uncle Sam."[84] This royal procession was also greeted by US flags hanging from the balconies of Americans' rooms at the Adlon, which transformed the colorscape of Unter den Linden into that of "Broadway or Michigan Boulevard," *The Times* correspondent joked. These flags signaled support for the monarchs on parade while alerting them to the presence of true republicans in their land.

The Times liked to announce a metaphoric invasion, Americans having "taken possession of 'Kaiserville.'" Indeed, "a look down the register

---

[83] "Berlin Draws Many Visitors," *The New York Times*, July 2, 1912.

[84] James Huneker, "Huneker Prowls around Kaiser's Jubilee City," *The New York Times*, June 22, 1913; "Americans Witness the Berlin Review," *The New York Times*, September 7, 1913; "Americans Cheer Royalty in Berlin," *The New York Times*, May 25, 1913.

of places like the Esplanade, Adlon, Bristol, or Kaiserhof" showed "an unending succession of New Yorks, Chicagos, Philadelphias, Bostons, San Franciscos, Wheelings, Leavenworths," leaving the Germans "hopelessly in the minority alongside the tailor-made, broad-hatted women and the padded-shouldered, wide-trousered men, whose make-ups betray their nationality unmistakably." Some of the wealthiest chose to sightsee by automobile, with small American flags affixed to the dashboards.[85] In this way, too, Americans used the flag to advertise their difference, their republicanism, adding a note of assertion to their ubiquity on the grand hotel scene.

The US holidays and commemorations occasioned more emphatic stagings of American exceptionalism. Since the 1890s, a small colony of American expatriates residing in Berlin had organized gatherings for Thanksgiving and the Fourth of July. In 1894, the grandest such event to date took place at the Kaiserhof, where the US ambassador, Theodore Runyon, delivered a Thanksgiving toast to the emperor's health and then to the "great republic" across the sea. He spoke of being "proud of our birthright" – freedom from monarchy, one imagines – while in the same breath he thanked the German people for their hospitality and praised the host country for "its splendid literature, its advanced art and science, and its military renown" – not, of course, its political culture. The biggest Independence Day celebrations happened at Grünau, on the banks of the Spree. Most attendees of the picnics and games were Americans living in Berlin, but as *The Times* reported in 1914, the "crowd" of "five hundred patriots ... was swelled during the day by the arrival of people, who came down from the hotels in automobiles or trains." At the celebration two years prior, the American colony had arrived in full ostentation by steamboat in order to celebrate, on the Kaiser's soil, the popular repudiation of monarchy and a heroic struggle against despotism.[86]

Americans flaunted their republicanism most during US presidential elections, when they threw raucous election parties at Berlin's grand hotels. The practice started as early as 1908 when the American ambassador and his staff decided to "camp out" on election night to await

---

[85] "Americans Cheer Royalty in Berlin"; "Germans Are Rare," *The New York Times*, July 25, 1909; "Ideal Weather in Berlin," *The New York Times*, July 14, 1912; "Berlin Attracting Many," *The New York Times*, May 21, 1911.

[86] "Thanksgiving in Germany," *The New York Times*, November 30, 1894; "Berlin Americans Enjoy Big Picnic," *The New York Times*, July 5, 1914; "Politics at Berlin Fourth," *The New York Times*, July 7, 1912.

news by cable from *The New York Times*. The Adlon had agreed to display returns as they arrived on a large board in the lobby. This was perhaps the first election party held "for the benefit of the Americans resident in the Kaiser's capital," as *The Times* put it. Two hundred men and women congregated to wait and consume champagne, sandwiches, cigarettes, and coffee – all provided by the Adlon. In the small hours of the morning, when Taft's victory seemed sure, "the assembly rose to its feet and broke into thunderous cheers." The women led everyone in patriotic song to the accompaniment of the orchestra, engaged to play "Yankee melodies" all night. Four years later, several hundred people attended the party on election night, when Lorenz and Louis Adlon had the Marble Hall draped with American flags, under which, when the time came, there issued "a frenzied outburst of cheering and handclapping." The orchestra, as before, played rags, marches, and other such "American compositions" until the party broke up after three o'clock in the morning. *The Times* had called the election for Woodrow Wilson.

When a *New York Times* correspondent wrote that "such scenes had never been witnessed in the memory of the oldest Berlin inhabitants," he was broadly correct. Yes, these events were Berlin's earliest American election parties, made possible by modern technologies of transoceanic telegraphy. At the same time, few Berliners would have recalled with clarity the last outburst of bourgeois enthusiasm for democracy: the Revolution of 1848.[87] Six and seven decades later, the election parties at the Adlon advertised the Americans' particular success with republicanism where the Germans had failed. Indeed, the election parties were jingoistic spectacles that flaunted before Berliners the privileges and rights unavailable to them in this, Germany's Second Reich. Ironically, the Americans' republican chauvinism found a comfortable home in the Kaiser's metropolis, itself famous, or notorious, for spectacular celebrations of national and imperial glory.

HOSPITALITY OF THE FORTRESS

The composition of these conflicting interests fell apart quite suddenly. Britain declared war on Germany on August 4, 1914, in the bloody culmination of a month-long diplomatic crisis. That night, August 4/5, a mob

[87] "Times Bulletins in Berlin," *The New York Times*, November 2, 1908; "Vigil in Berlin for Election News," *The New York Times*, November 10, 1912.

attacked the British embassy in Berlin and then descended on the Adlon next door, where an emergency meeting of American and British tourists was taking place. The US ambassador James Gerard was in the process of assuring British nationals that their interests would be protected by the American embassy when three policemen, sabers drawn, entered the hall, seized *New York Times* correspondent Frederick William Wile, and dragged him into the lobby. Ambassador Gerard raised his voice in protest as the men hauled Wile into the main reception hall and out the front door. There, in front of the hotel, members of an angry mob beat him with fists and blunt objects before the police pushed him into a waiting car and whisked him away. Some minutes later, a German woman appeared at the reception desk to ask for Wile. The Adlon's management had her arrested.[88]

She and Wile were victims of spy fever, which was being fed by German newspapers as mobilizations mounted to the east and west of the German Empire. On July 31, 1914, Berliners had learned that Germany was now at war with Russia and the Reich lay under siege. The socialist organ *Vorwärts* wrote then of the "leaden presentiment of an approaching and nameless calamity weigh[ing] upon the great multitude of those who wait for the latest news."[89] The announcement of Germany's mobilization on the following day, August 1, triggered a panic. With little to print in the way of details, editors opted for bogus stories of espionage against the fatherland – for example, that the country had been infiltrated primarily by Russians and their agents on the hunt for information and for ways to sabotage the fledgling mobilization. At the same time, hundreds, if not thousands, of people responded to government warnings that the French were secretly transporting gold in automobiles from France to Russia, across German soil, to finance the two-front war. In the first week of international hostilities, twenty-eight German motorists died from shots fired into their cars by excited patrolmen.[90]

Meanwhile, as German armies invaded Luxembourg, Belgium, and then France, many of the Reich's borderlands turned into war zones. The

[88] "Newspapermen Arrested," *The New York Times*, August 8, 1914; "Tales of Arrest," *The New York Times*, August 9, 1914.

[89] Quoted and translated in Jeffrey Verhey, *The Spirit of 1914: Militarism, Myth and Mobilization in Germany* (Cambridge: Cambridge University Press, 2000), 62–63.

[90] "Achtung, Spione!" *Kölnische Zeitung*, August 2, 1914, reprinted in Eberhard Buchner, ed. *Kriegsdokumente: Der Weltkrieg 1914 in der Darstellung der zeitgenössischen Presse* (Munich: Albert Langen, 1914), 1:83. See also Verhey, *Spirit of 1914*, 85–87.

rest were sealed. Ship berths sold out and travel by sea became perilous as Britain and then Germany declared naval blockades. But to stay put could be just as dangerous. Many foreign nationals – British, French, Russian, Belgian – lost consular representation in Germany and thus had to rely on the goodwill of other missions. Most travelers had no state-issued identification, to say nothing of passports. These conditions left thousands of hotel guests in Berlin at risk of being apprehended as suspected spies.

Soon, spy fever infected the Adlon's staff. Charles Tower, correspondent for the *Daily News* (London) was denounced by a chauffeur and arrested.[91] The following week, New Yorker John Davis was apprehended on the basis of a statement by a maid.[92] The porter, not the manager or a member of his staff, accompanied a police officer, his gun drawn, to Davis's room. The snooping maid, the call to the police, the absence of management, the drawn gun – all point to a breach in hotel decorum and a disturbance of hierarchy. Adlon staff members – in similar cases, also management – implicated themselves in a contest between a nativist mob and privileged tourists.

CONCLUSION

During the war, the Adlon and other grand hotels would become increasingly penetrable by outside demands, their hierarchies increasingly susceptible to internal instability. These vulnerabilities, latent in the prewar arrangement, burst forth at the first signs of external crisis. Huneker, in his 1913 critique of the capital, hinted at this latency. His discussion conjured two unstable balances: one, between nationalist and cosmopolitan imperatives; and the other, between guests and staff, in other words, between the social group that was granted liberal subjectivity and the social group that was denied it. "At times," Huneker felt "as if I was sitting over a big boiler that is carrying too much steam. If an explosion ever comes it will be felt the world over."[93] The explosion came in summer 1914 and rocked Berlin's grand hotels right away. It was the abrupt end to a relative golden age in grand

---

[91] "Army of Refugees," *The New York Times*, August 3, 1914; "Anxiety Endures," *The New York Times*, August 5, 1914; "Homecomers Sing Gaily," *The New York Times*, August 13, 1914.
[92] "Americans Out of Berlin," *The New York Times*, August 17, 1914.
[93] Huneker, "Huneker Prowls around Kaiser's Jubilee City."

hotel society – an age in which cosmopolitanism, nationalism, and the classes had coexisted in a delicate balance.

While the inciting incident came from outside, fatal flaws lay within. The staff hierarchies undergirding the cosmopolitanism of the elites buckled as cosmopolitanism itself became anathema to German society's new purpose. The war between empires buried the privileged cosmopolitanism and everyday liberalism of the grand hotel – the sense that elites could be trusted to behave and that workers could be pressured to cooperate – under a mountain of new, destructive imperatives: the imperatives of the fortress.

3

Grand Hotels at War

World War I felled Berlin's grand hotel industry in three blows. The first was a shortage of goods, services, and labor; the second, a decline in the quality of the goods and services still available; and the third, a resultant depletion of inventories and capital reserves as shortages drove prices out of reach. As the state made increasing demands on everyone's time and energy, managers found themselves unable to devote their full attention to shoring up systems and hierarchies. A grueling four years then ended in ignominy and danger when, in November 1918, political violence surged into hotel lobbies, restaurants, and guest rooms. In the meantime, shortages, regulations, and market dislocations of war made business at Berlin's grand hotels impossible and, in turn, prefigured the peace, when a return to normal conditions would likewise prove impossible. The fate of Berlin's grand hotels mirrors the fate of Germany's Second Empire, which also collapsed in the face of defeat and revolution in the fall of 1918.[1]

Shortages and dislocations had more complicated indirect effects on the grand hotels of Berlin. On the one hand, with a lack of food, material, and labor, plus the state's takeover of distribution, hotel staff were quite suddenly marshaled as gatekeepers between guests and the goods and services they demanded. Where there had been bounty, there was now scarcity; where there had been luxury, there was now austerity.

---

[1] See Belinda J. Davis, *Home Fires Burning: Food, Politics, and Everyday Life in World War I Berlin* (Chapel Hill: University of North Carolina Press, 2000); cf. Maureen Healy, *Vienna and the Fall of the Habsburg Empire: Total War and Everyday Life in World War I* (Cambridge: Cambridge University Press, 2004).

The culture of service and privilege gave way to limits and rationing as the hierarchical relationship between guests and staff was reversed. Nevertheless, those hoteliers who remained in business benefitted from full occupancy after 1914. The concentration of war industries and administration on the capital, as well as the elimination of competition through government takeovers of hotel buildings, simultaneously increased demand and reduced supply. Hotel after hotel became office space for the new war corporations charged with directing the German economy. Management tended to reap the rewards of this situation – and the workers, the consequences.

FULL OCCUPANCY

After the initial shock of hostilities, hotel registrations increased, an unexpected outcome of a war that concentrated the national economy on Berlin to an unprecedented extent. At the same time, the supply of rooms decreased as hotel corporations sold their properties to the state for use as office space. This dynamic inflated hotel revenues for the duration of the war, despite the eventual disappearance of foreign customers.

Grand hoteliers' client base shrank as soon as the war broke out, with western customers now cut off by a naval blockade and impassable trenchscapes. To Berlin hoteliers' surprise, however, occupancy increased as domestic demand came to the rescue. After a lull in late 1914, the number of hotel stays per year in Berlin increased by hundreds of thousands between 1915 and 1917. They came overwhelmingly from within the German Empire – 97 percent of all guests were German; by 1917, 99 percent. Closed borders, tightened restrictions on travel, the state takeover of the economy, and the steady impoverishment of the empire accounted for the disappearance of foreigners.[2] Even for travelers from neutral countries, it became more difficult to get into and out of Germany unmolested and with their possessions intact.[3] It also became harder to

---

[2] Berlin Police Presidium to the Association of Berlin Hoteliers, February 14, 1918, in LAB A Rep. 001-02, Nr. 2080, f. 38.

[3] Herbert Swope, *Inside the German Empire in the Third Year of the War* (New York: Century, 1917), 119–21; "Americans Pack Trains to Paris," *The New York Times*, August 4, 1914; "Tourists' Leaders Finding the Way," *The New York Times*, August 5, 1914; "10,000 Refugees Still in Berlin," *The New York Times*, August 8, 1914; "Newspaper Men Arrested," *The New York Times*, August 8, 1914; "Seized by Kaiser, Princes Escaped," *The New York Times*, August 8, 1914; "American Girls Insulted," *The New York Times*, August 9, 1914; "Many Send Word from War Zone," *The New York Times*, August 9, 1914; "Tells of Arrest as 'English Spy,'" *The New York Times*, August 9, 1914;

FIGURE 3.1 Men hawking German national flags and patriotic souvenirs
near the Central-Hotel, August 1914
Image credit: Landesarchiv Berlin

do business in Germany, as officials in the latter half of the war tightened
surveillance and regulation, especially of international commerce. While
foreign businessmen had flourished in Berlin in 1914 and 1915, they disappeared from its hotels after 1916.[4]

When foreigners did visit the capital, they usually came on military,
commercial, or diplomatic missions. German and non-German reporters,
along with German businessmen, money carriers, and couriers helped
fill the guest registers. Meanwhile, German holiday makers and country
elites, without access to foreign climes and uninterested in the largely
empty spa resorts, came to Berlin in good numbers. They filled the rooms
left by foreigners.

"How Germany Went to War," *The New York Times*, August 23, 1914; "Three Refugee
Ships Arrive with More Tales of Hardship," *The New York Times*, August 25, 1914;
"Passenger Ships Immune," *The New York Times*, January 29, 1915; "How Germany
Looks to George B. McClellan," *The New York Times*, September 20, 1915; Garet Gar-
rett, "How Germans React to War," *The New York Times*, January 26, 1916; "American
Tells of Berlin Conditions," *The New York Times*, February 9, 1917; "Many Americans
to Stay in Germany," *The New York Times*, February 9, 1917.
[4] Swope, *Inside the German Empire*, 78.

Americans returned a few months after the start of the war, not as pleasure seekers and society mavens but rather businessmen and journalists.[5] "Hotels again full," reported *The Times*: "The palm rooms of the Kaiserhof and Adlon are crowded at five o'clock coffee and whiskey time." Americans arrived "in increasing numbers," and they "gravitate[d] naturally to the American bar of the Adlon. About every other one is said to be 'writing for the magazines.'" American custom was unreliable, however. By spring, Americans were "conspicuously not among those present." Instead, military, diplomatic, and commercial attachés from the Central Powers, Germany's allies, formed the bulk of the hotel scene's foreign company. There was a particularly "large number of Austrian officers whom you now [saw] about the Berlin hotels."[6]

Foreign custom decreased again in 1916–17. Berlin had 2,625 fewer Austrian visitors in 1917 than in 1916, a reduction of 16 percent, on account of Austria's growing political and economic subordination to Germany. There were ever fewer opportunities for Austrians to make money in the capital and fewer instances in which Austrians were consulted by German decision-makers. The decrease in Dutch visitors was even more dramatic, down 53 percent in 1917. Visitors from Switzerland and Sweden decreased by 66 and 64 percent, respectively.

American visitors disappeared with the approach of their country's entry into the war. The year 1916 had produced 1,436 American registrations per year, an average of about 120 per month. That number fell to 87 in February 1917, after the departure of the American ambassador and the attendant break in formal diplomatic relations between Germany and the United States. In March, 50 Americans came to the city, many en route out of the country. In April, the month that the United States declared war on Germany, 31 Americans turned up. May saw 11.[7] Even before the disappearance of Americans from Berlin's grand hotel scene, a *New York Times* correspondent noted that the Adlon was perceptibly "less cosmopolitan" than it had been in the first three years of the war.[8] Full occupancy at Berlin's grand hotels persisted nonetheless,

---

[5] Annual report of the Berlin Hotel Corporation for 1914, in LAB A Rep. 001-02, Nr. 2080.

[6] "Berlin Nightlife under War Ban," *The New York Times*, January 31, 1915; Swope, *Inside the German Empire*, 167; "Berlin Calls Women to Tasks of Men," *The New York Times*, June 15, 1915.

[7] Annual reports of the Association of Berlin Hoteliers for 1916 and 1917, in LAB A Rep. 001-02, Nr. 2080.

[8] "Many Americans to Stay in Germany" *The New York Times*, February 9, 1917.

as hoteliers and hotel corporations sold their properties to the state for conversion to office buildings and reduced the overall supply of rooms.

DISAPPEARING HOTELS

Rooms became scarce over the course of the war, as Berlin lost twenty-one of its larger hotels to government bureaucracy and war corporations. Formed to manage the challenges of production and logistics that the war had wrought, these corporations proliferated. So too did government bureaucracy. Because of their locations and scale, hotels provided ideal office space. Taken together, the twenty-one hotels converted to offices during the war led to 164,615 fewer registrations, a more than 10 percent share of Berlin's total. Losses coalesced along Unter den Linden and Wilhelmstraße, around the Reichstag and Friedrichstraße station. This was the heart of the city, the heart of the hotel industry, and the heart of the imperial and Prussian governments. It was also where a disproportionate number of grand and luxury hotels did business. The larger the property, the more attractive it was to officials in search of office blocks.

The first hotels to fall under state control, in 1915, were the Royal and the Minerva, middling properties in scale and luxury. With about sixty rooms, the Royal had been in business since the 1850s and was Berlin's oldest luxury hotel, opulent but lacking in modern conveniences. Its closure might have occurred without the advent of war. The smaller Minerva, with only 30 rooms, did not excite comment when it disappeared. These two hotels, the only two to be purchased in 1915 for use by war corporations, contained a combined 90 rooms and expected an average of 31 registrations per day. These losses were easy for the market to sustain.

But in the following year, 1916, government bureaucracies took seven hotels out of commission and reduced the capacity for registrations by an average of 170 per day, 62,050 per year. These included five large and mid-sized hotels – the Windsor, National, Prinz-Albrecht, Saxonia, and Ermitage – in addition to two grand hotels, the Monopol-Hotel and the Grand Hotel Bellevue & Tiergarten, both less fashionable than their peers but still recognized by *Baedeker's* and other guidebooks as first-class properties.[9] The two latter establishments counted between them

---

[9] List of hotels in the city of Berlin closed during the war and transferred to war corporations, prepared by the Berlin Police Presidium, February 22, 1918, in LAB A Rep. 001-02, Nr. 2080, f. 29.

370 rooms and an average of 134 registrations per day. The loss of the Bellevue & Tiergarten put considerable pressure on other hotels near the Potsdam and Anhalt stations, particularly the Fürstenhof, Esplanade, and Palast-Hotel, all of which saw full occupancy from 1916 to the end of the decade.

In 1917, eleven hotel owners sold their properties to the state or its agents, depriving the market of another several hundred rooms. The Kleiner Kaiserhof, Hospiz (Budapester Straße), Reichstag, Terminus, Carlton, Kurfürstenhof, Heukulum, Wiesbadener Hof, Brandenburg, Victoria, and Lindenhof shut down. The last had been a grand hotel at Unter den Linden 17–18 with 120 rooms and nearly 15,000 registrations per year. The loss of the Lindenhof and the others reduced the city's capacity for hotel registrations by nearly 85,000 per annum.[10]

These closures and the resulting pressure on the hospitality industry came to the attention of the magistrate and city council in February of 1918, when the news broke that the state would purchase the Kaiserhof, Berlin's first grand hotel and among its two most famous. The Kaiserhof would be the largest property to close in this way. Its eminence, its location, its size, and its revenues gave councilors pause. They met on February 14, 1918, to decide whether to petition the Reichstag to cancel its deal. The debate made clear what was at stake: the maintenance of Berlin as a world city.

Since the police were in charge of permits for hostelries, an officer for the magistrate wrote to the Police Presidium on February 13, 1918: "The disappearance of a large number of hotels in Berlin, caused by the rental of space for various war corporations, fills us with concern about how to cover the need for accommodation for the flood of visitors sure to arrive with the end of the war."[11] The magistrate and his staff worried not only about the long-term effects of war on Berlin's economic health and tax base, but also about the nature of the peace and whether the city was even prepared for an end to hostilities.

In this view, the state should keep the doors of the Kaiserhof open for the good of all Berliners. The maintenance of Berlin as a world city depended upon the availability of suitable lodging for moneyed foreigners. By extension, the maintenance of the German Empire as a

---

[10] Ibid. One more hotel, the Altstädter Hof, would close in February 1918, reducing the count to 21.

[11] Magistrate to Berlin Police Presidium, February 13, 1918, in LAB A Rep. 001-02, Nr. 2080, f. 10.

world power depended in part upon the maintenance of its capital as a world city. This contention echoed prewar calls for the concentration of German national life in the capital. What had changed was the role of the state, which was now viewed as hindering, rather than facilitating, Berlin's rise. The council voted and resolved to "impede" the state's efforts to "strip the Hotel Kaiserhof of its extremely vital function" as Berlin's keystone grand hotel.[12]

Under these conditions, the magistrate petitioned the Reichstag and won. Lawmakers ultimately dropped their bid for the Kaiserhof.[13] The debate, the majority opinion of the magistrates, and the acquiescence of the Reichstag evinced the sea change in the state's understanding of its role with respect to its subjects.[14] By 1918, the state was not only responsible for mustering soldiers and prosecuting a war, as it had been for centuries, but also for provisioning the people in the broadest sense. This new charge was born of total war and the crushing burdens and painful deprivations it saddled on ordinary Germans.

SHORTAGES

On August 4, 1914, the Reichstag had passed an enabling act that transferred much of its power to the Bundesrat, an unelected body that would promulgate several hundred decrees by the end of the war. At the same time, the Prussian Law of Siege wrested executive power from civil authorities and placed it in the hands of one deputy commanding general for each of the 24 military districts of the empire.[15] Four days later, on August 8, 1914, the war ministry established the Department of Raw Materials for War (Kriegsrohstoffabteilung), which was supposed to coordinate the efforts of producers and manufacturers in the Reich. In turn, the state's slow, fitful takeover of the German economy during World War I would have an even greater effect on the grand hotel industry than did the shifts of demand and supply in the market for hotel rooms.

Hotel managers found themselves having to contend with the decrees of the Department of Raw Materials for War as well as the ordinances

---

[12] Minutes of a meeting of the Berlin City Council, February 14, 1918, in LAB A Rep. 001-02, Nr. 2080, f. 11.
[13] Decision of the Berlin City Council, February 14, 1918, in LAB A Rep. 001-02, Nr. 2080, f. 10; Magistrate to the Reichstag, petition of February 16, 1918, in LAB A Rep. 001-02, Nr. 2080, f. 8.
[14] Davis, *Home Fires Burning*, 238.
[15] Ibid., 9–10.

and regulations handed down from the military by way of the Police Presidium. Individually and collectively, Berlin's grand hoteliers tried to negotiate with their civil and military overlords. The main avenues open to them, however, were through the police, who rarely heard protests sympathetically, and through the magistrate and city council, who had very limited real power as compared with the military-backed police bureaucracy. This and other bureaucracies became powerful mediators in the German economy as shortages of raw materials and finished goods worsened in late 1914 and early 1915.

And yet, in the war's early months, grand hotel guests were spared the grind of war. A certain Clara Meyer of St. Louis reported to *The New York Times* that "the Berlin cafes are doing business as usual" and that things "had not advanced in price" – not as of late September 1914, that is. By November, the word from another American guest, at the Kaiserhof, was that "social life appear[ed] to be at a standstill." Although the restaurants were still full, the mood was sedate. Rising prices discouraged the consumption of several prewar delicacies and most of the expensive wines. Banquets, luncheons, and parties became fewer and smaller. Hoteliers, accustomed to a flood of Americans for the Berlin social season, lost out in the fall and winter of 1914/15, when an American correspondent observed not "one American ... in the Hotel Adlon." On New Year's Eve 1914/15, there were none of the customary "horns" or "bells," "nor could any other noise-making contrivances be heard."[16]

Early in the new year, 1915, the authorities extended rationing to the city's grand hotels, obliging waiters to enforce a 2 kg per week limit on the individual consumption of bread. Upon returning to their rooms the night before enforcement, guests would have seen a card pasted over the headboard that read:

The BREAD CARDS instituted by the authorities are to be found for each of our honored guests and good for ONE DAY ONLY at the Bread Card Desk in the lobby, to be obtained daily. The honored guests are reminded that from Feb. 22 bread may only be given at meals on presentation of this official bread card. We therefore beg guests always to keep this BREAD CARD by them and to give it back when paying the bill on the day of departure.[17]

---

[16] "Wartime Scenes in German Cities," *The New York Times*, September 29, 1914; "Says Berlin Feels the Pinch of War," *The New York Times*, November 28, 1914; "Berlin Silent City on New Year's Eve," *The New York Times*, January 2, 1915.
[17] "Berlin Cheerful on Bread Ration," *The New York Times*, February 23, 1915.

This notice was extraordinary. Behind the obsequious language lay a transformation in the political economy of luxury hotels. For the first time, consumption would be limited. By what factor, guests would find out the next morning.

On the way to breakfast stood a man behind a table, the bread-card clerk, in fact an official of the state. The Kaiserhof's clerk, Wilhelmine patriotism personified, had a handlebar mustache and medals pinned to his chest.[18] Guests lined up in front of him to have their names recorded in his ledger, whereupon they would receive from him a ration ticket that dispensed with the finer expressions of the previous night's notice: "Not transferable. Only valid for Feb. 22, 1915. Not valid unless bearing date. See back!" The reverse side contained information about what constituted bread under ration and what did not. The edges of the card were perforated and could be removed in pieces marked 25 g each, adding up to the full ration for the day.[19] This card, its presentation, and the regulations it communicated represented a reversal of grand hotel dynamics. The cards and new practices admitted and responded to the reality of scarcity, a reality anathema to the culture and business model of the grand hotel. Moreover, this new system, requiring guests to wait in line to speak to a government official, rather than a staff member, breached the hotel's defenses against outside interference.[20] Finally, and most radically, the new dynamic positioned hotel waiters, who would distribute the rations in exchange for coupons, as gatekeepers between guests and the objects of their demands. In this new crisis, the heaviest burden of enforcement landed on the worker.

Some four months later, in June 1915, a new decree banned fixed-price menus, which had always guaranteed at least three courses. The new à la carte bills of fare limited guests to one dish. Later paragraphs of the new decree went so deep as to change the word order in individual menu items, with restaurateurs now having to list the vegetable before the meat, which had to be boiled rather than roasted or fried – to save on fat. Once again, it fell to individual waiters to explain and enforce the

---

[18] On these officials' condescending airs, see Roger Chickering, *The Great War and Urban Life in Germany: Freiburg, 1914–1918* (Cambridge: Cambridge University Press, 2007), 465, 482.

[19] Cf. Swope, *Inside the German Empire*, 118, 163–70.

[20] Belinda J. Davis, "Food Scarcity and the Female Consumer," in *The Sex of Things: Gender and Consumption in Historical Perspective*, eds. Victoria de Grazia with Ellen Furlough (Berkeley: University of California Press, 1996), 297–99. See also Healy, *Vienna and the Fall of the Habsburg Empire*, 73–86.

latest restrictions. Ernst Barth, director of the Association of Berlin Hoteliers, protested to the police against these measures, particularly the ban on fixed-price menus and the limit to one dish per guest, but to no avail.[21]

Regulations expanded again in October 1915 with the arrival of meatless and fatless days. Immediately, hoteliers and restaurateurs registered lower profits and struggled to dispel widespread confusion about the new definitions.[22] On two days of the week, certain meats were banned from appearing on the menu. On two other days of the week, certain kinds of fat were banned. On the fifth day, the sale of pork was forbidden, pork not considered a meat under the "meatless day" decree. On any day, however, guests could order offal, game, poultry, and fish, none of which fell under the category of meat. Nevertheless, in contrast with the outside world, grand hotels still offered enough to eat. "You get your daily bread card [and] it gets you good bread," wrote one correspondent for *The Times*. "It is a meatless day, the waiter tells you. For lunch there is sole and other fish, with plenty of potatoes, and dainty things in sauce."[23] Another American observed that the urban food supply was neither "varied" nor "abundant," but sufficient.[24]

As foreign goods and foodstuffs – grains from Russia, exotic ingredients from the British Empire, fruits and vegetables from points south, and eggs, milk, butter, lard, and meat from neighboring countries – passed out of reach, local replacements for many such items proved "extraordinarily" expensive, as executives at Aschinger's Incorporated reckoned, and drove up costs.[25] In response, hoteliers and restauranteurs became creative with the menus. Game and fish proliferated; sausage, offal, and other déclassé proteins became the norm. Portions shrank. The bread ration dropped by one-eighth. The number of meat dishes on menus fell and then came under rationing. By summer, shortage and want had become the defining experience of a hotel restaurant.[26]

The mix of regulations became ever more complicated in 1916. Many customers found the new regime impossible to navigate, but some learned quickly and ordered to advantage. When hotel restaurants started printing on menus the gross raw weight of the meat on offer, guests turned bargain hunters could identify the heaviest courses for the

[21] "Vereinsnachrichten: Verein Berliner Hotelbesitzer," *Das Hotel*, June 18, 1915.
[22] Annual report of Aschinger's Incorporated for 1915, in LAB A Rep. 225, Nr. 635.
[23] "No Starvation in Germany," *The New York Times*, January 18, 1916.
[24] Swope, *Inside the German Empire*, 162.
[25] Annual report of Aschinger's Incorporated for 1915, in LAB A Rep. 225, Nr. 635.
[26] "Simplified Menu Bewilders Berlin," *The New York Times*, June 9, 1916.

fewest coupons, according to a *New York Times* correspondent. Waiters helped with calculating and strategizing, "putting their heads together" with the guests "to figure out which dishes did or did not require the production of meat cards."[27]

Meanwhile, prices continued to rise. The cost of food, heat, textiles, and labor particularly burdened hoteliers. Meat, fish, flour, potatoes, coffee, tea, chocolate, eggs, sugar, and beer were in extremely short supply. Block ice was harder to import. Widespread copper confiscations in 1916 left hotels with too few pots; replacements were too expensive. By November, clothing would be rationed, too, putting a strain on the appearance of the staff. Scarcity of materials for cleaning and for clerical work made day-to-day operations difficult. Paper shortages led hotel managers to withhold the complimentary stationery. In general, it now required a good deal of "effort" to come up with goods of even "middling quality," hoteliers reported.[28]

With rising costs, city authorities established a board of price monitoring, the Price Auditing Bureau of Greater Berlin (Preisprüfungsstelle Groß-Berlin), to chart and limit inflation, though to insufficient effect.[29] By late summer 1916 and through the end of the year, shortages, hoarding, and inefficiencies continued to drive prices up.[30] In September, the Department of Potato Distribution (Abteilung für Kartoffelversorgung) under the magistrat of Berlin made things worse by announcing that "owners of hotels, pubs, bars, restaurants, cafeterias, and similar businesses who intend to store potatoes for the winter will be given the opportunity to buy their winter supplies, for the period from November 20 to March 11, in advance."[31] Grand hotels and other large concerns with ample storage space now enjoyed a particular advantage. This system of sanctioned hoarding also signaled an unequal distribution of resources that favored factory workers and the wealthy – those who ate in grand hotels and large restaurants and cafés or who took their lunch from an office cafeteria or shop canteen.[32]

---

[27] "12 oz. Meat Week's Ration for Berliners," *The New York Times*, June 7, 1916.

[28] Annual report of Aschinger's Incorporated for 1916, in LAB A Rep. 225, Nr. 635.

[29] Davis, *Home Fires Burning*, 117.

[30] Thierry Bonzon and Belinda J. Davis, "Feeding the Cities," in *Capital Cities at War: Paris, London, Berlin, 1914–1919*, eds. Jay M. Winter and Jean-Louis Robert (Cambridge: Cambridge University Press, 1997), 1:321; Davis, *Home Fires Burning*, 30–32, 50, 162.

[31] Notice sent by the Department of Potato Distribution (Reichskartoffelversorgung) to hoteliers, plus resulting correspondence, in LAB A Rep. 013-01-08, Nr. 14.

[32] Davis, *Home Fires Burning*, 24–32; Jonathan Manning, "Wages and Purchasing Power," in Winter and Robert, *Capital Cities at War*, 1:257–60.

That winter, 1916/17, the potato crop failed, and new shortages overwhelmed the government's ad hoc measures for transporting, rationing, and pricing foodstuffs and materials.[33] There would be so little to eat that the period became known as the Turnip Winter, after the "Swedish roots" that Germans and particularly Berliners had to eat in lieu of food fit for human consumption. ("Swedish roots" are largely indigestible without the accompaniment of fats, which were mostly off the market by December 1916.) At the same time, Berlin faced an acute coal shortage. In mid-December, the Bundesrat responded to the emergency by decreeing various coal-conservation measures.

Public transportation, much of it dependent upon coal, became scarce during the day and stopped at night. Illuminated advertisements went dark, and it took months for hoteliers to persuade the authorities to allow entrance lighting, at least, for safety reasons during Berlin's notoriously dark winter – darker, now, since the city had cut municipal lamps. To make matters worse, the limited daylight hours in which Berliners could see enough to market and purchase goods contributed to the upward pressure on prices, especially for services. These dislocations would multiply and widen after the winter of 1916/17, the coal shortage still a year from its climax in 1917/18.[34]

The lack of heat, light, and transportation removed the last opportunities for conspicuous consumption and bourgeois self-display at grand hotels. The shortage of coal limited heat and light in the restaurants, bars, and ballrooms. With the near disappearance of motorized transportation and the dispatch of horses and other beasts of burden to the fronts, hotels farthest from train stations had to lower prices. Well-heeled guests chose second- and third-class establishments if a first-class railroad hotel could not accommodate them. Few visitors braved the windswept, pitch-black streets to find a grand hotel in the urban interior.[35] Then the national rail network itself broke down. By April 1917, with the food crisis worsening, railroad planners found themselves unable to answer civilian needs for calories and coal. The result was another cut in the bread ration for Berliners – and that on top of the potato ration of January 1917, which had limited effect since there were almost no

[33] On the authorities' apparently abject failure to provision the capital, see Bonzon and Davis, "Feeding the Cities," 1:339.

[34] Armin Triebel, "Coal and the Metropolis," in Winter and Robert, *Capital Cities*, 1:353.

[35] Annual report of the Association of Berlin Hoteliers for 1917, in LAB A Rep. 001-02, Nr. 2080.

potatoes to buy, anyway.[36] Despite hoteliers' best efforts, life in hotels became far less comfortable than during the first half of the war.

MANAGERS, SALARIED EMPLOYEES, WORKERS

Hotel employees' salaries and workers' wages increased during the war, though unevenly and not always in proportion to prices.[37] The salaries of hotel managers and corporate officers rose fastest throughout the war, however, and did keep pace with inflation. Boards of directors were quick to grant these wealthy men's requests for raises. Chief Financial Officer Hans Lohnert's 1917 appeal to the board of Aschinger's Incorporated was typical: "In light of the considerable increase in my activities ... of the unusual growth of my responsibilities on account of myriad laws and regulations, and of annual profits having far exceeded those of all past years, I am ... requesting an augmentation of my income by way of [a bonus] in proportion to gross annual profits."[38] Although Lohnert was correct – profits had indeed risen – he had not accounted for the need, under these conditions, to divert those profits from salaries and dividends to procurement and capital projects.

In real terms, in fact, profits were paltry, and given wartime inflation as well as the uncertainty of the future, there was good reason to invest profits immediately in aging plants and furniture, as some hoteliers already understood.[39] Yet Lohnert and other elites at Berlin's largest hotel corporations saw and seized the opportunity to argue for bonuses.[40] Indeed, it became standard during and after the war for a portion of a Berlin grand hotel manager's pay to be tied to annual profits. The 1918 contract of Ewald Kretschmar is representative, promising him a salary-plus-one-percent package at war's end.[41] Kretschmar and others

---

[36] Jay M. Winter, *The Experience of World War I* (Oxford: Equinox, 1988), 15.

[37] Richard Bessel, *Germany after the First World War* (Oxford: Clarendon, 1993), 26.

[38] Lohnert to the board of Aschinger's Incorporated, May 2, 1917, in LAB A Rep. 225, Nr. 396.

[39] "Notstandsmaßnahmen für die deutsche Hotelindustrie," *Das Hotel*, December 31, 1915; "Notstandsmaßnahmen für die deutsche Hotelindustrie," *Das Hotel*, April 13, 1917; "Die neuesten Vorschläge zur Umwandlung unseres Wirtschaftslebens," *Das Hotel*, January 31, 1919.

[40] On the uneven effects of wartime economic dislocations, see Matthias Blum, "War, Food, Rationing, and Socioeconomic Equality in Germany during the First World War," *Economic History Review* 66 (2013), 1065.

[41] Employment contract between Kretschmar and the Hotel Management Corporation, February 10, 1918, in LAB A Rep. 225, Nr. 987.

justified their requests for higher salaries and profit-sharing by claiming that with so many clerks, bookkeepers, and secretaries called up, managers now had to work longer hours.

Although only a few of the managers and corporate officers of Berlin's grand hotels served in the field, many of their white-collar subordinates did. Their absence proved a major difficulty. The mobilization of bookkeepers, for example, made for hazy accounting.[42] With the onset of conscription, still more white-collar employees of fighting age left for the front. Women replaced a small number of these men but usually in back-office positions.[43] (The Kaiserhof presented an exception, however, with female reception clerks.[44]) Among hotel managers, the replacement of men with women was an act of desperation. The consensus was that a trained man would always be preferable to a woman.[45] In practice, moreover, hoteliers opted for an untrained man over a trained woman.

For those male white-collar workers who retained civilian status and their jobs, salaries rose but did not keep pace with the mounting cost of living, nor did they reflect the extra hours that understaffed managers demanded. What is more, these white-collar workers who, unlike much of the hotel staff, lived off-site and had to contend with associated deprivations, fell through the net of wartime relief directives. To make matters worse, men such as these, of the petty bourgeoisie, were least inclined to accept support from the state. They went home to communities, some to wives, some to families, feeling cold, hungry, frightened, and proud.[46]

The war was even more disruptive at the next level down, among workers. Harsh conditions and punishing hours aside, hotel workers had the advantage of upward mobility, however limited and slow. Present hardships could pay off later, when a floor servant might be promoted to assistant waiter, an assistant waiter to waiter, a waiter to senior waiter, a senior waiter to headwaiter, a headwaiter – in extremely

---

[42] Central-Hotel management to the board of the Hotel Management Corporation, June 10, 1915, in LAB A Rep. 225-01, Nr. 1.

[43] Report on employment figures, 1911–1917, n.d., prepared by the Association of Berlin Hoteliers, in LAB A Rep. 001-02, Nr. 2080. On women replacing men at work, see Karen Hagemann, introduction to *Home/Front: The Military, War, and Gender in Twentieth-Century Germany*, eds. Karen Hagemann and Stefanie Schüler-Springorum (New York: Berg, 2002), 3; Birthe Kundrus, "Gender Wars: The First World War and the Construction of Gender Relations in the Weimar Republic," in *Home/Front*, 159–79.

[44] "Berlin Calls Women to Tasks of Men."

[45] Report on employment figures, 1911–1917.

[46] Davis, *Home Fires Burning*, 78–86.

rare cases – to a restaurant manager with an income to rival that of the hotel manager himself. Leaving a job in hotel service thus had a high opportunity cost for some – while cashing in on short-term opportunities, one cheated oneself out of long-term rewards. High-paying munitions factory jobs lured few workers away from the grand hotel's ladder, steep and truncated as it was. In most cases, when workers left, they went to the fronts.

By 1915, sourcing labor became a hotelier's "most difficult task by far," according to an Aschinger's Incorporated annual report.[47] The reports of all the major hotel corporations cited labor shortages as their greatest difficulty, above even food and fuel shortages and government regulations. As workers vanished, hoteliers scrambled to replace them, only to find that "equally [capable] replacements were not possible," according to the employers at Aschinger's Incorporated.[48] Many of the new workers lacked the skills of the regular staff.

The disappearance of experienced workers placed strains on interactions between staff and guests. When familiar waiters left service, the loss of longstanding relationships, cemented through the practice of tipping, were felt keenly by customers. For a *New York Times* correspondent, it was as if the war had robbed him of the return on his investment. Relationships had to be built anew, this time with a "frail," "old," or "young" ersatz-servant, as yet untrained, sufficiently malleable in the case of the young ones – at a price – but nonetheless wanting. "This mustering-out process," wrote a *New York Times* correspondent of the disappearance of workers from a Berlin hotel in mid-1915, "has been speeded up to such an extent that for the first time you can observe here and there a slight strain on the complicated machinery of modern life."[49]

The *New York Times* correspondent noted that "familiar faces have been disappearing with increased frequency. The elevator boy at your hotel grins hopefully and announces that this is his last night on duty. He has been 'eingezogen' or pulled into the army."[50] Five months later, in November 1915, the conscription age dropped to eighteen, making cannon fodder of still more elevator boys, servants, and trainees. In December 1916, the Auxiliary Service Law introduced compulsory labor service for boys and men aged sixteen to sixty. Experienced hotel porters now

[47] Annual report of Aschinger's Incorporated for 1915.
[48] Annual report of Aschinger's Incorporated for 1917, in LAB A Rep. 225, Nr. 635.
[49] "Berlin Calls Women to Tasks of Men."
[50] Ibid.

left in disquieting numbers. The Auxiliary Service Law and regular conscription ensured that the bulk of the staff of a grand hotel stood to be conveyed either to the front or the factory.[51]

By the implementation in 1917 of the Hindenburg Program, the state's effort to channel the entirety of the German economy into the war effort, 300,000 more workers were drafted into munitions production. The ensuing pressure on the labor market revealed itself in short order to the Association of Berlin Hoteliers, which had to raise premiums charged to employers to cover the costs of its employee-placing service now that workers were so hard to find.[52] Meanwhile, in spring 1917, on the heels of the Turnip Winter, 200,000 Berliners went on strike; the following January, when coal briquettes ran out, 500,000 would leave their posts.[53] These disturbances were rehearsals for the massive, uncontained strikes in autumn 1918 that helped bring down the regime. Yet, even as the economy approached and attained full employment, and workers came to demand more in this newly advantageous labor market, hotel workers refrained from agitating for higher pay or better working conditions.

There are a few explanations for hotel workers' docility during World War I. They were faring relatively well, after all, with food on their plates and heat in their quarters. Yet even if they had wanted to organize, their remoteness from other communities of workers and from the imaginations of labor union leaders kept hotel workers outside the mainstream of solidarity movements. Most importantly, the proportion of workers of foreign extraction, recruited from neutral or allied countries, shot up during the war.[54] A staff divided by nationality, in addition to gender, age, and skill, would not organize easily. Stratified and diverse, hotel workers lacked a common standpoint until the mass strikes of late 1918 and early 1919 extended to every industry in the country.

THE CARTEL AS A SOLUTION

Where workers declined to organize, their employers jumped at the chance. The Association of Berlin Hoteliers provided the forum and framework. A creation of the prewar period, the association continued to

---

[51] Bessel, *Germany after the First World War*, 8, 14.
[52] Annual report of the Association of Berlin Hoteliers for 1917.
[53] On the strikes in 1917 and 1918, see Hagemann, introduction to *Home/Front*, 7; and Bessel, *Germany after the First World War*, 41.
[54] "Vereinsnachrichten: Verein Berliner Hotelbesitzer," *Das Hotel*, May 21, 1915.

bring hoteliers together to set prices, standardize policies, lobby against regulations, and find staff. In its early days, the association's members were generally owners of the city's mid-sized hotels; owners of grander establishments such as the Adlon tended to opt out. Grand hoteliers began to join only after the outbreak of war. In 1914, the directors of the Hotel Management Corporation signed up. By 1916, the association's roster included representatives of all the city's grand hotels.[55] Their participation ensured a united front toward the authorities as well as the possibility of benefitting from and influencing collective negotiations and decision-making. The war had transformed the Association of Berlin Hoteliers into the governing body of a cartel that kept prices stable and consistent while also restricting competition.

Officials communicated with hoteliers through notices to the association, which in turn bundled the concerns and grievances of all hoteliers and brought them to the government as resolutions.[56] Through its leader, Ernst Barth, the association also engaged in formal and informal negotiations with the police, the magistrate, and the military command for the Berlin region. To accomplish all of this, in 1917 representatives began to meet monthly rather than yearly and assumed increasing authority over members.[57]

The association mostly failed in its efforts to help members manage wartime difficulties. Even the grand hotels, with far better access to capital, inventory, and economies of scale than their middling counterparts, became subject to the avalanche of regulations and ordinances that the Bundesrat, the magistrate, and the police heaped on the economic life of Berlin and especially the hospitality industry. In the course of the war, authorities placed legal limits on "celebrations": The timing, outlay, and magnitude of these events would now be prescribed by rules and susceptible to official scrutiny.[58] The authorities also curtailed nightlife, reduced public transportation, and banned many kinds of advertisements. These measures – in addition to the ordinances and regulations around food, materials, fuel, and labor – prompted the board of Aschinger's Incorporated to declare that "the practical transfer of the

---

[55] Annual report of the Association of Berlin Hoteliers for 1916, in LAB A Rep. 001-02, Nr. 2080.

[56] On cartels and the state, see William O. Henderson, *The Industrial Revolution on the Continent: Germany, France, Russia, 1800–1914* (Oxford: F. Cass, 1961), 60.

[57] Minutes of a meeting of the Association of Berlin Hoteliers, February 2, 1917, in LAB A Rep. 001-02, Nr. 2080.

[58] Ibid.

private economy to the state economy" by way of "the pileup of laws and directives" had made it "impossible" to do business as usual.[59]

Where Barth, the hotelier association's leader, did succeed against the state, it was usually in the case of decrees that excessively inconvenienced guests. For example, he managed to persuade the police to postpone the implementation of a proposed requirement that foreigners go in person to the police station to register rather than fill out the customary police registration card at reception. The police even dropped the proposed requirement that guests, foreign and domestic, go to offsite offices of the Bread Commission (Brotkommission) to obtain daily ration cards. But with the arrival and progress of the dictatorship of the German Army Supreme Command (Oberste Heeresleitung) in 1916 and 1917, Barth lost room to maneuver. Most of his appeals to the authorities in 1917 and 1918 went "unheard," he reported.[60] By 1918, the authorities extended their activities into the business of the association itself. Most of its decisions now had to be approved by the police.[61]

The cartel of hoteliers, such as it was, could not protect the industry when the Hindenburg Program was implemented in spring 1917.[62] This dictatorship of the Army Supreme Command enjoyed popularity among the public, who hoped that autarky might ease shortages of fuel, food, and materials.[63] The effects were rather more mixed than had been hoped, however. The program called for the requisition of most of the horses, few at this point, still in private service. Thus, in addition to having no fuel for motor trucks and vans, hoteliers were forced to rely on a skeleton crew of starving beasts or else pay steeply rising delivery costs.[64] Meanwhile, to save coal, the authorities declared that all restaurants and cafés would close at 11:30 p.m., when the trams stopped running.[65]

---

[59] Annual report of Aschinger's Incorporated for 1916.

[60] Minutes of a meeting of the Association of Berlin Hoteliers, February 2, 1917.

[61] Barth to the Berlin Police Presidium, September 13, 1918, in LAB A Pr. Br. Rep. 030, Nr. 1594.

[62] On the Hindenburg Program and the advent of total war in Germany, see Jürgen Kocka, *Facing Total War: German Society, 1914–1918*, trans. Barbara Weinberger (Cambridge, MA: Harvard University Press, 1984), 36.

[63] Davis, *Home Fires Burning*, 114–15; Robert Asprey, *The German High Command at War: Hindenburg and Ludendorff Conduct World War I* (New York: W. Morrow, 1991), 320–21.

[64] Annual report of Aschinger's Incorporated for 1917.

[65] Annual report of the Association of Berlin Hoteliers for 1917.

Further regulations gummed up the works in the cellars. Bones, for example, had to be separated from the remaining gristle, boxed, labeled, and sent to the magistrate. The Bureau of Clothing (Reichsbekleidungsstelle) reduced hotels' access to new linens. Bedsheets frayed and blankets went threadbare. As paper, too, came under tighter control, chefs de reception complained of a lack of bill forms and bookkeepers scrounged for scraps.[66] All these difficulties caused the Association of Berlin Hoteliers to recommend price increases. Placards were distributed to member hoteliers with the words, "In accordance with the decision of the Association, a cost-of-living supplement of 10% of the room price will be added to hotel bills." The rarified, hyper-polite culture of the grand hotel had slowly but surely chipped away over the course of the war to reveal a business model that could not survive the ordeal intact.

HIDDEN COSTS

Shortages, regulations, and hoarding remade hotels' balance sheets and business practices. As the black market expanded over the course of the Turnip Winter (1916/17), anything a hotel purchased elsewhere became the exception to the rule, according to the business reports of Aschinger's Incorporated, which owned the Fürstenhof and, by now, the Palast-Hotel.[67] Other hospitality and gastronomy corporations would be prosecuted after the war for black marketeering.[68] To pay for goods and materials largely unavailable by licit means, hotels moved money from funds budgeted for the regular purchase of new furniture, further depleting the value of their assets, and sold off the choicest bottles in their extensive wine stores.[69] These were short-term solutions with long-term consequences.

Such deleterious business practices began in the first months of war, when rising wholesale prices for foods, and the attendant efforts not to pass these costs on to consumers, occupied the attention of chefs,

[66] Ibid.

[67] Annual report of Aschinger's Incorporated for 1917.

[68] Internal report submitted to the board of directors of the Hotel Management Corporation, January 13, 1920, in LAB A Rep. 225-01, Nr. 2; Heinrich Kreuzer, transcript of a speech, "Preispolitik im Hotelgewerbe: Vortrag gehalten auf der I. Hauptversammlung des Verbandes der Hotelbesitzervereine Deutschlands am 7. Dezember 1920 in Berlin," in LAB A Rep. 225, Nr. 893, f. 10.

[69] Annual report of the Berlin Hotel Corporation for 1916, in LAB A Rep. 001-02, Nr. 2080.

restaurant managers, and corporate boards of directors. Meanwhile, the initial dip in the number of guests – which lasted only a few months – limited hoteliers' ability to raise prices to cover mounting expenses. The industry-wide response was to hunker down for the duration by reducing liabilities and halting investment. Carpets frayed, beds sagged, paint crumbled, facades cracked, roofs leaked, machinery broke. Instead of upgrading any one of these features or systems, owners paid off loans, paid down mortgages, and even postponed previously funded renovations until "the arrival of normal conditions."[70] When normal conditions never came, and credit became tighter, hoteliers found themselves standing empty-handed amid broken furniture, rusting radiators, and inoperative machines.

The officers of Berlin's hotel corporations consistently failed to account for the insidious impact of the conflict on the long-term value of assets. Managers who sold much of their wine stores at the latest, highest prices to replace revenue lost from dining concessions realized only after the war that they might never again be able to afford the bottles they had offloaded. Those who reallocated cash from funds for new furniture to offset losses in food and drink sales, moreover, diminished the total assets of the corporation. And with the exception of the Palast-Hotel, which did have its renovations finished during the war, all renovations halted, yet managers failed to predict the long-term costs their aging plants would incur. Finally, and most damagingly (though it was beyond the control of managers and owners) was the personnel problem. The loss of armies of trained, experienced workers and white-collar employees was irredeemable. Short-term successes, such as full occupancy, obscured the trouble that lay ahead for Berlin's grand hotels.

The last year of the war, November 1917 to November 1918, was a disaster for Berlin's hotel industry, even as properties continued to maintain full occupancy. Increasing hardships – resulting from shortage, regulation, and government interference; skyrocketing prices; steadily falling revenues; and mass closures of hotels as they were converted to the offices of an engorged state bureaucracy – all helped dismantle the prewar grand hotel. To make matters worse, the winter of 1917/18 saw a complete breakdown in the coal supply. The coke and hard coal that most hotels needed to fire their furnaces fell to one-third of their required levels.[71] Although supplies reappeared at the end of January 1918, the

[70] Annual report of the Berlin Hotel Corporation for 1914.
[71] Triebel, "Coal and the Metropolis," 354.

shortage of brown coal briquettes, required to heat most of the city's residential buildings, persisted.[72] The worst ensued: coal hoarding, a crisis of confidence, and widespread unrest. Half a million workers went on strike in January 1918, exacerbating the labor shortage that had presented the single greatest challenge to hoteliers in wartime.

CONCLUSION

The scarcity of labor, food and materials, and the government's rationing schemes and decrees, brought mounting – eventually insupportable – difficulties for hoteliers. Rationing and government regulations around all matters of commercial life meant increased interference from the authorities. Enforcement was left up to hotel staff, however. This new role for waiters and others effectively upended relations between staff and guests. Then, the disappearance of skilled, experienced workers and employees further disrupted relations not only between staff and guests but also internally, among staff, management, and the corporations that owned most of the hotels. Owners and managers' business strategies, which included cartelization, black marketeering, and the sale of precious inventories, were short-term solutions that compromised the viability of the businesses in the long run. While at present the managers could enjoy the elimination of competition after waves of hotel closures, they failed to see that this situation would not outlast the decade and that its effects were detrimental to the health of the industry. The steady breakdown of grand hotels' defenses continued until, by the end of the war, the hotels' cultures of cosmopolitanism, luxury commercial hospitality, and spectacular conspicuous consumption had fallen away.

At war's end, Berlin's grand hoteliers got a nasty surprise. Instead of something approaching normal conditions, the peace brought violence and destruction.[73] In the Kaiserhof banquet hall, drunken vigilantes swung from chandeliers. In the Adlon dining room, a prince of Prussia and his supporters beat a diplomat senseless. In the vestibule of the Eden Hotel, a soldier bludgeoned a woman in front of a crowd. She fell to the floor – it was Rosa Luxemburg – but someone hauled her up again.

---

[72] Jon Lawrence, "The Transition to War in 1914," in Winter and Robert, *Capital Cities at War*, 1:155.

[73] On the violent peace more generally, see Robert Gerwarth, *The Vanquished: Why the First World War Failed to End* (New York: Farrar, Straus and Giroux, 2016), especially 118–32.

4

Hoteliers against the Republic

In defeat, the grand hotel scene became a microcosm of misery. Shortages, loss of property, financial insecurity, the breakdown in social relations, and political violence characterize the first several months of peace. All the city's hotels were subject to at least some of these phenomena; a few withstood them all: the Kaiserhof, the Eden, and the Adlon. They are uncommonly good vantage points for viewing Berlin and Germany's painful transformation from empire to republic.

World War I had left behind an exhausted and newly vulnerable grand hotel industry. The niceties were gone; so was the relative equipoise among management, white-collar employees, workers, guests, and the authorities. Incrementally, outside forces had corroded hotels' defenses and animated conflicts. Staff–management hierarchies trembled, service suffered, the labor force revolted, the state intervened. Each of these developments, any and all of which would have been inconceivable in the prewar period, posed an existential threat to the industry. Berlin's hoteliers responded by trying to form a cartel, that quintessentially illiberal formation.

Fresh threats assembled against them – from the left in the form of revolution, the January Uprising, and strikes; from the right in the form of vandalism, looting, atrocity, and an unsuccessful coup d'état. Then came the threats that originated neither on the right nor the left: material and labor shortages, high crime, inflation, hyperinflation, and rising taxes. Between 1918 and 1923, hoteliers began blaming the left and the state for all these misfortunes – a tendency that pushed them into the camp of the anti-republican right, Weimar's enemies. With the hyperinflation of 1923, a catastrophe for Berlin's grand hotels, that tendency became the rule. The republic, they had come to believe, was bad for business. The efforts of Berlin's grand hoteliers to manage the crisis of the postwar era, 1918–23, reveal a progression from quotidian struggles to political decisions that led farther and farther from the liberal path.

REVOLUTION AND THE JANUARY UPRISING

The social and political tensions of the Weimar period (1919–32) came early to Berlin's grand hotels. On November 9, 1918, bullets broke the windows of the Hotel Adlon's most luxurious corner suite facing the Brandenburg Gate and Unter den Linden, according to Hedda Adlon, the wife of Louis Adlon Jr.[1] Then, in early January, a battlefield formed at the Adlon's front door, with pro-government Freikorps (paramilitary) exchanging fire with communist revolutionaries.[2] Volleys of bullets riddled the facade. Explosions shattered the plate glass.[3]

Upon the abdication of Emperor Wilhelm II and the dissolution of his regime in November 1918, the leader of the Social Democratic Party of Germany (Sozialdemokratische Partei Deutschlands or SPD), Friedrich Ebert, assumed control as Philipp Scheidemann, another SPD politician, proclaimed a republic from the balcony of the Reichstag. All of this occurred on November 9, 1918, the same day that bullets hit the Adlon. The next day, November 10, Ebert agreed to exclude the far-left wing of his party from the government in exchange for the support of the army under Wilhelm Groener. In opposition, the left-radical Communist Party of Germany (Kommunistische Partei Deutschlands or KPD) formed on New Year's Day 1919. In the so-called Spartacist Revolt, KPD supporters took to the streets to effect another revolution, this one on behalf of the proletariat, and fight against the pro-government Freikorps. The Freikorps, in turn, commandeered the Kaiserhof as their headquarters, fortress, and impromptu jail on January 6. The end for the Spartacists came shortly thereafter, on January 15/16, when army officers arrested their leaders Rosa Luxemburg and Karl Liebknecht, interrogated and beat them at another grand hotel – the Eden – and then proceeded to

---

[1] Adlon, *Hotel Adlon*, 71.

[2] On the composition of the Freikorps, see Peter Keller, *"Die Wehrmacht der Deutschen Republik ist die Reichswehr": Die deutsche Armee, 1918–1921* (Paderborn: Ferdinand Schöningh, 2014), 51; Robert Gerwarth and John Horne, "Vectors of Violence: Paramilitarism in Europe after the Great War, 1917–1923," *Journal of Modern History* 83 (2011), 489–502.

[3] "When Revolution Stalks Streets of Berlin," *The New York Times*, January 19, 1919.

murder them both. These revenge killings introduced extreme political violence into Berlin's grand hotels, which became staging grounds in the transition from foreign war to civil war.

Rosa Luxemburg had arrived in Berlin on November 10, 1918, where she checked in to the Excelsior and got right to work with her co-revolutionary, Karl Liebknecht, who had been in town since late October. She wanted to be close to events and close to the presses recently seized for use as organs of the revolution. Until November 17 or 18, Luxemburg's hotel room at the Excelsior doubled as the Spartacists' headquarters. For Luxemburg, Liebknecht, and their opponents, Berlin's grand hotels would serve as sites of revolutionary and counterrevolutionary planning and execution.[4]

All but one of the hotels continued operations through the November 9 revolution, despite the dangers. On the 10th, shots rang out in the night "like an intermezzo" outside the Excelsior, according to the writer Harry Kessler, who was dining there.[5] Upstairs, Luxemburg and Liebknecht might have heard the shots, too. The next morning, a firefight broke out around the Central-Hotel. From turrets and windows, by some reports even from the hotel's windows, machine-gun fire tore across the dawn, but nobody was hurt. When the shooting abated, pro-revolutionary soldiers entered the building and arrested several counterrevolutionary officers.[6] There, and at other hotels, pro-revolutionary soldiers, before they left, charged managers with disarming all officers on the premises.[7] For the most part, however, guests and staff carried on as usual, even when late morning brought more shooting near the Central, this time at Wolff's Telegraph Bureau, which the revolutionaries had already occupied. At some point, too, several revolutionaries occupied the Viktoria and Astoria cafés in Friedrichstadt. A person or group broke windows there and at Wertheim's department store, but they left the hotels intact.[8]

In the coming weeks (November–December 1918), huge crowds descended on the city center, where most of Berlin's hotels were located. Tens of thousands marched through on November 20 in the funeral

---

[4] Elżbieta Ettinger, *Rosa Luxemburg: A Life* (Boston: Beacon, 1986), 233.

[5] Harry Kessler, *Das Tagebuch, 1880–1937*, vol. 6, *1916–1918*, ed. Günter Riederer (Stuttgart: Cotta, 2006), 629.

[6] Mark Jones, *Founding Weimar: Violence and the German Revolution of 1918–1919* (Cambridge: Cambridge University Press, 2016), 58.

[7] I found no evidence of a manager complying with this request.

[8] Jones, *Founding Weimar*, 58–59.

cortege for fallen revolutionaries.[9] Two days later, across the river and to the northeast of the hotels, sentries shot and killed two demonstrators at the Police Presidium. December brought an increase in violence.

The Kaiserhof stood most seriously exposed because of its location across from a focal point in revolutionary and counterrevolutionary action, the chancellery. In the late afternoon of December 6, soldiers and sailors forced Chancellor Ebert from his office and into Wilhelm-platz. Rows of revolutionary soldiers faced him in formation against the backdrop of the Hotel Kaiserhof. Nearby, another group of soldiers breached the Prussian parliament building and tried to arrest their own representatives. Spartacists demanding a temporary dictatorship of the proletariat demonstrated farther north; in an attempt to kill them all, government forces machine-gunned a crowded tram. They slew an estimated sixteen people and hurt eighty more, mostly bystanders. In response, revolutionaries and socialists organized a protest the following day. A crowd of thousands made its way through the hotel district and returned to the Kaiserhof after nightfall.

Demonstrations continued apace until the next explosion on December 24. At the palace and in its vicinity, artillery fire resounded at around 8 a.m. The government's soldiers were fighting bands of sailors who had been entrusted to protect important buildings in central Berlin but whose loyalty had come into question (Figure 4.1). By 11:30, the square in front of the city palace looked a wreck: tram lines down, rubble on the pavement, rows upon rows of broken windows and smashed muntins – smoke billowing from inside the erstwhile royal and imperial residence. By noon, the government's soldiers had lost the battle, a blow to the regime that cast doubt on its staying power.

Yet for all the fears among hoteliers and guests about the left, the real danger came from the right. By the end of January, the balance sheet would show that hoteliers, especially, only ever had the government's forces to fear. The revolutionary left, despite its soaring rhetoric, never tried to take ground from grand hotels. There is no evidence even to suggest that the Spartacists and their co-revolutionists had any interest in interfering with a single hotel. As damage to the city center and grand hotels escalated in January, with aftershocks later in 1919 and in 1920, almost all the attacks – and indeed all the devastating ones – came from

---

[9] I have distilled the rest of this section – shifting the focus to grand hotels – from Mark Jones's meticulous reconstruction of the sequence of events from newspaper accounts, memoirs, police testimony, and official reports. See Jones, *Founding Weimar*, 58–59, 151, 167–68, 180–86.

FIGURE 4.1 Sailors on patrol on Friedrichstraße in front of the
Central-Hotel, December 1918
Image credit: Scherl/Süddeutsche Zeitung

the right, not the left. In trusting the government's forces to protect commercial establishments in the central districts against bolshevist revolution, hoteliers and their class miscalculated.

In the three weeks after December 24, the failure of the government's soldiers to retake full control of the city center became apparent, and the revolution reached its crisis point, with Social Democrats committed to halting its progress toward bolshevism and the far left increasing its radical demands for the transfer of property and power to the working class. On Christmas Day, Karl Liebknecht and some 3,000 of his far-left supporters marched through central Berlin and took brief control of the Social Democrats' newspaper, *Vorwärts*, a frightening action, however inconsequential, from the perspective of the Social Democrats.

Funerals for the pro-revolutionary victims of the December 24 melee at the palace motivated perhaps the largest mass gathering to date, including supporters of almost every party, on December 29. Again, hundreds of thousands descended on the city center. The Social Democratic (moderate socialist) and German Democratic (left-liberal) contingent converged at the chancellery and Kaiserhof. There, they chanted, "Down with bolshevism! Spartacus out!" and "Deutschland, Deutschland über alles!"

The following week, on the night of January 5/6, Chancellor Ebert called on the crowd again, urging his supporters to meet at Wilhelmplatz, the site of the chancellery and the Kaiserhof, and protect it from the radical revolution that seemed to be underway. In what came to be known as the January Uprising, Spartacist and other anti-government actors took control of key sites: the *Vorwärts* offices, Wolff's Telegraph Bureau, four large publishing houses, and the printing facilities of the *Berliner Tageblatt*. At Wilhelmplatz, Philipp Scheidemann (SPD) addressed the crowd that Ebert had summoned: "This dirty mess has to be brought to an end," he pleaded. "We appeal to the entire people, especially those who are armed, the soldiers, that they remain available to the government." The listeners cheered and demanded weapons. Another speaker ascended the dais to tell women and children to go home, for "the work of the men has begun!"[10] The Social Democrats' incitement to violence across the square had direct and devastating consequences for the Kaiserhof, now at the center of a literal turf war.

THE SACK OF THE KAISERHOF

On January 6 at 4 p.m., the speeches at Wilhelmplatz having come to an end, Harry Kessler took a room at the Kaiserhof. Inside, it was business as usual. Pages sat in a row in the vestibule, he wrote in his diary. The elderly cloakroom attendant took his coat. In the atrium, waiters served tea to the clientele, a smaller group than usual. At five, Kessler went upstairs to his room to write, and as he put pen to paper, he heard gunshots, then solders calling out on the street below. He heard them running down the pavement for cover, "then silence."

Some several minutes later, shots rang out again. To Kessler, this round sounded more explosive, like a real battle. When the firing died down, he left his room for information and found soldiers on the stairs. Guests and staff were collecting in the corridors and discussing plans of action in the event of a Spartacist takeover of the building. Rumors reverberated around the hotel: *The Spartacists have surrounded us on three sides; the Spartacists are planning to storm the hotel; the Spartacists have taken the entire city center.* "Because it looked as if the hotel could

---

[10] Quoted in Jones, *Founding Weimar*, 186.

be completely cut off, I decided to go home," Kessler wrote in his diary. Once outside, he heard more shooting and fled the scene.[11]

There is no evidence to suggest that the Kaiserhof was ever under threat from the Spartacists or that the shooting came from guns other than those of the government's own forces. The *Berliner Börsen-Zeitung* reported the next day that teenage boys had come to Wilhelmplatz with guns and started firing in front of the Kaiserhof at about the time Kessler heard the first shots, but we cannot know who these boys were or whether they even existed.[12] It is just as likely that the sound of gunfire far away caused the government's stressed, excited, and trigger-happy soldiers to assume the worst and start firing into the night, beginning a vicious cycle that fed on rumor, impulse, and incitements to violence. Exaggeration of the threat from the far left likewise prompted the government to use whatever means available to lock down the city center.[13]

Shortly after Kessler's departure from the Kaiserhof, the government's soldiers there ejected the manager, the staff, and the guests. Having commandeered the hotel, the soldiers took posts in the guest rooms and fired on Spartacists – real or imagined – from the windows.[14] Even as the neighborhood returned to normal after January 7, the Kaiserhof lay in a cordon sanitaire and continued to serve as a barracks for the government's soldiers in the city center. "Government troops in the Kaiserhof, closed up and dark," Kessler reported on January 8. He then made the short walk to the Fürstenhof, open for business but with its shutters down for protection. On the sidewalk, merchants plied their wares: cigarettes, malt candy, and soap. Despite Kessler's sense that shooting could start again at any moment, peace prevailed.[15]

The uprising's final curtain on January 11 restored normalcy to most places but not inside the Kaiserhof. There, the ranks of government soldiers had swollen to 1,200. Their commanders would not give up the hotel until the end of the month. In the meantime, their men broke most of the windows, wrecked textiles and furniture, and swung from chandeliers, which eventually came crashing down. They clogged toilets, bidets, and baths, flooding the building and damaging the floors, ceilings, and

---

[11] Harry Kessler, *Das Tagebuch, 1880–1937*, vol. 7, *1919–1923*, ed. Angela Reinthal (Stuttgart: Cotta, 2007), 81.

[12] "Der Zug der Arbeitslosen," *Berliner Börsen-Zeitung*, January 7, 1919.

[13] Jones, *Founding Weimar*, 138.

[14] Minutes of meetings of the board of directors of the Berlin Hotel Corporation, January 30, 1919, and March 24, 1919, in LAB A Rep. 225, Nr. 1046.

[15] Kessler, *Tagebuch*, 7:85–87.

walls. In the restaurant and café, they smashed china and glasses, broke up the tables, and stole all the silver. They ate everything in the kitchens and storerooms and quaffed all the wine. When they finally pulled out, taking most of the Kaiserhof's remaining property, they left a sopping wreck.[16] The hotel never quite recovered.

Its ground floor reopened first, after several months, with cheaper replacements of its imperial-era furniture and finishes. The rest of the hotel required years of work and incalculable sums. Impossible to repair was the Kaiserhof's reputation. The owners tried to obscure the memory of its role in the atrocities of January 1919 with the help of an extraordinarily expensive advertising campaign, but the violence had broken the hotel's association with prestige and power. To make matters worse, when the state finally compensated the Berlin Hotel Corporation for damages to this, the crown jewel of its properties, the sum was too little, too late. The mark was so heavily devalued by 1922 that the payment amounted only to a few thousand prewar marks, not enough even to repaint the guest rooms.[17] The government declined to pay for the damages its own forces had inflicted in pursuit of counterrevolution.

The only attacks reportedly launched from the far left in 1918–19 happened at the Central and the Bristol – if these attacks happened at all.[18] The newspaper coverage is inconclusive, and no harder evidence survives. At any rate, if they are true, the stories tell of broken windows only. Compare that to the Kaiserhof, its sacking well documented, and the Eden, which hosted the most notorious atrocities of the whole uprising. There, on the night of January 15/16, amid witnesses and supporters, the government's soldiers beat Karl Liebknecht and Rosa Luxemburg nearly to death and finished them off in revenge killings nearby.

OUT OF THE EDEN

The Eden Hotel fell under partial control of the Guard Division just after New Year's Day 1919. Unlike the Kaiserhof, however, the Eden functioned more as an officers' club and headquarters, with some allowances

---

[16] Minutes of a meeting of the board of directors of the Berlin Hotel Corporation, January 30, 1919.

[17] Ibid.; minutes of meetings of the board of directors of the Berlin Hotel Corporation, October 8, 1919, October 18, 1919, March 3, 1920, March 30, 1920, September 16, 1920, and April 1, 1921, in LAB A Rep. 225, Nr. 1046.

[18] See Kurt Wrobel, *Der Sieg der Arbeiter und Matrosen: Berliner Arbeiterveteranen berichten über ihren Kampf in der Novemberrevolution* (East Berlin: Bezirksleitung der SED Groß-Berlin, 1958), 30.

made for the rank-and-file who served their commanders. Some of them became accomplices to murder on January 15/16. The staff stayed on, too, as did some of the guests, who became witnesses.

Liebknecht and Luxemburg arrived by car at the Eden Hotel on January 15. They had been arrested in their hideout in Wilmersdorf, a nearby district, and would be executed for their failed attempt to overthrow the government. The executioners of the Guard Division were convinced of Liebknecht and Luxemburg's guilt; they lived in a subculture of right-wing violence fueled by rage at the war's outcome and the outbreak of revolution in November.[19] One such soldier confirmed the identities of Luxemburg and Liebknecht at the Eden before having them escorted to separate parts of the building.

Here the narrative sequence grows murky, with conflicting testimony and several lies circulating just after the event and in the weeks, months, and years since.[20] One version has it that Luxemburg was beaten once or twice over the head, put in a car, and shot in the head, and that Liebknecht escaped blows altogether. But a recent, exhaustive assessment of all the available sources by Mark Jones, who relies in part on accounts by hotel personnel that confirm the grisliest version of the story, reveals the Eden as a site of greater atrocity than that.

The grisly version would fit the pattern of escalating violence perpetrated by the government's counterrevolutionary forces. A few days prior, on January 11, government soldiers captured the occupiers of the *Vorwärts* offices, brought them to the Dragoon Barracks south of the city center, and set upon them with horsewhips and fists. Seven prisoners were shot dead – some in the face, and with such ballistic force as to obliterate their features. Of the hundreds of revolutionaries arrested, one received extra-special treatment: a Frau Steinbring, whom the government's soldiers mistook for Rosa Luxemburg. They began hitting her as soon as she came out of the *Vorwärts* building. They kicked her and bludgeoned her with their rifle butts. Only the intervention of an officer stopped the assault, a dress rehearsal for the real performance of January 15/16 at the Eden. Stage directions had

---

[19] Jones, *Founding Weimar*, 235.

[20] Elisabeth Hannover-Drück and Heinrich Hannover, eds. *Der Mord an Rosa Luxemburg und Karl Liebknecht: Dokumentation eines politischen Verbrechens* (Frankfurt am Main: Suhrkamp, 1967), 36–58; statement of Hermann Wilhelm Souchon, June 4, 1925, in LAB A Rep. 358-01, Nr. 464, f. 45–46; report on the interrogation of Wilhelm Souchon, Landgericht II, Berlin, June 5, 1925, in LAB A Rep. 358-01, Nr. 464, f. 50.

been posted all over town, in the form of signs urging Germans to "beat [the Spartacists'] leaders dead."[21]

Liebknecht's murder played out first. Two officers and a soldier brought him out of a side door to a waiting, open-topped car, but before they reached it, a mob of military men assailed him. The beating was severe and continued as Liebknecht got into a vehicle. A waiter, among others, saw someone climb onto the chassis and bludgeon Liebknecht one more time as the car made its way out. The driver proceeded to the Tiergarten, where Liebknecht received three shots at close range. The killers then delivered his body to the morgue as that of an unknown man.

Back at the hotel, soldiers led Luxemburg into the lobby, full of officers. "Beat her to death!" they cried, according to testimony by a soldier, but Luxemburg made it all the way to the revolving door before Otto Runge, one of Liebknecht's assailants, brought a rifle butt down on her head, probably twice. And then, either at the door or just outside it, more assassins attacked. When they were done, Luxemburg lay bloody, broken, and dying. She had to be carried to the next conveyance, a small truck, and might already have been dead when the vehicle lurched into gear and someone shot her through the head. Luxemburg's killers then drove to the nearby Landwehr Canal and tipped her over the railing.[22]

The coverup began immediately, with Luxemburg and Liebknecht's killers issuing statements early on January 16 (Figure 4.2). They claimed to have shot Liebknecht as he attempted an escape and to have seen Luxemburg get beaten and shot to death by a mob of her own comrades, the Spartacists, while the government's soldiers tried in vain to save her. The problem for the story was that the assassinations had occurred in public and when the Eden Hotel was still open for business. Hotel staff and guests corrected the record in Berlin's daily papers, adding to the confusion and mystery attending such lurid reports.[23]

As the last building Luxemburg and Liebknecht ever set foot in, the Eden Hotel became an important site of anti-communist, anti-feminist, and anti-Semitic violence.[24] Later, the association proved to be a major

---

[21] Volker Ullrich, *Die Revolution von 1918/19* (Munich: C. H. Beck, 2009), 48: "Schlagt ihre Führer tot! Tötet Liebknecht! Dann werdet ihr Frieden, Freiheit und Brot haben."

[22] Jones, *Founding Weimar*, 213–14, 236.

[23] Kessler, *Tagebuch*, 7:112; Hannover-Drück and Hannover, *Mord an Rosa Luxemburg und Karl Liebknecht*, 36–58.

[24] On anti-feminism and the demonization of Luxemburg in the revolutionary period, see Matthew Kovac, "'Red Amazons'? Gendering Violence and Revolution in the

FIGURE 4.2 At the Eden Hotel shortly after the murders of Rosa Luxemburg
and Karl Liebknecht on January 15/16, 1919
Image credit: Franz Gerlach/Bundesarchiv (SAPMO), Bild Y 1-330-1485-76

public relations liability for the Eden's owners, who decided to claim in
their promotional materials that the Eden had not even existed before
1922.[25] Better to hide the property's vulnerability to the vicissitudes
of recent history, which had to be expunged if the Eden was to turn
profits in the 1920s.

THE KAPP PUTSCH AND A DINING ROOM BRAWL

In March 1919, the government gained full control of the city center, but
conditions in the grand hotels did not return to normal. The naval blockade continued into the summer, and food shortages persisted into the
1920s. Meanwhile, as demobilization proceeded, the labor market failed
to absorb returning soldiers. Those released from foreign internment

---

Long First World War, 1914–23," *Journal of International Women's Studies* 20 (2019),
71, 78; Paul Fröhlich, *Rosa Luxemburg: Ideas in Action*, trans. Joanna Hoornweg
(London: Pluto, 1994), 190.
[25] Promotional book for the Eden Hotel, n.d. (1920s), 9–10, in HAT Soz/420.

in 1919 and 1920 pushed unemployment rates even higher. Ostensibly good news for hoteliers, such high unemployment threatened their businesses in other ways. Economic dislocation bred social strife, which in turn shook the political status quo and compromised the security of the city center again.

In March 1920, Wolfgang Kapp, a nationalist politician, and Walther von Lüttwitz, a general, attempted a right-wing coup, and the city center erupted. On March 13, after the insurgents managed to occupy Friedrichstadt, where the government and grand hotels were located, the ousted cabinet called a general strike. Workers across the city abandoned their posts in support of the republic. By the evening on March 15, the lights were out. Then the gas and water supplies collapsed. Kapp and Lüttwitz's battalions stalked the streets in disarray, orders having failed to reach them from the central command since phones and cables were dead. Berlin as an urban system ceased to function, and four days into the strike, the coup foundered.[26] The moment of its failure occasioned a massacre in front of the Adlon.

George Renwick, a foreign correspondent for *The New York Times*, was stationed at the Adlon on March 18, the day Kapp and Lüttwitz's army, in retreat, processed past the hotel to the Brandenburg Gate and out of town. "Huge crowds" gathered in front of the hotel to witness the sorry parade. From a corner window at the Adlon at 5 p.m., Renwick saw a group of civilians push their way into the hotel, but they departed moments later, voluntarily. The group passed back out the doors and turned left toward Pariser Platz, into a hail of bullets fired by one of Kapp and Lüttwitz's battalions in retreat.

Renwick then saw the onset of a mass panic. Many of "the people ... thickly packed on both sides of the Pariserplatz [*sic*]" ran in all directions. Others fell on their faces to protect themselves from bullets, or as a result of being knocked to "the muddy ground," Renwick explained. The soldiers now began to shoot from all sides of the square. "Suddenly, volley after volley rang out," remembered Leonard Spray, another American journalist on the scene. Artillery horses fled in terror with their loads, careering into the backs of fleeing civilians. Amid smoke and screams, survivors rushed toward side streets, doorways, and windows. Hundreds of people pushed their way into the editorial offices of the

---

[26] "Fünf Tage Kapp Regierung," *Berliner Illustrirte Zeitung*, March 28, 1920. The *Berliner Illustrirte Zeitung* was generous in this account, giving the putschists an extra day of rule.

Lokal-Anzeiger, while "the hall of the Adlon Hotel was transformed until it looked like a hospital ward," according to Renwick. Several wounded were brought in and placed on divans to be attended by doctors and nurses, probably guests of the hotel who had volunteered their services. Two of the victims turned out already to be dead and were laid on the floor.[27] This was the second spate of violence to visit the Adlon that month. On March 6, 1920, a prince of Prussia had attacked representatives of the French government during dinner in one of the hotel's public dining rooms.

In early 1920, many of the highest-level delegates of the Entente Commission, charged with reckoning Germany's reparations obligations, had found accommodation at the Adlon. At the same time, the Adlon was becoming the favorite spot for the losers of recent events: the royals, major and minor, and their associates, especially military men like Kapp and Lüttwitz. Many of these archconservatives resented the presence of the Entente Commission and sought insidious ways to show displeasure. By early March 1920, the situation in the Adlon was explosive.

On the night of March 6, diners filled the hotel's main restaurant. Most of them were German, but a small party of French nationals – two Frenchman in town with the commission and one of their wives – had been seated on the terrace, near the table of Prince Joachim Albrecht of Prussia, a cousin of the deposed emperor. At some point, the orchestra struck up and began to play "Deutschland über alles," just as it did every night in compliance with a standing request from the prince. A soprano began an impromptu performance, and soon almost everyone in the room was standing. The French guests remained seated. As the music swelled, Prince Joachim cried to the French, "Aufstehen!" ("Stand up!"). As the crowd hushed and turned to face him, Joachim repeated himself: "Aufstehen!" Others began to shout the same – "Aufstehen! Aufstehen!" – until the music died down.[28]

Seeing that the French meant to defy him, Joachim hurled a saucer at their table. Other diners followed suit. A wine bottle fell behind the

---

[27] George Renwick, "Junker Farewell a Berlin Tragedy," *The New York Times,* March 20, 1920.

[28] Statement of Alfred Körner (sommelier) March 11, 1920, in LAB A Rep. 358-01, Nr. 2039; statement of Prince Victor Salvator of Isenburg, March 8, 1920, in LAB A Rep. 358-01, Nr. 2039, f. 5; statement of Alexi von Harfeld, March 8, 1920, in LAB A Rep. 358-01, f. 7; statement of Richard Augur, March 8, 1920, in LAB A Rep. 358-01, Nr. 2039, f. 20; statement of Wilhelm Back (waiter), March 11, 1920, in LAB A Rep. 358-01, Nr. 2039; statement of Georg Seiser (waiter), in LAB A Rep. 358-01, Nr. 2039, f. 17.

chair of one of the Frenchmen, a champagne flute into the seatback of the other. En masse, men and women in evening dress began to ascend the steps to the terrace to assail the foreigners. The one woman in the French party managed to escape unscathed, the headwaiter having spirited her out just in time. The two men had less luck. Members of the mob began to pummel them about the head, face, and torso. One of the Frenchmen succeeded somewhat in defending himself, though he was hit many times. Eventually, a waiter managed to drag him from the room to safety. Alone, the second Frenchman faced the brunt of the attack. He was pulled out of his chair and thrown to the floor, whereupon his fellow diners kicked him in the back and sides. Two men pulled him up and held him fast by the arms so that others could take turns delivering blows. He would at times manage to free his arms to guard his abdomen, but then a volley of punches to the face would knock him from his feet. His attackers kept pulling him up from the floor to begin again. They also tried to pull his hair out. Eventually, mercifully, they let him go. Bleeding, his dinner jacket torn, his tie ripped, and his cigarette case and money stolen, he reconvened with the other members of his party in the safety of the directors' office, where Lorenz and Louis Adlon, the father and son, apologized profusely for what had happened.[29]

Such a scene had never played out in a grand hotel in Berlin. The image of this descent into barbarity in the finest public dining room in the country, occupied by over a hundred men and women in evening dress and jewels, was great fodder for the press. Louis Adlon himself referred to the event as a "scandal."[30] What had been like a second Berlin residence to the royal family in prewar years was by 1920 a terrain that required violence to defend. The prince's ejection from the premises (he was arrested shortly after the attacks) mirrored his cousin Wilhelm's disgrace sixteen months prior.

There were enough accounts from disinterested observers of the brawl – particularly lower-ranking waiters and hapless diners – for the police to complete a full investigation. All the royals or aristocrats interviewed

---

[29] Ibid.; statement of the victims, a Captain Rougevin and a Captain Klein, March 7, 1920, in LAB A Rep. 358-01, Nr. 2039, f. 36–38; statement of Louis Adlon, in LAB A Rep. 358-01, Nr. 2039; statement of Oberleutnant Wilhelm Bartels, March 8, 1920, in LAB A Rep. 358-01, Nr. 2039, f. 15.

[30] "Prince Joachim, Ex-Kaiser's Cousin, Attacks French Party in Berlin Hotel," *The New York Times*, March 8, 1920; "Germany Disavows Joachim's Actions," *The New York Times*, March 20, 1920.

vigorously denied the charge that the prince had had anything to do with the disturbance, but damning testimony from the prince's waiter and from several people seated nearby, as well as the testimony of the victims, pointed to the prince's guilt. The state prosecutor eventually charged him with incitement to violence and culpability in the crime of assault, for which he was ultimately fined 500 marks – a slap on the wrist.[31]

The events of March 6 at the Adlon signaled the vulnerability of foreigners and cosmopolitans even in the city's most rarified venues. Now more than a year in the past, the end of the war had not returned conditions to normal. Equipoise between cosmopolitan and nationalist imperatives had not returned, nor had the stability of social relations specific to the grand hotel hierarchy. On the contrary, conditions for grand hotels and more generally, for social, economic, cultural, and political life in Berlin, were more poisonous than they had been in generations. Into the 1920s, grand hotels would figure as crucibles in which tensions reached the breaking point, arenas where groups with irreconcilable differences contested one another's right to enter and enjoy, as well as to profit from, or simply earn a living within, the city's economy of elite hospitality.

STRIKES

In light of the Kaiserhof sacking, the Eden murders, and the Adlon massacre and dinner brawl, hoteliers' visions of the future were grim in 1919/20. At the meeting of the board of directors of the Berlin Hotel Corporation on January 30, 1919, one member stated the obvious. Since the "outbreak of the revolution," business had dried up. In addition to the dangers of going out and traveling during an incipient civil war and amid widespread street fighting, Germans' lower incomes and the continuation of the wartime blockade made it "impossible" to resume the "luxury services of former times." Wilhelm Rüthnik, member of the board of the Berlin Hotel Corporation and general manager of the ruined Kaiserhof, tendered a solution: to dissolve the accommodation concession entirely. After some discussion, the directors opted for exploratory steps toward other sources of revenue, in this case in the form of a five o'clock tea dance. "With amusements like these," Rüthnik reasoned, "we might again find at least a modicum of profitability."[32] Yet the

---

[31] "Hohenzollern Prince Fined for Assault," *The New York Times*, April 17, 1920.

[32] Minutes of a meeting of the board of directors of the Berlin Hotel Corporation of January 30, 1919, in LAB A Rep. 225, Nr. 1046.

main problem from the hoteliers' perspective was the workforce, not the violence or the blockade or the impoverishment of the clientele. The very day of the occupation of the Kaiserhof, the rest of Berlin's hotels had also descended into chaos. Effective January 6, 1919, the city's waiters were on strike.[33]

Leaders of the Union of Hospitality and Gastronomy Workers (Verband der Gastwirtsgehilfen) coordinated the strike and demanded the abolition of tipping as well as the institution of a weekly wage of 90 to 130 marks, the immediate implementation of an eight-hour workday, and a prohibition on firing a waiter without the express approval of the union. The issue of tipping had been fraught since before the war but came to a head now that custom had collapsed and with it a waiter's chance of earning enough in tips to feed himself.

Das Hotel, the leading trade publication for hoteliers, described unruly crowds at restaurants across the city. The fashionable Café Keck fell to demonstrators who destroyed all the breakables, "from plates to champaign coolers." The Adlon's restaurant was one of the few to remain open during the strike, thus prompting a demonstration of 1,500 waiters and their sympathizers in front of the hotel, according to *Das Hotel*. Some members of the crowd apparently even forced their way into the restaurant; as the dining room filled with demonstrators, patrons made for the exits. The publication reported that the demonstrators "thrashed" a diplomat and "violently attacked" either Lorenz or Louis Adlon.[34]

In increasing numbers, hoteliers responded to the strike, which *Das Hotel* called "this terror," by trying to move together against the strikers. Occurring at the same time as the January Uprising (early January 1919), the waiters' strike became another example of a world turned upside down and a case in point for the argument that forces of the liberal order should come together and crush the radicalism of workers-turned-activists. Echoing language from pro-government speeches during the uprising, Ernst Barth, still chairman of the Association of Berlin Hoteliers, told a reporter for *Das Hotel* that he believed it was the "duty" of all hoteliers to come together "in solidarity."

---

[33] On confrontational labor politics after World War I, see Petra Weber, *Gescheiterte Sozialpartnerschaft – Gefährdete Republik? Industrielle Beziehungen, Arbeitskämpfe und der Sozialstaat: Deutschland und Frankreich im Vergleich, 1918–1933/39* (Munich: Oldenbourg, 2010), 179–90; Sean Dobson, *Authority and Upheaval in Leipzig, 1910–1920: The Story of a Relationship* (New York: Columbia University Press, 2001), 189ff.

[34] "Kellnerausstand in Berlin," *Das Hotel*, January 10, 1919.

Ernst Rachwalsky, managing director of the Interest Group for the German Hospitality and Gastronomy Trades (Interessenverband für deutsche Gastwirtsgewerbe), which represented the hoteliers and restaurateurs in negotiations with the Union of Hospitality and Gastronomy Workers, urged a punishing form of collective action on the part of owners: Close every restaurant for the duration of the strike to produce infighting between waiters who wanted to return to work and waiters who did not. Although the shuttering of restaurants and cafés large and small proceeded almost without exception, the strategy failed.[35] Hoteliers and restaurateurs' balance sheets could not sustain the closures. On January 10 and 11, just as the January Uprising was meeting its atrocious end, the Association of Berlin Hoteliers gave in. It notified hotel employees, by means of large placards, of the hoteliers' decision to abolish tipping for waiters and non-waitstaff, raise wages to make up the difference, and shift almost everyone to an eight-hour day. To cover the expense, restaurant prices would go up 20 percent.[36]

Within four days, the Union of Hospitality and Gastronomy Workers had gotten what it wanted. By January 15, 1919, the agreement would come into force at every hotel except the Kaiserhof, which was still out of its owners' control and in the process of being sacked by the government's forces.[37] Soon, kitchen workers got their due. On March 26 and 27, 1919, in Frankfurt, the Coalition of Hoteliers' Associations of Germany (Verband der Hotelbesitzervereine Deutschlands) and its member organizations, including the Association of Berlin Hoteliers, met with various service workers' unions to standardize wages for kitchen staff across the Reich. The talks succeeded. The standardization of wages ushered in what *Das Hotel* called "a new era for the German hotel industry."[38]

---

[35] Ibid.

[36] "Beschlüsse des Vereins Berliner Hotelbesitzer," *Das Hotel*, January 24, 1919. The eight-hour working day had become the law of the land for industrial workers on November 23, 1918, and extended to most other workers, including white-collar employees, on March 18, 1919. See Ben Fowkes, trans. and ed. *The German Left and the Weimar Republic: A Selection of Documents* (Leiden: Brill, 2014), 21–22. On labor unions' efforts to get the eight-hour day enshrined in law, see Gerard Braunthal, *Socialist Labor and Politics in Weimar Germany: The General Federation of German Trade Unions* (Hamden, CT: Archon, 1978), 255–56.

[37] E. Kiefer and H. Bieget, "Nottarif im Berliner Hotel- und Gastwirtgewerbe," *Das Hotel*, January 17, 1919.

[38] "Der erste Reichstarif im deutschen Hotelgewerbe," *Das Hotel*, April 4, 1919.

And yet, labor relations remained stormy. Strikes broke out again in May 1919.[39] Disputes with "our more than 2,000 employees," Aschinger's Incorporated reported in its 1919 annual report, "have not settled down even for a second."[40] The language here fits a pattern. Since the end of the war, the board of Aschinger's had used hyperbole to get the point across to shareholders that the workers needed to be brought to heel. Rising wages threatened "to attain undreamed-of dimensions and will serve in the end to bury" the business, read the annual report for 1918 (drafted in April and May of 1919).[41] Wages for 1918 had imposed a total cost of 3,273,578 marks, while the sum of all dividends did not exceed 120,000. The situation had been "uncommonly favorable" to the workers, Aschinger's top brass reasoned.

Many white-collar employees agreed and took sides against the workers. The Combined Associations of Hotel Employees (Hotel-angestelltenverbände), the umbrella organization for various associations of clerks, accountants, salesmen, procurers, and management staff, had made its position clear on the pages of the *Deutsche Gastwirte-Zeitung* back in February 1919.[42] The Combined Associations of Hotel Employees wanted nothing to do with what they and their employers called, again, the "terror" tactics of hotel workers. The best thing to do was to have white-collar employees join their own unions, which would use "Christian" principles to exorcise the workers of their bolshevism.[43] This anti-Bolshevik, anti-labor rhetoric had echoes in the liberal and right-wing pro-government newspapers, which responded to strikes, such as the general strike of March 3–7, 1919, with increasing militancy.[44]

In their 1919 report (written in early 1920), Aschinger's directors weighed in on the government's labor policy. If the reduction of unemployment was the aim, they argued, then the state would have to freeze wages and force workers' acquiescence. The report went on to claim that the survival of grand hotels and related businesses depended on workers

---

[39] "Vereinsnachrichten: Verein Berliner Hotelbesitzer," *Das Hotel*, May 18, 1919.

[40] Annual report of Aschinger's Incorporated for 1919, drafted in 1920, in LAB A Rep. 225, Nr. 635.

[41] Annual report of Aschinger's Incorporated for 1918, in LAB A Rep. 225, Nr. 635.

[42] "Hotelangestelltenverbände gegen den Terror," *Das Hotel*, February 7, 1919.

[43] Ibid. On Christian labor unions and the Stinnes–Legien Agreement (November 15, 1918), see William L. Patch Jr., *Christian Trade Unions in the Weimar Republic, 1918–1933* (New Haven: Yale University Press, 1985), 36–37; on Christian unions' anti-socialism, see the same volume, 47–49.

[44] Jones, *Founding Weimar*, 259–64.

"merely recognizing that their movement for higher wages must be kept within the bounds of what is bearable."[45] Wages and salaries had indeed increased. The total expenditure on payments to staff for the year 1920 topped 18 million marks, up from 8.5 million in 1919 and 3.5 million in 1918.[46] What the board did not recognize, or refused to recognize, in its arguments against the workers, was that inflation, mounting since 1914, easily outstripped this increase in wages and salaries.[47]

Agreements about wages started to fall apart in 1921, and not only because inflation threatened to wipe out the recent raises. On May 25, 1921, the *Berliner Tageblatt* reported that both employers and some waiters were in the process, however quietly, of rolling back the abolition of tipping.[48] This illicit yet widespread practice of accepting tips resulted in another strike on October 1, 1921.[49] *Das Hotel* accused union leaders of exhibiting a "flippancy without parallel." Were their "eyes closed" to the weakness of the industry and the paucity of its resources? Yes, it seemed: The strike was nothing more than the invitation to a "trial of strength." A victory for the workers, should the hoteliers and restaurateurs surrender, would prove pyrrhic, according to *Das Hotel*. No industry and therefore no jobs would be left.[50] Stalemate ensued; the strike lasted weeks.

In some cases, to offer a tip was to stake a position against the workers' movement, socialism, and the republic. In October 1921, Prince Joachim Albrecht, who was allowed back into the Adlon after having been arrested the year before for assaulting the French delegates to the Entente Commission, tried to force his waiter to accept a tip. Cyril Brown of *The New York Times* tried it, too, and met the same "adamant refusal."[51]

---

[45] Ibid.

[46] Annual report of Aschinger's Incorporated for 1920, in LAB A Rep. 225, Nr. 1162.

[47] Cf. Bessel, *Germany after the First World War*, 30–35.

[48] "Die Gesellschaft für soziale Reform und das Trinkgeldproblem," *Berliner Tageblatt*, May 25, 1921.

[49] "Die 'schlagenden' Argumente der streikenden Gastwirtsgehilfen," *Das Hotel*, October 14, 1921.

[50] "Gastwirtsgehilfenstreik in Berlin," *Das Hotel*, October 7, 1921. On an important exception, among many, to this anti-labor stance among business owners, see Werner Plumpe, "The End of World War I," in *Business in the Age of Extremes: Essays in Modern German and Austrian Economic History*, eds. Hartmut Berghoff et al., (New York: Cambridge University Press, 2013), 41.

[51] Cyril Brown, "Berlin Waiters, Striking for Higher Pay," *The New York Times*, October 4, 1921; "Lifts Ban on Joachim," *The New York Times*, December 11, 1920. On the leniency of the judiciary in cases of right-wing criminality, see Anthony McElligott, *Rethinking the Weimar Republic: Authority and Authoritarianism, 1916–1936* (London: Bloomsbury, 2014), especially chapters 5 and 7.

The situation was almost explosive. Reports abounded of union saboteurs who punished strikebreaking by sneaking into hotels at night to
hang threatening signs and steal or destroy property, food, and wine.[52]
Das Hotel hoped that these retaliatory actions would be a "wakeup call
to everybody" and show that such strikes could not go on unabated.[53]

Yet the strike did go on. By its third week, scarcely any hotel rooms
could be found in Berlin. Where one did happen to be available, the traveler might contend with "strikers driving guests from the hotels, sometimes with violence." The Paris edition of the *Chicago Tribune* recounted
breathlessly the experience of two American women who, after "a week
in the Kaiserhof without food, light, or heat ... [,] were forced to flee
from the hotel" all the way to Paris.[54]

By this point in 1921, Berlin's hotels already presented the precon-
ditions for the eventual crisis of German democracy, the collapse of the
Weimar Republic. A propertied class – the hoteliers – established close
associations among each other to control labor by whatever means necessary. These associations would turn into cartels and other illiberal formations. Meanwhile, the leaders of the working class seized the moment
to tip the balance in their favor. And finally, the petty bourgeoisie, the
white-collar employees, adopted radical language and a radical tone that
took issue not with the machinations of their betters but with the exer-
tions of their inferiors. Fearful of downward social mobility and unsure
of how to respond to the political culture of the new republic, these
white-collar employees of the lower middle class turned increasingly to
the splinter parties of the radical right.[55]

---

[52] "Sabotage in Berlin's Hotels," *The New York Times*, October 15, 1921.

[53] "Die 'schlagenden' Argumente der streikenden Gastwirtsgehilfen."

[54] "Berlin Waiters' Strike," *Chicago Tribune*, Paris edition, October 20, 1921.

[55] Detlev J. K. Peukert, *The Weimar Republic: The Crisis of Classical Modernity*, trans.
Richard Deveson (New York: Hill and Wang, 1992), 156–58, 233; Thomas Childers,
"The Social Language of Politics in Germany: The Sociology of Political Discourse
in the Weimar Republic," *American Historical Review* 95 (1990), 332–33. On the
"negative self-definition" of the *Mittelständler*, somewhere between proletarian and
bourgeois, see Eley, *From Unification to Nazism*, 237–38; Benjamin Lapp, *Revolution from the Right: Politics, Class, and the Rise of Nazism in Saxony, 1919–1933*
(Boston: Humanities Press, 1997), 136–83; Michael L. Hughes, *Paying for the German
Inflation* (Chapel Hill: University of North Carolina Press, 1988), 48–50, 107–9. On
the historiography concerning the Nazis' social base, see Frederick L. McKitrick, *From
Craftsmen to Capitalists: German Artisans from the Third Reich to the Federal Republic, 1939–1953* (New York: Berghahn, 2016), 12–14; Patch, *Christian Trade Unions*,
199–201.

RIGHTWARD DRIFT

However tenaciously hoteliers attempted to cling to laissez-faire liberalism, in their political statements, they began to drift to the right. The mainstream of their politics between 1919 and 1924 flowed into a synthesis of anti-republicanism and National Liberalism. Anti-labor liberalism had been easier to sustain in the prewar period, when the Social Democrats had scant access to power, than it was now, with the Social Democrats in control of a governing coalition of left-center parties. In this new era, hoteliers supported the Social Democrats so long as they cracked down on worker militancy, a "grave danger," one hotelier wrote, against which everybody had to "stick together" – to defeat "these radicals" and their "terroristic principles."[56] "The world war may have ended," read an opinion piece of August 1919, "but the war of Germany with itself has yet to find its end."[57]

Many men of the hotel industry made clear whose side they were on. A lawyer writing for *Das Hotel* in January 1921 referred to the economy under state control as the "sword of Damocles … hanging over the head of every hotelier and restaurateur" in Germany. Or, if not a sword over the head, the managed economy was a shackle around the ankle, heavy and "unbearably" tight.[58] In this sense, hoteliers perceived the outcome of the war as having little to do with the present economic peril, which they believed was the product of larger, more obscure forces acting on a fledgling republic, pushing it toward illiberal economic policies that had to be stopped.

This logic, which associated the republic and unseen forces behind it with Germany's present woes, extended to foreign relations. The rejection of the Treaty of Versailles and subsequent ancillary agreements became an increasingly popular position among hoteliers – disadvantageous agreements for which hoteliers blamed the republic alone. Here, liberalism entered the conversation, for revision would usher in an era of free trade, and only through free trade – that is, the self-correcting capacity of the free market – could inflation be halted.[59] Yet this liberalism expressed itself in the treaty-revisionist terms of the anti-republican right.

---

[56] "Kellnerausstand in Berlin."
[57] "Mit- und nicht gegeneinander," *Das Hotel*, August 1, 1919.
[58] "Das schiefe Gleis unserer Zwangswirtschaft," *Das Hotel*, January 21, 1921.
[59] Annual report of Aschinger's Incorporated for 1921, in LAB A Rep. 225, Nr. 636. On liberals and the politics of reparations, see Andrew Williams, *Liberalism and War: The Victors and the Vanquished* (New York: Routledge, 2006), especially chapters 3 and 6.

On July 12, 1920, Heinrich Kreuzer, chairman of the so-called Hotel Trust Cooperative (Hoteltreuhandgenossenschaft), in his address to the first annual meeting of the Coalition of Hoteliers' Associations of Germany, pulled together the strands of anti-republicanism and National Liberalism. Identifying a litany of disasters and blunders that had brought the hotel industry to its knees, Kreuzer told everyone who was to blame:

The people, who have no understanding [of the problem], as well as the government and the municipalities, who sit by in silence as one fine hotel after the other is stripped of its identity, are all guilty. It is they who will be held responsible if in the foreseeable future the German hospitality and travel industries collapse and thus forfeit every competitive advantage to foreign countries, which never could have happened in the old days.[60]

Examples in recent months had indeed proved the indispensability of the hotel industry to German culture, society, and politics. After all, hotels had accommodated and continued to accommodate delegates to the Entente Commission meetings, where the details of reparations were hammered out. National and international business likewise depended on the capacity of Berlin's grand hotels to accommodate investors, salesmen, and money carriers. But fewer examples supported the belief that responsibility for the hotel industry's woes lay primarily with the Weimar state and society.

Kreuzer's was an accusation that took its cues from the legend of the "stab in the back" (*Dolchstoßlegende*), then making rounds among right-radicals, conservatives, and other Germans, positing that proponents of the illegitimate republic had undermined the army and lost the war for Germany. Thereafter, Jewish, socialist, and effeminate republicans had disgraced the German people by signing the "war guilt clause," had degraded the German state by dismantling the military, had dismembered the German nation by ceding territory, and had crippled the German economy by agreeing to pay reparations in cash, gold, and kind.[61]

---

[60] Transcript of a speech given in Berlin by Heinrich Kreuzer, managing director of the Hotel Trust Cooperative, at the First Executive Convention of the Coalition of Hoteliers' Associations of Germany in Düsseldorf, December 7, 1920, in LAB A Rep. 225, Nr. 893.

[61] See George S. Vascik and Mark R. Sadler, eds. *The Stab-in-the-Back Myth and the Fall of the Weimar Republic: A History in Documents and Visual Sources* (London: Bloomsbury, 2016), especially chapter 8. See also Boris Barth, *Dolchstoßlegenden und politische Desintegration: Das Trauma der deutschen Niederlage im Ersten Weltkrieg, 1914–1933* (Düsseldorf: Droste, 2003); Sally Marks, "Mistakes and Myths: The Allies, Germany, and the Versailles Treaty, 1918–1921," *Journal of Modern History* 85 (2013), 635; Corey Ross, "Mass Politics and Techniques of Leadership: The Promise and Perils of Propaganda in Weimar Germany," *German History* 24 (2006), 188.

And now, Kreuzer charged, these internal enemies had trained their sights on the grand hotels of Berlin. In 1920, Kreuzer's was an extreme position for a hotelier to take. By the end of 1923, it was commonplace. The war having cut short their forty-year commitment to liberalism and cosmopolitanism, hoteliers embraced increasingly conservative and xenophobic explanations for the postwar disaster as their worldview swung ever further toward the anti-republican right.

Against this trend, some hoteliers nonetheless clung to the vestige of prewar liberalism that emphasized the capacity of the free market to correct all imbalances. "Experience teaches us," argued Richard Weser, the chairman of the board of Aschinger's Incorporated, "that free trade alone is capable of delivering the necessary quantities of foodstuffs, cheaply and unspoiled, to where they are wanted." The problem, he felt, was not shortage itself but the regulations imposed to mitigate it. The tendency of raw materials rationing and wage-setting to increase the cost of domestic goods was threatening to do "monstrous damage" to the German economy, he warned. Regulation of domestic production gave the advantage to foreign suppliers – and here Weser would have meant Germany's old foes. This time, the way to beat them was not to dig in but to reach out. Let the world market determine prices and Germany would prosper; turn its back on the world and on free trade and nothing could "save our national economy."[62]

Yet the German government was not the only party responsible for the interruption of free trade. The Entente, having declined to disband, continued its blockade, "view[ing] us still as opponents in the field," according to the annual report of Aschinger's Incorporated for 1920. The report went on to complain about Entente members "casting us, whom they hate ... as the counterpoint to their humanitarianism, to their love of freedom and justice." The Entente had not considered the "consequences of this line of thinking": continued hostility and the danger of another war.[63] A contributor to *Das Hotel* took the same view when he complained about the deleterious effects of the symbolic "action" (*Akt*) at Versailles.[64] Like so many of his compatriots, he refused to use the document's title phrase, "Treaty of Peace."

As German businessmen, liberal and otherwise, Berlin's hoteliers found themselves in a difficult position. Wanting to get on with the

---

[62] Annual report of Aschinger's Incorporated for 1920.
[63] Ibid.
[64] "Der Friede und die internationale Hotelindustrie," *Das Hotel*, July 11, 1919.

West and restart international streams of custom and credit, they would have advocated for the settlement of the reparations question at once. In other words, reparations and the Treaty of Versailles would be the cost of doing business with France, Britain, and the others. Yet, as Germans in Germany, Berlin's hoteliers were subject to an extensive campaign of misinformation about the treaty, reparations, the nature of the peace, and the reality of defeat.[65] In the main, hoteliers added to the confusion by agreeing and arguing in public that reparations would bankrupt Germany and therefore should not be paid. In reality, these hoteliers were prolonging their own pain, having lost sight of their original priority, the resumption of normal relations with Britain, France, and the United States.

Between 1918 and 1924, bitter recriminations against Germany's erstwhile foes became a common feature of hoteliers' comments, annual reports, and editorials for *Das Hotel*. In his opinion piece for that publication, Harry Nitsch, an authority in the field of advertising in the hotel industry, singled out the French for special opprobrium.[66] To him, Germans telling their downtrodden and pessimistic compatriots to summon "our people's inner strength and efficiency" to pay up – to find "Germany's star," to submit to the "healing power of Reason" – was not only useless but also un-German; indeed, it was a prototypically French thing to do, a pragmatic, cynical, yet foolhardy approach to negotiations that rested on a delusion. The worship of reason and the belief in the nation's capacity to overcome all challenges captured the spirit of the French Revolution in the days "of Robespierre and Danton," Nitsch argued.[67] Railing against the French machine state while praising the German genius for freedom had become current as early as the 1790s, shortly after the Reign of Terror. In offering this familiar opposition, Nitsch lent a historic and spiritual importance to the question of reparations.[68]

---

[65] See Marks, "Mistakes and Myths," 644.

[66] Nitsch's book appeared in 1927 under the title *Das Hotel- und Gastgewerbe: Moderne Propaganda-Methoden* (Düsseldorf: Floeder, 1927). By 1933, the same press (Friedrich Floeder Verlag) was printing Nazi propaganda, such as *Das Ehrenbuch des Führers: Der Weg zur Volksgemeinschaft* (The Führer's Book of Honor: The Path to the National [Aryan] Community) by Heinz Haake (1933).

[67] Harry Nitsch, "Die neue Zeit: Einführung und Ausblicke," *Das Hotel*, November 7, 1919.

[68] On the origins of this German vision of French civilization, see Frederick C. Beiser, *Enlightenment, Revolution, and Romanticism: The Genesis of Modern German Political Thought, 1790–1800* (Cambridge, MA: Harvard University Press, 1992), 1–7ff.

Nitsch had nothing to offer in the way of advice, however, and could propose no way out. Deliverance from the present disaster depended on a change of heart among the alleged authors of Germany's misfortune in Paris and London, he suggested. They were the culprits. Other hoteliers extended these assignments of guilt to the Weimar coalition parties, especially the Social Democrats who, as Kreuzer put it in the speech to his colleagues, had sabotaged the German economy by abetting the Entente's program of extortion.[69]

Nonetheless, many hoteliers saw the pitfalls of expressing widespread resentment of Germany's enemies. After all, former foes made for reliable guests flush with foreign currency. As soon after the war as January 1919, a contributor to *Das Hotel* asserted that hoteliers must be "neutral," or at least appear to be neutral, in all matters including foreign relations. "The visitor of those nationalities" made to feel unwelcome here will prefer to "clear out and stay away." Moreover, deprivations resulting from the continued blockade needed to be hidden lest they evoke uncomfortable feelings of guilt among French and British guests. Guests, when in the hotel, should forget the unpleasantness. They "would not like to see that the hotel industry suffered acutely because of the war, nor indeed that it still suffers from the effects of the war, nor that it is because of these effects that not every wish of the traveling public can be fulfilled to satisfaction." Still, the writer recognized that some acknowledgment of the difficulties would be in order, perhaps a nicely worded notice about postwar scarcity.[70]

SCARCITY, CONSPIRACY, CRIMINALITY

Hoteliers' rightward drift happened in the context of poor labor relations and mounting shortages of materials and fuel. Scarcity was most severe during mass strikes, but at no time before 1924 did the pressure on supplies quite relax. Hoteliers had not expected the continuation of the blockade much past the armistice. Even after it lifted, cooks lacked adequate supplies of flour, butter, sugar, milk, meat, and potatoes into 1920 and in some cases beyond. With cream deliveries intermittent, guests often had to take their coffees black. In September 1919,

---

[69] Transcript of a speech by Heinrich Kreuzer, December 7, 1920. On the politics of reparations in the German People's Party (Deutsche Volkspartei, successor to the National Liberal Party), see Raffael Scheck, *Mothers of the Nation: Right-Wing Women in Weimar Germany* (Oxford: Berg, 2004), 34. See also Lothar Gall, *Walther Rathenau: Porträt einer Epoche* (Munich: Beck, 2009), 223.

[70] "Der Hotelgast der neuen Zeit," *Das Hotel*, January 31, 1919.

managers reported a perilous shortage of coal, as well. To keep people alive through winter, the state imposed limits on the consumption of gas, electricity, water, and certain foodstuffs. Only later in 1920, when poultry, fish, game, meat, and potatoes came off rationing, did hoteliers observe a turning point for the gastronomy side of the business.[71]

Throughout the difficult period, however, there remained one shortage that turned out to be a major advantage to Berlin's hoteliers. In April 1919, *Das Hotel* reported that the "lack of housing" had resulted in "a severe state of emergency" in the capital. "Thousands of people without apartments" were coming to the hotels for relief, and most hotels, at full capacity, were turning people away.[72] In October 1919, Ewald Kretschmar, manager of the Bristol, responding to government proposals to force the conversion of hotels into apartment houses, beseeched city officials to recognize that the acute shortage of apartments had produced an equally acute shortage of hotel rooms.[73] As the magistrate moved to compel the sale of many of Berlin's small and medium-sized hotels, a group of hotel and restaurant staff held a protest against the disappearance of their workplaces. The protest, at the headquarters of the Teachers' Union (Lehrervereinshaus) on April 29, 1921, descended into chaos and effectively stopped the magistrate from taking any further action.[74] Still, the specter of requisition remained present. In October 1921, a new law enabled the municipality of Vienna to claim a full quarter of the city's hotel rooms for use as apartments.[75] Increasingly, in Vienna as well as Berlin, chefs de reception had to act as gatekeepers, explaining to guests time and again, and with increasing insistence, why no rooms could be made available today, tomorrow, or even at any near-future date.

The shortage of apartments and rooms, a result of underinvestment in residential real estate and the closure of so many hotels during the war, ensured the survival and even profitability of many hotel businesses.[76] The gift of full occupancy saved most of Berlin's grand hotels

[71] Report of the managing directors to the board of directors of the Hotel Management Corporation, January 13, 1920, in LAB A Rep. 225-01, Nr. 2; annual reports of Aschinger's Incorporated for 1919, 1920, and 1921; "Kohlennot und Polizeistunde," *Das Hotel*, September 12, 1919.

[72] "Die Hotels und die Wohnungsnot," *Das Hotel*, April 18, 1919.

[73] "Hotelnot," *Berliner Tageblatt*, October 4, 1919.

[74] "Protest" (editorial), *Das Hotel*, May 6, 1921.

[75] "Requisition von Hotels," *Neues Wiener Journal*, October 30, 1921.

[76] See Thomas Koinzer, *Wohnen nach dem Krieg: Wohnungsfrage, Wohnungspolitik, und der Erste Weltkrieg in Deutschland und Großbritannien, 1914–1932* (Berlin: Duncker & Humblot, 2001), 24–28, 233–48.

from closure in the face of the labor and materials crisis.[77] Room rates stayed high – so high, in fact, that guests threatened to call the Anti-Profiteering Office (Wucheramt). Hoteliers responded by developing a blacklist. At a 1922 meeting of Berlin's hoteliers, attendees decided to notify each other, by means of a circular letter, of guests who had ever threatened to call the authorities. Moreover, they promised to bar anyone who "otherwise makes difficulties for the hotelier and restaurateur."[78] In hotel restaurants, management called on headwaiters to observe guests' demeanor and to take in hand anyone disgruntled enough to threaten the house with exposure to the authorities for any perceived infraction, usually having to do with pricing. If the exchange between headwaiter and guest soured, the restaurant manager would be called. In December 1922, five people identifying themselves as "longtime guests" of the Fürstenhof complained to head manager Franz Kessels that his colleague in the restaurant had "harassed us" and otherwise exhibited "improper behavior" (*ungebührendes Verhalten*), all on account of a breakfast bill.[79]

Upstairs, hoteliers learned to be creative, accommodating more and more guests with fewer and fewer resources. Kessels decided to convert the Fürstenhof's extra bathrooms to bedrooms, but finding funds for the furniture became difficult as prices continued to rise.[80] On September 1, 1922, he reported to his boss, Chief Corporate Officer Hans Lohnert of the parent company Aschinger's Incorporated, that the Fürstenhof was now in the position of having to turn away even the most important and loyal guests. The bathroom conversions, as well as the use of six small single rooms as doubles, no longer sufficed. Kessels was now preparing to make doubles out of the rest of the singles, and that meant finding extra blankets, sheets, pillows, and beds "of any kind." To increase the number of beds, he had chaises longues broken down and reassembled to lie flat.[81]

The task was not made easier by the fact that "*so much bedding has been stolen recently.*"[82] Further difficulties ensued as inflation and

---

[77] Annual reports of Aschinger's Incorporated for 1918, 1919, 1920, and 1921.

[78] Minutes from a confidential meeting of the Berlin Hotels Commission (Kommission der Berliner Hotels), Group A and B, November 7, 1922, in LAB A Rep. 225, Nr. 1174.

[79] Ferdinand Goldschmidt, G. Meyer, and three other guests of the Hotel Fürstenhof to the management of Aschinger's Incorporated, December 15, 1922, in LAB A Rep. 225, Nr. 1174.

[80] Kessels to Lohnert, May 17, 1922, in LAB A Rep. 225, Nr. 1174.

[81] Kessels to Lohnert, September 1, 1922, in LAB A Rep. 225, Nr. 1174.

[82] Emphasis in the original: Kessels to Lohnert, September 1, 1922.

shortages mounted and especially after corporate officers rescinded managers' purchasing authority. Managers now had to write to a corporate officer for permission, which slowed the process of procurement. To buy as few as ten telephones, for example, Kessels had to send a formal letter to the managing directors of Aschinger's Incorporated.[83]

At the nexus of the shortages of goods, space, and currency, hotels attracted the sustained attention of the Anti-Profiteering Office. In the popular imagination, too, hotels stood for the evils of hoarding and price gouging. *Das Hotel* reported in 1921 that a good number of "thoughtless newspaper readers" believed sensationalist reports of "extortionate pricing" (*Wucherpreise*) in hotels and were being swayed by fiery opinion pieces that called for immediate "state intervention."[84] Some hoteliers responded that the recent spate of trials of profiteers amounted to a witch hunt that aimed simply to destroy the hotel industry once and for all.[85] Not only hotels but also individual hoteliers and restaurateurs came under investigation. According to *Das Hotel*, in May 1921, the owner of a restaurant in Frankfurt was called before the court for having charged 54 marks for two portions of lobster mayonnaise, 50 marks for two rump steaks, 8 marks for two portions of fried potatoes, and 14 marks for two servings of bread and butter. The court found the restaurateur guilty and sentenced him to three days in prison and a fine of 1,500 marks.[86]

Hotel corporations also had to dispel rumors, some of them true, that the grand hotel industry was making purchases on the black market.[87] On January 13, 1920, the board of the Hotel Management Corporation met to discuss the urgent matter of "pending proceedings ... against hotels, and in particular against ours, for alleged offenses against the so-called 'Decree on Illicit Trade.'"[88] But without access to basic necessities, hoteliers wondered what to do. They were losing business to nearby pubs (*Kneipen*), which, as small gastronomy enterprises, were not under the same rationing regime as grand hotels, nor did pubs seem to attract the attention of the authorities. Where grand hotels "were forced"

---

[83] Kessels to Lohnert, August 18, 1922, in LAB A Rep. 225, Nr. 1174.

[84] "Die Preise der Hotels und die Öffentlichkeit," *Das Hotel*, June 24, 1921.

[85] "Kampf der deutschen Hoteliers und Wirte gegen die Wuchergerichte," *Das Hotel*, December 19, 1919.

[86] "Drei Tage Gefängnis und 1500 Mk. Geldstrafe," *Das Hotel*, May 3, 1921.

[87] Diary entry of March 27, 1919, in Kessler, *Tagebuch*, 7:211.

[88] Report of the managing directors of the board of directors of the Hotel Management Corporation, January 13, 1920, in LAB A Rep. 225-01, Nr. 2.

(*zwangsweise*) to offer coffee without milk, bread without wheat, tea without sugar, and pastries without butter, pubs next door leveraged the luxury and lure of the real thing.[89]

Meanwhile, pricing was becoming increasingly complicated, a result of the tendency toward industry-wide agreements among hoteliers. In 1922, they all decided to charge one price for Germans and another price for foreigners. As of October 18, a single room at the Fürstenhof, for example, would be 1,000 marks for Germans and 3,000 marks for foreigners.[90] In late October, Berlin's hoteliers met again to increase room prices among the city's grand hotels and, for foreigners, peg those prices to the US dollar; under this scheme, Germans would receive a discount of around 25 percent.[91] Then, on November 7, a smaller group of hoteliers – industry leaders only – met in secret to deal with the sensitive issue of pricing by nationality which, as things stood, disadvantaged ethnic Germans resident outside Germany, whether in Austria, Switzerland, or territories ceded to France and newer states in Central and Eastern Europe. After a long discussion, the hoteliers landed on ethnicity as a better distinction than nationality. Ethnic Germans still resident in ceded territories would enjoy the price for all other Germans (except Austrians who, even if they were ethnically German, at first were to get half the foreign rate but lost the advantage in the last round of talks). For purposes of pricing, therefore, German hoteliers chose not to recognize the new map of Europe. Any ethnic German resident inside the borders of Germany as they had been in 1914 was entitled to a discount. Everyone else, "*without exception*," would be charged the foreigners' price on the dollar basis.[92]

Hoteliers tried to keep the price differences a secret but failed. At the front desk, chefs de reception were supposed to inquire about nationality before giving the rate, a move that aroused suspicions. In the restaurants, a waiter likewise had to ask for patrons' nationalities before handing them the correct menus. Tables of mixed ethnicity could therefore

---

[89] "Das schiefe Gleis unserer Zwangswirtschaft."

[90] Price list of the Hotel Fürstenhof, October 9, 1922, in LAB A Rep. 225, Nr. 1174.

[91] Minutes from a confidential meeting of the Berlin Hotels Commission, Group A and B, October 22, 1922, in LAB A Rep. 225, Nr. 1174.

[92] Emphasis in the original: Minutes from a confidential meeting of the Berlin Hotels Commission, Group A and B, November 7, 1922. On Germans and Austrians, see Erin R. Hochman, "Ein Volk, ein Reich, eine Republik: Großdeutsch Nationalism and Democratic Politics in the Weimar and First Austrian Republics," *German History* 32 (2014), 29–52. On immigration in the Weimar Republic, see Jochen Oltmer, *Migration und Politik in der Weimarer Republik*, (Göttingen: Vandenhoeck & Ruprecht, 2005).

compare prices. This practice, and guests' dishonesty about their nationalities, put the headwaiter in the uncomfortable position of asking to see
passports before the cashier could compute the bill. In cases of indeter-
minate or suspect ethnicity, headwaiters had to adjudicate and execute
procedures of discrimination accordingly.[93]

More and more guests were pretending to be who they were not. The
master criminal Wilhelm Blume, "one of the most refined and scrupu-
lous murderers in the last decade," according to police, checked into
the Adlon under the name Baron von Winterfeldt on New Year's Day
1919 and then robbed and strangled a money carrier there. Blume had
already distributed leaflets around most of the city's banks warning of
the Spartacists' plans to confiscate all assets by January 4. The leaflets
advised depositors to withdraw their money and hide it at home (the
better for Blume to steal it and dispatch the owners).[94] Even after the
end of the January Uprising in 1919, criminals found new opportunities
to use the political situation to their advantage.[95] At the Grand Hotel
Alexanderplatz on February 21, 1919, two men dressed as a counterrevolutionary soldier and civilian entered through the front door and
announced themselves as agents of the state in search of Spartacists on
the run. Then, the two men robbed a guest of 8,000 marks. In the same
week and at the same hotel, a civilian and an armed man in an army
uniform came on a mission to find a certain salesman, Zokolowski
of Łódź, who was wanted, they said, on charges of trading chocolate
on the black market. Management showed the soldier and civilian to
Zokolowski's room, where they seized one of his suitcases containing
20,000 marks as "evidence," and then, after a tussle, shot and wounded
him. Although hotel employees managed to apprehend the counterfeit
soldier, the civilian got away.[96]

---

[93] Minutes from a confidential meeting of the Berlin Hotels Commission, Group A and B,
November 7, 1922.
[94] File summary in the Central Register for Murder Cases (Zentralkartei für Mordsachen),
n.d., in LAB A Pr. Br. Rep. 030-03, Nr. 1712; interview transcripts for Richard Black-
burn (chef de reception); Max Zingel (servant); Minna Leber (maid); Hugo Neubauer
(page); and a waiter named Flocker, in LAB A Pr. Br. Rep. 030-03, Nr. 1714. Cf. Vicki
Baum, *Menschen im Hotel* (Cologne: Kiepenheuer & Witsch, 2002), 12, first published
in serial form in 1929.
[95] Although the murder rate increased in Germany after World War I, it was still low
compared to the United States at the same time, according to Sace Elder, *Murder Scenes:
Normality, Deviance, and Criminal Violence in Weimar Berlin* (Ann Arbor: University
of Michigan Press, 2010), 21.
[96] "Die Schadenersatzfrage bei Plünderung und Raub in Hotels," *Das Hotel*, February 21,
1919.

Across the Reich, in fact, all sorts of criminals attacked hotels and their guests. In May of 1919, the wine merchants J. Langenback & Sons, of Worms, gave notice to *Das Hotel* of a "female swindler" making the rounds at hotels and restaurants, posing as a saleswoman for the firm and taking money for goods that she said would be delivered at a later date.[97] In the face of staggering losses of their own and guests' property, hoteliers throughout Germany took a radical step. They began to renege on the promise to guests, which had been commonplace in the prewar period, that their property would be safeguarded.[98] In the summer of 1922, Kessels notified guests upon registration that the Fürstenhof no longer accepted responsibility for items lost or stolen.[99] Notices in the rooms were more elaborate. In German, English, and French, they explained that "on account of present conditions, we are forced ... to refuse all responsibility for personal effects." For a fee, safes would be made available. Furthermore, guests now had to carry a "room card to be shown upon request when asking for room keys" at reception.[100] *Inspectricen* (female inspectors), one for each of the guest floors, were to keep watch over linens and other vulnerable items belonging to the hotel.[101] Not only did the Fürstenhof and other houses roll back their commitment to securing guests' property, they also stepped up their commitment to protecting their own property, even if this required spying on guests.

INFLATION TO HYPERINFLATION

Criminal activity, scarcity, strikes, and violence put Berlin's grand hoteliers in a weak position on the eve of the Weimar Republic's first economic catastrophe, the hyperinflation of 1923. Despite full occupancy, conditions had failed to improve since 1918, and as the situation worsened, corporate officers had to find new explanations for shareholders. Annual reports after 1918 became increasingly dismal. Revenues were shrinking, and board members stressed that it was on account of the weak economy, and not on account of mismanagement, that dividends had to be curtailed. Blaming the business cycle rather than structural

---

[97] "Warnung!" *Das Hotel*, May 9, 1919.
[98] "Die Haftpflicht bei Raubanfällen in Hotels," *Das Hotel*, September 5, 1919.
[99] Registration card for a room at the Hotel Fürstenhof, n.d., ca. 1922, in LAB A Rep. 225, Nr. 1174.
[100] Notice to guests of the Hotel Fürstenhof, n.d., ca. 1922, in LAB A Rep. 225, Nr. 1174.
[101] Kessels to Lohnert, September 1, 1922.

weaknesses of the business model also reinforced the perception that in this economy, any alternative was as bad as the other: Shareholders, the reports' principal audience, might as well keep the shares they already had. Authorities constituted a secondary audience for the annual reports. If officials could be convinced of the industry's plight, they might lay off hotels for a while. These conflicting messages to different audiences produced reports that contradicted themselves and confused the issues as the corporate board of directors tried at once to deflect blame, downplay some weaknesses, and exaggerate others.

Das Hotel warned of the "total collapse of our economy" as early as December 1919, yet hoteliers found some surprising advantages in inflation.[102] One was in the opportunity to pay off prewar loans with postwar marks. The Berlin Hotel Corporation announced in July 1919 that it would pay its 1911 obligations of 5,218,000 marks in full, at a small fraction of their prewar value, by October.[103] Other corporations tried for the first time to raise money by selling shares on the open market. One of them, the Esplanade Hotel Corporation, in going public on May 16, 1919, picked up a new majority shareholder who promised to save the hotel from insolvency.[104]

In 1920, however, as new liabilities mounted, Aschinger's and others considered taking out new mortgages on their properties, but credit was too tight.[105] Typical was the predicament of the Kaiserhof in 1921, still in disrepair two years after the government's forces had sacked it. Apparently saddled with a hopeless case and thus without access to credit, the Kaiserhof's owner, the Berlin Hotel Corporation, discussed raising money through the sale of shares in order to add two stories to the building, which could be filled with cheap guest rooms to allow the business better to capitalize on being at full occupancy. The scheme came to naught.

Some corporate chairmen, such as Richard Weser at Aschinger's, ventured cautious optimism in annual reports of 1920 and 1921. Healthy reserves, the result of "conservative budgeting" in the years of full occupancy, might help businesses overcome most difficulties.[106] These reserves

[102] "Kohlennot und Polizeistunde."
[103] "Hotelberichte," *Das Hotel*, July 25, 1919.
[104] "Hotelberichte," *Das Hotel*, May 30, 1919.
[105] Annual report of Aschinger's Incorporated for 1920; minutes of a meeting of the board of directors of the Berlin Hotel Corporation, September 16, 1920.
[106] Minutes of a meeting of the board of directors of the Berlin Hotel Corporation, April 1, 1921.

could now cover the costs of capital improvements delayed since 1914. But Weser's optimism was misplaced. By 1922, as prices for goods and labor reached dizzying heights, the board began to channel its reserves into seizing every opportunity of "filling our stores." By the beginning of 1923, what reserves remained were worthless.

For hoteliers, the emergency had become evident back in March of 1922, when bookkeepers started to register inflation by the day, after a year of particularly fast rising prices. As machinery and furniture wore out, the money was not there to repair them. In the spring of 1922, for example, the cost of replacing the water tanks at the Kaiserhof was 670,000 marks "and rising." The final settlement for damages from the sacking of the hotel, received about the same time, came to one-third of that sum.[107] "Extraordinary increases in operation costs" ensued as a result of rapidly rising expenditures on labor, laundry, and coal.[108] By September 30, 1922, runaway gas prices were already causing bills for cooked meals to change multiple times a week.[109]

When the Entente Commission declared Germany to be in default on its reparations payments and the French and Belgians occupied the Ruhr in early 1923, the worst finally happened. To counter the inflationary effects of its policy of passive resistance to French and Belgian efforts at extraction, shutting down much of the German economy in the process, the German government printed more and more money. The currency collapsed, bringing down with it Berlin's hospitality industry.[110]

Hotels' official price lists could not be reprinted fast enough. From February 1, 1923, Aschinger's Incorporated added to the frenzy by changing the menus without any advance warning.[111] Overnight, prices for coal would rise 160 percent; soap, 200 percent; and laundry, 350 percent.[112] In mid-March, taxes followed suit, now climbing "not only

[107] Minutes of a meeting of the board of directors of the Berlin Hotel Corporation, March 2, 1922, in LAB A Rep. 225, Nr. 1046.

[108] Annual report of Aschinger's Incorporated for 1921.

[109] Kessels to Lohnert, September 30, 1922, in LAB A Rep. 225, Nr. 1174.

[110] See Conan Fischer, *The Ruhr Crisis, 1923–1924* (Oxford: Oxford University Press, 2003), 290; Gerald D. Feldman, *The Great Disorder: Politics, Economics, and Society in the German Inflation, 1914–1924* (New York: Oxford University Press, 1993), 669ff.; Carl-Ludwig Holtfrerich, *The German Inflation, 1914–1923: Causes and Effects in International Perspective*, trans. Theo Balderston (Berlin: Walter de Gruyter, 1986).

[111] Beverages price list of February 1, 1923, in LAB A Rep. 225, Nr. 1174.

[112] Price list sent from the Association of Laundry and Linen Services of Greater Berlin (Verband Groß-Berliner Wäsche-Verleihgesellschäfte), February 27, 1923, in LAB A Rep. 225, Nr. 1174.

from month to month but from week to week – no, day to day, even."[113] Profits withered and then disappeared.

Workers, managers, and their corporate bosses became overwhelmed. Letters from Kessels to Lohnert from the week of January 15, 1923, point to chaos. On January 16, Kessels pleaded with Lohnert to find funds to fix the flagpole over the main entrance, which was drooping to the breaking point.[114] Two days later, Kessels importuned Lohnert for money to mend the kitchen roof, which leaked buckets of water every day, and to hire an exterminator to dispatch the rats in the guest-level pantries, the dumbwaiters, and the elevators, the baseboards of which had been "nibbled" to splinters.[115] The letters also indicate infighting among Aschinger's different branches. The company's café concessions, independent of the hotels, had apparently made off with the Fürstenhof's hors d'oeuvre trucks.[116] As an acknowledgment of the new reality, Kessels dispensed with the cash economy altogether when, in advance of a business trip, he asked Lohnert for a box of cigars, a few dozen small bottles of cognac, and 100 napkins so that he might bribe "corrupt police officers and officials" along the way.[117]

Compensation became an even bigger problem under hyperinflation. Many white-collar employees had to be rewarded for extra time and effort, including the chief buyer for the Hotel Management Corporation, whose job it was to source supplies for all the company's hotels, including the Bristol and Central-Hotel, and gastronomy concerns, including the Kranzler and Bauer. The board agreed to give him a bonus equaling 60 percent of his April wages. But how much money would that be, exactly? By the board's own estimate: 23 million marks.[118] Other employees had to be let go; there was not enough cash on hand to pay them. The cost of leasing telegraphs, for example, had consumed the wages of the Fürstenhof telegraph girl, so the corporate office ordered that her post be eliminated.[119] Staff who remained at the hotel saw their real wages dwindle by the hour. The Fürstenhof's musicians started going from table to table asking guests for money. Such "pestering"

[113] Annual report of Aschinger's Incorporated for 1922, in LAB A Rep. 225, Nr. 636.
[114] Kessels to Lohnert, January 16, 1923, in LAB A Rep. 225, Nr. 1174.
[115] Kessels to Lohnert, January 18, 1923, in LAB A Rep. 225, Nr. 1174.
[116] Kessels to Lohnert, January 19, 1923, in LAB A Rep. 225, Nr. 1174.
[117] Kessels to Lohnert, April 16, 1923, in LAB A Rep. 225, Nr. 1174; Lohnert to Kessels, April 18, 1923, in LAB A Rep. 225, Nr. 1174.
[118] Minutes of a meeting of the board of directors of the Berlin Hotel Corporation, May 30, 1923, in LAB A Rep. 225, Nr. 1046.
[119] Müssigbrodt to Kessels, March 1, 1923, in LAB A Rep. 225, Nr. 1174.

must stop under all circumstances, Lohnert wrote to Kessels. Longtime American guests, angered by the scene, had decided to check out and cancel their lavish farewell dinner, such as it would have been under the circumstances. Disciplined just short of being fired, the musicians had their hours reduced and were told that they would be dismissed without compensation should they ever go "begging" again.[120]

If begging did not work, then stealing would. When, in February 1923, 5,000 marks went missing from a package containing 1,169,257 marks, the Fürstenhof management first blamed Fräulein Klüger, a cashier. She denied any wrongdoing and pointed to all the other people who had laid hands on the money en route to its final depository. These included the head cashier, Fräulein Klückmann, the clerk, Herr Pfitzner, and finally the bookkeeper, Herr Werth. At any rate, as the value of 5,000 marks approached zero, the matter soon would not be worth pursuing.[121] In the end, morale was more important than a few stolen marks, especially considering recent, cost-prohibitive increases in the premiums for a riot insurance policy.[122]

In April, upward pressure on wages and salaries exploded. Managers threw money at staff and workers with abandon.[123] On April 14, 1923, the chairman of the Hotel Management Corporation, on behalf of the Berlin Chamber of Commerce (Handelskammer zu Berlin), sent waiter Fritz Haas the customary notice of congratulations on twenty-five years of service to the Central-Hotel. The "certificate of honor" came with no less than 50,000 marks in cash, which would lose much of their value by sunset.[124] In fact, in four days, 50,000 marks would not have bought five napkins, now costing 12,000 marks apiece.[125]

The board of the Hotel Management Corporation looked for cuts everywhere and then took drastic measures. Plans materialized early for alterations that might reduce costs. In April 1923, the board discussed shrinking the hotel kitchens to accommodate fewer machines and workers. Without any way of reckoning the cost of these alterations, however,

---

[120] Corporate management of Aschinger's Incorporated to the management of the Hotel Fürstenhof, August 21, 1923, in LAB A Rep. 225, Nr. 1174.

[121] Report on money missing from the Fürstenhof, February 8, 1923, in LAB A Rep. 225, Nr. 1174.

[122] Minutes of a meeting of the board of directors of the Berlin Hotel Corporation, April 23, 1923, in LAB A Rep. 225, Nr. 1046.

[123] Annual report of Aschinger's Incorporated for 1922.

[124] Managing directors of the Hotel Management Corporation to Fritz Haas, waiter at the café of the Central-Hotel, April 14, 1923, in LAB A Rep. 225-01, Nr. 150.

[125] Lohnert to Kessels, April 18, 1923.

the board suspended its decision and looked instead to the simpler project of fixing the roof, a much more pressing problem, at the cost of "several hundred million." On this proposal, too, the board reached no conclusion, and discussion moved to linens and how to replace them.[126] In May, out of desperation for cash, the board of the Berlin Hotel Corporation decided unanimously to sell all foreign currency and apply the proceeds to the purchase of textiles, goods, and wine.[127] Since the onset of hyperinflation, the strategy had been to "settle up every day," including with guests, and then put every bit of the proceeds immediately toward laying in supplies. Hoarding was now so common that the Berlin Hotel Corporation referred to the practice without euphemisms in its annual report.[128]

It became impossible to keep account of inventories as the stores filled and emptied so fast. In fact, when Price Waterhouse came to audit Aschinger's Incorporated, owner of the Fürstenhof, a few years later, they found that the "schedules relating to the Inventories of Merchandise at Hand on January 1, 1924, have been mislaid."[129] Had they been available, if indeed they had ever existed, the inventories would not have shed any light. Money values meant nothing. Where it was necessary to reckon in cash, firms did so with little sense of what the money was worth or would be worth in a few hours.

Aschinger's Incorporated had tried in early 1923 to fashion its own imaginary "Goldmark," expressed in British pounds, for valuing assets and inventories but had little success with this solution.[130] The books still conveyed nonsense. For other assets, the corporation used gold. Dividends received a different treatment, with corporate accountants using several modes of translation for the values of a prewar mark, a present-day mark, a 1918 mark, gold bullion, and the exchange rate of marks to US dollars[131] With stabilization and a new temporary currency in late 1923 and then the introduction of a new permanent currency, the reichsmark, the following year, hoteliers were able to catch their breath and shifted their attention to a different, related problem – taxes – and this, with a bitterness borne of the experience of hyperinflation.

[126] Ibid.
[127] Minutes of a meeting of the board of directors of the Berlin Hotel Corporation, May 30, 1925, in LAB A Rep. 225, Nr. 1046.
[128] Annual report of the Berlin Hotel Corporation for 1923, in LAB A Rep. 225, Nr. 1048.
[129] Audit report of the Berlin Hotel Corporation and "Geka" Corporation (Geschäfts- und Kontorhaus AG) for 1923, in LAB A Rep. 225, Nr. 626.
[130] Minutes of a meeting of the board of directors of the Berlin Hotel Corporation, June 20, 1923, in LAB A Rep. 225, Nr. 1046.
[131] Annual report of Aschinger's Incorporated for 1922.

It had been the terrible result of a policy that no one felt ready to excuse, pursued by a government that few would find cause to forgive.[132]

TAXES AND RECKONINGS

In the midst of hyperinflation, tax rates had indeed reached astronomical proportions. The accommodation tax for foreigners in early 1923 was 80 percent (40 percent for Germans). Along with all the other taxes, the resulting payments pushed hoteliers' and restaurateurs' contributions up to about 50 percent of all revenue. The worst of these taxes abated in 1924 but stayed higher than prewar levels. Sales tax now entailed an accommodation tax, a 10 percent state tax, a tax on wine, an additional tax on sparkling wine, and a tax on profits. The state also collected on bonds, mortgages, ground rent, and land use. And finally, there was the tax on commerce in the state of Prussia.[133]

Even before the hyperinflation, Aschinger's Incorporated predicted that taxes would result in the demise of the hotel industry. The accommodation tax, then higher for foreigners, would keep American and other investors from visiting Germany. Such taxes on commercial hospitality, the board argued, would surely sink "the whole of our national economy." To the people's detriment, then, the hotel industry suffered – and worse than any other industry, "not one" of which was "saddled with so many and such heavy taxes," as the hoteliers saw it.[134] Complaints like these spilled easily into demonization of the republic, the "tax hydra" that reached farther and wider by the day.[135] But after the hyperinflation, this hyperbolic language around taxes became more common among hoteliers.

A second set of complaints, also contending that the republic was singling out the hotel industry for punishment, revolved around the institution of the Price Auditing Bureau of Greater Berlin. In July 1924, the Association of Berlin Hoteliers wrote to the magistrate in protest against the bureau's recent decision to compel the reversion of room prices to their prewar values, since such prices failed to account for the tax rate and cost of living having gone up 40 to 60 percent since July 1914.[136]

---

[132] On stabilization and new taxes, see Holtfrerich, *German Inflation*, 301–3.
[133] Annual report of the Berlin Hotel Corporation for 1923.
[134] Annual report of Aschinger's Incorporated for 1922.
[135] Georg Persisch, "Gegen die Steuerhydra," *Das Hotel*, December 12, 1921.
[136] Association of Berlin Hoteliers to the Price Auditing Bureau of Greater Berlin, July 30, 1924, in LAB A Rep. 001-02, Nr. 2390, f. 108; Annual report of the Berlin Hotel Corporation for 1923.

Moreover, the "incessant pestering of our members by your officials' pointless inquiries" was taking up valuable time and energy. The Association of Berlin Hoteliers also wrote to the Office of Statistics (Statistisches Amt der Stadt Berlin) to complain that questionnaires issued by the Price Auditing Bureau exhibited flaws in procedure. In the association's words, "the Price [Auditing] Bureau has neither the competency nor the prerogative" to conduct its own surveys, which should be the exclusive purview of the Office of Statistics.[137]

These exchanges point to hoteliers' two-pronged strategy when dealing with state and municipal regulations. First, complain to the relevant authority about the unfairness and deleterious effects of the policy in question; second, contact a rival authority that might intercede to your benefit. Increasingly, hoteliers, hotel corporations, and hotel industry combinations tried where possible to complicate, confuse, and frustrate the state's efforts to extract revenue from commercial hospitality. As these instances of evasion and protest mounted, they converged with anti-republican currents in hoteliers' thinking and actions.

CONCLUSION

In the Weimar Republic's early years, 1919–1923, hoteliers in the main buried their prewar affiliations with the National Liberal Party and embraced the language and politics of conservatism and even right radicalism. They did so in the context of quotidian disasters that befell Berlin's luxury hospitality industry. With the advent of peace, material and labor shortages got worse, not better. High crime, inflation, hyperinflation, and the effects of a decade of underinvestment stripped veneers in the metaphorical and literal sense. Labor relations deteriorated as hospitality workers awakened to their collective power and the swift efficacy of direct action. They joined demonstrations on bloodstained pavements many times in the course of the successive tumults of the early Weimar period: revolution, communist revolt, counterrevolution, and a failed coup d'état. For these political, social, and economic dislocations, many hoteliers blamed foreigners, workers, labor organizers, and the republic itself – that is, almost all the scapegoats of the anti-republican right. But in resorting to anti-republican tropes, Berlin's hoteliers compromised and then broke their commitment to the reinstatement of the liberal culture

---

[137] Association of Berlin Hoteliers to the Price Auditing Bureau of Greater Berlin, July 30, 1924.

on which grand hotel society had depended. The expensive practices of elite cosmopolitanism, which depended on everyone else submitting to class domination, no longer functioned amid widespread conflict among classes and nations in the first five years of peace.

Hoteliers thus compromised their liberal commitments. The language of their annual reports, trade publications, and internal memos in the early 1920s developed a semantic affinity to the anti-republicanism of the right. Hoteliers' incorrigible pessimism regarding the economy, society, and polity, in turn, would one day make them willing to countenance the destruction of the republic and its replacement with an authoritarian regime.

5

Abdication of the Liberals

William Meinhardt, chairman of the board of the Hotel Management Corporation, made his decision about Hitler on September 15, 1932. The manager of the Kaiserhof had come to Meinhardt with a complaint against the Nazis, who had been using the hotel as their Berlin headquarters for the better part of a year and were scaring away the Jewish clientele. The manager wanted permission from the board to throw Hitler and his men out. Meinhardt declined, and the Nazis stayed. Four and a half months later, on January 30, 1933, Hitler became chancellor.

Before the end of 1933, Meinhardt was on a ship to England, fleeing for his life, never to return to Germany. Why did Meinhardt, Jewish and a member of the German Democratic Party, allow the Nazis to stay in what was, in some sense, his house – a largely Jewish house, too, since the board of the Hotel Management Corporation was Jewish by a majority?

The minutes of the board meeting of September 15 are a highly mediated source, to put it mildly. Any number of persons might have tampered with the transcript; the secretary might even have done so as he or she generated it. Certain things, too, might easily have gone unsaid. But the paper trail from summer and autumn 1932, read in the context of grand hoteliers' pessimism of 1924–29 and fatalism of 1930–32, contains clues that help explain why the September 15 decision made sense to the people involved.

Why, indeed, did a group of the country's financial, industrial, and commercial elites, led by a Jewish German, cast their lot with Hitler in 1932? Several factors played into the decision, but the most important was an unshakable pessimism, born of the chaos of 1918–23 and never quite dispelled in the years of relative prosperity of 1924–29, which after 1929 hardened into fatalism – that is, absolute certainty that business would fail under present conditions. Under the influence of a contagious fatalism endemic to his milieu by 1932, Meinhardt would not have seen or understood the ramifications of his decision to let Hitler stay. It at least kept open the possibility of a different future under the next regime. The alternative, ejecting Hitler, would have brought the threat of immediate and violent retaliation by the Brownshirts.

MODEST IMPROVEMENTS

In the Weimar Republic's years of relative stability (1924–29), the period between hyperinflation and the Great Depression, the instability of social relations and economic conditions persisted but also lessened. From on high, the owners of Berlin's grand hotels continued to abide by a series of broken relationships across classes, genders, nations, industries, and political institutions. The impossibility of a return to the relative equipoise of prewar arrangements deepened hoteliers' pessimism, regardless of the improvements evident after 1923.

The first area of improvement was in labor relations. The last major strike of the era happened in March 1924, when the cooks' walkout laid up scores of hotel restaurants large and small. The conflict made national and international headlines when the Adlon served President Ebert a dinner prepared by strikebreakers.[1] But the Adlon was the exception to the new rule. In the main, Berlin's grand hoteliers wanted to be seen as cooperative partners in the negotiation of wages and conditions. Now, as at other workplaces, the workers of the properties of the Berlin Hotel Corporation formed a committee (*Betriebsrat*) that sent two delegates, the waiter Peter Saftig and the painter Gustaf Haseloff, to join the corporate board of directors. Saftig and Haseloff's first request was for a modest increase in winter bonuses. The board declined to take up the issue, recommending instead that they try again in better times.[2] Accordingly, Saftig and Haseloff's presence proved to be ceremonial, resulting in no appreciable material gains. Nevertheless, the rancor in labor relations of 1918–23 had passed.

In the more peaceful, prosperous years after 1924, hoteliers caught up on renovations that had been delayed since 1914. In 1925 and 1926,

---

[1] "German President Eats Dinner Cooked by Strikebreakers," *The New York Times*, March 18, 1924.

[2] Minutes of a meeting of the board of directors of the Berlin Hotel Corporation, April 28, 1924, in LAB A Rep. 225, Nr. 1046.

the Excelsior added more public rooms and expanded the lobby.[3] The Coburger Hof, a large hotel near Friedrichstraße station, installed telephones in every room and increased the number of en suites.[4] A smaller but luxurious property, the Hotel am Tiergarten in Charlottenburg, spread the benefits of a 16-million-mark renovation over its seventy rooms, each now with its own bathroom – a first for Berlin.[5] Yet any single modification had at best a thirty-year run before it would become "completely outdated," according to a contemporary analysis in the *Berliner Wirtschaftsberichte*.[6]

Tastes and priorities had shifted since the inception of Berlin's grand hotels in the imperial period. More guests now prioritized a new standard of cleanliness, referred to as "hygienic," which signaled an especially virtuous mode of domestic living. Grand hotels had always been clean in a Victorian sense: dusted, washed, polished. Clean, in the hygienic sense, demanded more – the design and selection of furnishings, fixtures, and textiles that gave dirt and dust no safe harbor. In the 1920s, Berlin's grand hotels therefore accentuated what they had deemphasized before, the tiled bathroom. A mid-1920s promotional book for the Hotel Esplanade left the lavatory door wide open. "Elegant and comfortable, convenient and hygienic" were the "watchwords" of the day, the book declared.[7]

New bathrooms were part of an expensive program of modernization that followed the designs of ocean liners.[8] An article for *Das Hotel* in 1925 observed that "the shipbuilding industry and the hotel industry are closely connected" through the exchange of design personnel and ideas. The ocean liner and the grand hotel designer both had to combat "the sense of confinement and crowdedness [by] deploying all possible technological and organizational means," the article continued. Both were charged with the safety of property and people. Both had to accommodate and please a heterogeneous, transient population. Yet ship designers had pulled ahead of hotel architects when it came to marrying technology and luxury, the author conceded: "It is in the cabins of the modern steamer where H. G. Wells's futuristic conception of the hotel room is being realized."[9]

---

[3] "Hotel Excelsior Berlin," *Deutsche Bauzeitung* 63 (1929), 65.
[4] "Hotel Coburger Hof, Berlin," *Das Hotel*, August 14, 1925.
[5] "Internationale Hotel-Messe," *Das Hotel*, March 25, 1921.
[6] "Berlin als Hotelstadt," *Berliner Wirtschaftsberichte*, December 8, 1928.
[7] Promotional book for the Hotel Esplanade, 1926, in HAT 96-211.
[8] On ocean-liner design and international competition, see Anne Wealleans, *Designing Liners: A History of Interior Design Afloat* (New York: Routledge, 2006), 78.
[9] "Das moderne Schiffshotel," *Das Hotel*, December 18, 1925.

The article spent more words on the kitchens than on guest rooms, however, because the former offered new and appealing labor-saving, cost-cutting technologies. Patents for devices like cheese-cutting and potato-slicing machines, champagne swizzle sticks with built-in thermometers, and mechanical egg-grabbers came to light every month in a new insert to *Das Hotel* called *Technik im Hotel* (Technology in the Hotel), which advised readers on how best to find, afford, and profit from the latest inventions.[10] The most important of these was the walk-in refrigerator.[11] Finally, wrote a professor at a hospitality trade school in Düsseldorf, "the latest technologies in refrigeration have minimized the risks that storing foodstuffs had until recently" presented.[12] Although refrigerators, refrigeration rooms, and other such technologies tended to land in spaces off limits to guests, hoteliers still found ways to publicize these latest of backroom acquisitions. A 1926 advertisement in Paris's *Le Matin* for the Hotel Excelsior in Berlin promised "the most modern in hotel technologies," including an electric generator of 920 horsepower and pumps capable of discharging 75,000 liters of water per hour.[13]

This new emphasis on scale and technology reflected the ascent of the American model of commercial hospitality, which underwrote a technological revolution by accessing the potential of economies of scale – a model that fascinated German hoteliers and plenty of other business leaders.[14] Early in the 1920s, *Das Hotel*'s editors had begun to devote large amounts of space in almost every issue to the American hotel industry. Hoteliers' visits to the United States received particular attention. Scarcely two years after the end of the war, two contributors to *Das Hotel* filled three pages with details of a recent trip to the United States, where they were received "with open arms" at the annual banquet of the New York Hotel Men's Association. Having visited dozens

---

[10] On hotels in the history of technology, see Molly W. Berger, *Hotel Dreams: Luxury, Technology, and Urban Ambition in America, 1829–1929* (Baltimore: Johns Hopkins University Press, 2011).

[11] "Patentbericht," *Technik im Hotel*, March 2, 1928.

[12] Richard Glücksmann, "Die Betriebswirtschaft des Hotels," in *Fremdenverkehr*, ed. Industrie- und Handelskammer zu Berlin (Berlin: Georg Stilke, 1929), 382.

[13] Advertisement in *Le Matin* (Paris), December 18, 1926.

[14] Charles S. Maier, "Between Taylorism and Technocracy: European Ideologies and the Vision of Industrial Productivity," *Journal of Contemporary History* 5 (1970), 29; Mary Nolan, *Visions of Modernity: American Business and the Modernization of Germany* (New York: Oxford University Press, 1994), 58–69. See also de Grazia, *Irresistible Empire*, 97–98.

of hotels and interviewed several American hoteliers, they wrote in awe of the quantities they witnessed and heard about. There was one hotel where "two to three thousand oysters are opened per day," a fact almost as impressive as the refrigerators on hand to keep so many bivalves alive. The highlight, however, was a meeting with E. M. Statler, whose singular vision, these German visitors insisted, made such immensity possible.[15] *Das Hotel* cast Statler as a man with an original, wholly American way of doing business. He was charismatic, the "most pleasant of people," always willing to share his experience and expertise.[16] The results of his genius, *Das Hotel* reported breathlessly, were manifold: "Nearly three hundred thousand rooms a month are occupied. Three and a half million individuals stop at Statler hotels during the course of a year. What an army of pleased and comforted human beings!"[17]

In 1928, another new regular insert to *Das Hotel* appeared, entitled "Hotels in America" and edited by Hans Ullendorff, the liaison between the North American and German hoteliers' associations. Ullendorff projected the modern American hotel as the model of "simplicity and clarity ... particularly in its technical and organizational aspect." This image reflected a characteristically "American functionalism and practicality" that nonetheless allowed for elegance and ornament.[18] The owners of the Esplanade, the Eden, and other grand hotels in Berlin tried to market their properties similarly, as luxurious and practical, cozy and hygienic, traditional and modern. At the same time, in their promotional materials, these Berlin hotel owners downplayed their properties' prewar associations with aristocratic and royal personages in favor of a new association with the "modern hotel system," a reference to Statler's genius. Having learned from his example, the promotional materials argued, the Esplanade's owners went further and "combined" the Americans' lessons in "art, technology, and hygiene" to outdo the masters. The Americans had set the "pattern," the Germans had "perfected" it.[19] In reality, however, the Esplanade and its sister properties lacked the credit to make investments on the American scale.

[15] "Amerikanische Reise-Eindrücke," *Das Hotel*, March 11, 1921. On visits by Germans to American firms in the 1920s, see Nolan, *Visions of Modernity*, 18–22.

[16] "E. M. Statler," *Das Hotel*, May 4, 1928. See also Sandoval-Strausz, *Hotel*, 127–33.

[17] "Statler's Hotel Theory in Action," *Das Hotel*, April 6, 1928. In the late 1920s, *Das Hotel* experimented with dual language editions, in English and German.

[18] Gustav Leonhardt, "Das amerikanische Hotel," *Das Hotel*, January 6, 1928.

[19] Promotional book for the Hotel Esplanade, 1926.

A "shortage of capital," according to *Das Hotel*, endemic to the German economy, limited the ability of German hoteliers to approach such American heights.[20]

RATIONALIZATION AND COMBINATION

The difficulty in finding sources of credit animated the tendency "toward combines, mergers, and programs of corporate reorganization," according to an economist writing in *Das Hotel*.[21] Having already acquired the controlling interest in the Berlin Hotel Corporation in 1924, Aschinger's Incorporated purchased a majority stake in the Hotel Management Corporation the following year.[22] Then, in 1927, Aschinger's took a step toward what its corporate officers understood as "rationalization" at the managerial level and merged its two new subsidiaries under the name of the Hotel Management Corporation, further concentrating the ownership and oversight of Berlin's grand hotel industry.[23] Only the Adlon, Esplanade, Eden, Continental, and Excelsior hotels operated as competitors to the new Aschinger's conglomerate. Fewer hotel corporations meant simplified negotiations with competitors in the attempt to set prices and wages. In the middle of the 1920s, such coordination paid off in the standard non-competition clauses that began to appear in managers' contracts.[24] At the same time,

---

[20] Leonhardt, "Das amerikanische Hotel."

[21] Emil Theilacker, "Die Bedeutung der Wirtschaftswissenschaften für die Hotelindustrie," *Das Hotel*, September 25, 1925. On Germany in international credit markets, German industry's reliance on credit for investment, and the tendency among German corporations to consolidate, in part a function of their reliance on American credit, see Peukert, *Weimar Republic*, 122, 194, 197–98, and 251. On corporate consolidation in Europe in the 1920s, see Derek H. Aldcroft, *The European Economy, 1914–2000*, 4th ed. (London: Routledge, 2001), 30. See also Frank Costigliola, "The United States and the Reconstruction of Germany in the 1920s," *Business History Review* 50 (1976), 477–502; Charles H. Feinstein, Peter Temin, and Gianni Toniolo, "International Economic Organization: Banking, Finance, and Trade in Europe," and Gerd Hardach, "Banking in Germany, 1918–1939," in *Banking, Currency, and Finance in Europe between the Wars*, ed. Charles H. Feinstein (Oxford: Clarendon, 1995), 131–50 and 269–95.

[22] Audit report by Price, Waterhouse & Co., February 5, 1926, in LAB A Rep. 225, Nr. 626.

[23] Copy of the contract for a merger of the Berlin Hotel Corporation and the Hotel Management Corporation, March 28, 1927, in LAB A Rep. 225, Nr. 985; annual report of the Hotel Management Corporation of 1928/29, in LAB A Rep. 225-01, Nr. 94.

[24] Contract between the Hotel Management Corporation, the Hotel Adlon, and Ewald Kretschmar, January 9, 1925, in LAB A Rep. 225, Nr. 987; minutes of a meeting of the board of directors, October 3, 1924, in LAB A Rep. 225-01, Nr. 2.

the Hotel Management Corporation (Aschinger's) struck an agreement with the competition at the Esplanade, the Excelsior, the Adlon, and the Continental to set the minimum price for wine and champagne.[25] These developments fell under the rubric of rationalization and modernization as Berlin's grand hoteliers understood the terms. (The moves also continued a tradition of cartel capitalism in which Meinhardt was a key player.[26])

Rationalization and modernization could not generate demand, however, and therefore failed to support any hotel project as large as those in the United States. The real estate developer Heinrich Mendelssohn did try and persuade the chief officers of Aschinger's Incorporated and the Hotel Management Corporation that there was still a hotel shortage and thus a need for a new, giant hotel.[27] In November 1927, he sent plans for a property of 650 rooms, 900 beds, and 8,000 square meters of reception rooms, restaurants, and ballrooms.[28] Two years later, in 1929, the proposed room count for this fantasy project had ballooned to 1,200.[29] "When it is finished," Mendelssohn wrote, "the Excelsior might very well feel the pinch," a favorable eventuality for Aschinger's, which now owned most of the Excelsior's competition.[30] But even before the Wall Street crash, Mendelssohn's attempts to get the new hotel built were bound to fail. The shortage of rooms, evident in the immediate postwar period, had abated, hoteliers agreed.[31] A full third of all rooms in grand hotels now tended to sit empty on any given night. The Association of Berlin Hoteliers took the position that the city's number of beds ought to be reduced, and the way to do that was by closing hotels.

---

[25] Hotel Management Corporation to Aschinger's Incorporated, November 30, 1927, in LAB A Rep. 225, Nr. 644.
[26] Andries Heerding, *The History of N. V. Philips' Gloeilampenfabrieken*, vol. 2, *A Company of Many Parts*, trans. Derek S. Jordan (Cambridge: Cambridge University Press, 1989), 331; Renate Tobies, *Iris Runge: A Life at the Crossroads of Mathematics, Science, and Industry* (Basel: Springer, 2012), 342; Robert Jones and Oliver Marriott, *Anatomy of a Merger: A History of G.E.C., A.E.I. and English Electric* (London: Cape, 1970), 32–36; Levy, *Industrial Germany*, 77–80.
[27] Hans Lohnert to Hans Friedmann, February 11, 1929, in LAB A Rep. 225, Nr. 920.
[28] Annual report of Aschinger's Incorporated for 1929, in LAB A Rep. 225, Nr. 636; "Allerlei aus aller Welt," *Das Hotel*, February 4, 1921.
[29] Lohnert to Friedmann, February 11, 1929.
[30] Heinrich Mendelssohn to Kurt Lüpschütz, September 23, 1929, in LAB A Rep. 225, Nr. 920.
[31] Kurt Lüpschütz, "Organisation der Hotels," in Industrie- und Handelskammer zu Berlin, *Fremdenverkehr*, 412.

In 1926, Berlin's grand hoteliers were pleased to hear that the Reich government, once again, wanted to purchase the Kaiserhof. The acquisition was part of the drive to pull government offices, still spread out across the capital, into the Friedrichstadt and Tiergarten districts. This move would save the government money on "physical and human resources," and the Kaiserhof was "most suitable" on account of its location and size, from the government's perspective. From the perspective of the Berlin Hotel Corporation, with the Kaiserhof operating at a loss, selling it made sense. In a previous round of attempts to purchase the building, in 1917 and 1918, the hue and cry of the city council had forestalled the deal (see Chapter 3). This time, in 1926, to keep the hotel running, the city of Berlin offered the Berlin Hotel Corporation a mortgage at cut-rate interest.[32]

The city's opposition to the latest proposal to sell the Kaiserhof had two justifications. First, the hotel provided valuable tax revenue. As a Reich government office building, it would contribute nothing. Second, the Kaiserhof, with its historical and cultural importance and its central location, anchored the surrounding palaces, government offices, department stores, shopping arcades, cafés, restaurants, and theaters. Much more imposing and impressive than any structure in the immediate vicinity, the Kaiserhof attracted thousands of moneyed visitors a week and then dispersed them, pocketbooks in hand, to the four corners of Friedrichstadt.

Still wanting to drive up prices by limiting supply, Berlin's grand hoteliers came down on the side of the Reich government and the sale. On behalf of the Association of Berlin Hoteliers, a lawyer wrote to Reich Minister of Finance Peter Reinhold in October 1926 in support of the latter's attempts to buy the Kaiserhof. "In the interest of rationalization," leaders of the association reasoned, hotels that were failing to turn a profit should close. For its part, the city was wrong to try and block the sale, and its effort to do so suggested underlying inconsistencies and hypocrisies, the association claimed. Although city council members were now decrying the loss of 300 jobs through the sale of the Kaiserhof, the very same members remained silent when their "friends" decided to close factories with workers in the thousands. At any rate, in the case of the Kaiserhof's workforce, the labor market "should have no trouble absorbing" the surplus.

In the same letter, the association then attacked another of the city's arguments against the sale of the Kaiserhof: that it would hinder the

[32] Report on the sale of the Kaiserhof, October 21, 1926, in LAB A Rep. 225, Nr. 1031.

growth of the city's tourism industries. To the contrary, with so many empty rooms, the hotel scene would benefit from reducing its inventory. Finally, the association revealed where its members thought the subtext of the debate lay: in party politics. The city of Berlin, the association charged, was using the Kaiserhof issue as an opportunity to criticize the Reich minister of finance and the coalition government, which fell to the right of the government of Berlin.[33] The city wanted to cast the Reich government as anti-Berlin by drawing attention to the latter's attempt to rob Berliners of one of their greatest hotels.[34]

Despite the association's appeals, the city ultimately won and the Kaiserhof survived – but not because the Reich minister of finance relented. Rather, the Hotel Management Corporation swooped in and purchased the Kaiserhof's parent company, the Berlin Hotel Corporation. The advantage to the Hotel Management Corporation was two-fold: First, the takeover eliminated a significant source of competition, which had put downward pressure on prices; second, the acquisition gave the buyer, with its greater portfolio of properties, a chance to direct investment into the Kaiserhof and then turn a profit, something the Berlin Hotel Corporation was too small and too beleaguered to afford.

Nonetheless, the hoteliers' outlook was gloomy. Consensus was forming between 1924 and the onset of the Great Depression that the market could not sustain the grand hotel scene any longer, at least not at its present scale. Consolidation and rationalization would only delay the inevitable collapse. This pessimism pervaded annual reports and left little room for acknowledging positive, or even ambiguous, developments in the city's luxury hospitality industry during Weimar's interval of relative stability.

THE POLITICS OF PESSIMISM

The annual reports of the Hotel Management Corporation, approved if not co-authored by Meinhardt, declared a lack of confidence in the governments of Germany, Prussia, and Berlin, even as economic

---

[33] See Christopher Clark, *Iron Kingdom: The Rise and Downfall of Prussia, 1600–1947* (Cambridge, MA: Belknap Press of Harvard University Press, 2006), 651; Thomas Friedrich, *Hitler's Berlin: Abused City*, trans. Stewart Spencer (New Haven: Yale University Press, 2012), 204ff.

[34] Report on the sale of the Kaiserhof, October 21, 1926.

and political conditions improved after 1923.[35] Surprisingly, the annual reports of the Hotel Management Corporation concealed the company's relatively good health in the period between 1924 and 1928. And by the end of the decade, the reports no longer served the purpose of informing shareholders and the public of the corporation's financial state; rather, these documents' principal function became to convey complaints and demands to the authorities – to lobby, not to testify. This was a curious choice.

In these reports, the directors established a consistent pattern of pessimistic argumentation that minimized consideration of what was actually going well in these years of relative stability and prosperity. But whose argumentation was this? The question has no simple answer. The reports, which always had to be approved by the chairperson of the board, in this case Meinhardt, were the product of collaboration among the managing directors of the corporation: Kurt Lüpschütz, Jakob Voremberg, and Carl Pelzer, later replaced by Heinz Kalveram. More precise information about the authorship of the annual reports is missing from the archive. Nevertheless, the content of the annual reports had to reflect the wishes of the managing directors – Lüpschütz, Voremberg, Pelzer, Kalveram – and Meinhardt, chairman of the board. The reports were in their names and bore their signatures.

Lüpschütz was a businessman in four industries: electricity, gas, entertainment, and hospitality.[36] By the time of the war, in which he served, Lüpschütz held the title of "*Direktor*" in the Hotel Management Corporation.[37] He was also the artistic director of the Central-Hotel's Wintergarten variety theater and served on the advisory board of the Association of Berlin Hoteliers.[38] In the 1920s, he developed a reputation for expertise in the field of commercial hospitality. A 1926 visit to the United States furnished him with information that became part of an exegesis, published in 1929 in an edited volume on the hospitality

---

[35] Peukert, *Weimar Republic*, 12–14. Cf. Rüdiger Graf, *Die Zukunft der Weimarer Republik: Krisen und Zukunftsaneignungen in Deutschland, 1918–1933* (Munich: R. Oldenbourg, 2008), 83–133.

[36] "Veränderungen," *Licht und Lampe: Zeitschrift für die Beleuchtungsindustrie*, no. 15 (July 20, 1917), 485.

[37] Annual report of the Association of Berlin Hoteliers for 1916, in LAB A Rep. 001-02, Nr. 2080.

[38] "Vereinsnachrichten," *Das Hotel*, February 2, 1917; Ruth Freydank, ed. *Theater als Geschäft: Berlin und seine Privattheater um die Jahrhundertwende* (Berlin: Hentrich, 1995), 55.

and gastronomy industries, on how to set up and run a grand hotel.[39] In 1931, Lüpschütz, "in accordance with his own wishes," stepped down from the board of managers and retired.[40] Evidence of Lüpschütz's politics has not survived, though a strand of cultural conservatism is visible in his response to the Wintergarten renovation in 1928. In a letter to the architects, whom Lüpschütz accused of a spree of vigilante redecoration, he railed against what he saw as "gratuitous modernism [*unnötige Moderne*]" more suited to a "minor cinema" than the city's most famous variety theater. Lüpschütz demanded the immediate restoration of the traditional sconces and the banishment of anything he deemed to be "hypermodern."[41]

Voremberg and Pelzer might have been less directly involved than Lüpschütz in the day-to-day business of the Hotel Management Corporation, or perhaps the demise of documents inscribed with their names has obscured their roles. In the case of Voremberg, we do know that he served as one of the three managing directors from 1925 to 1933. In that period, Aschinger's Incorporated purchased the Hotel Management Corporation, but Voremberg continued to serve on its board until Hans Lohnert, Aschinger's highest-ranked corporate officer, forced him out for being Jewish after the Nazis assumed power in 1933. By that time, Voremberg had worked for the Hotel Management Corporation for twenty-five years.[42] Pelzer had also given a quarter-century to the Hotel Management Corporation by the time he was through. He served as a managing director until his death in 1928 or 1929.[43] Like Voremberg, Pelzer appears to have been less involved in daily operations. Both men, however, would have shared responsibility with the others for finishing the annual reports.

[39] Lüpschütz, "Organisation der Hotels," 412.
[40] Annual report of the Hotel Management Corporation for 1931/32, in LAB A Rep. 225-01, Nr. 189.
[41] Kurt Lüpschütz to Bielenberg & Moser, August 20, 1928, in LAB A Rep. 22, Nr. 1002.
[42] Lohnert to the NSDAP local group leader (*Ortsgruppenleiter*) of Berlin-Dahlem, October 10, 1938, in LAB A Rep. 225-01, Nr. 59; minutes of a meeting of the Management and Personnel (Ausschusses für Direktions- und Personalangelegenheiten, previously called the Commission for Personnel), Hotel Management Corporation, November 8, 1933, in LAB A Rep. 225-01, Nr. 64; minutes of a meeting of the Commission for Personnel (Personalkommission), Hotel Management Corporation, July 15, 1933, in LAB A Rep. 225-01, Nr. 60; annual report of the Hotel Management Corporation for 1926/27, in LAB A Rep. 225, Nr. 644; annual report of the Hotel Management Corporation for 1927/28, in LAB A Rep. 225, Nr. 645; annual reports of the Hotel Management Corporation for 1928/29 and 1931/32; minutes of the meeting of the board of directors of the Hotel Management Corporation, September 15, 1932, in LAB A Rep. 225-01, Nr. 39.
[43] Annual report of the Hotel Management Corporation for 1928/29.

The tone of the annual report for fiscal year 1924/25 changed little from that of 1923/24, which had been a disastrous fiscal year for the hotel industry. Points of information that could have generated optimism about the near future of a German economy now blessed with a stable currency were nonetheless tempered by dark prognoses based on what Lüpschütz, Voremberg, and Pelzer characterized as the "poor general condition of the German economy." German guests could no longer afford to patronize luxury hotels in the midst of "Germany's impoverishment," they lamented in the 1924/25 annual report. The report did not quite lay blame for this impoverishment, but it did acknowledge geopolitical forces at work. Foreigners were staying away, the argument went, largely on account of advertisements abroad that cast a visit to Germany in a negative light. Lüpschütz and the others were quick to blame Germany's local governments for the bad press. Foreign visitors to Germany learned not to expect "some of the entertainments" to which they might be accustomed "on account of officials' wrongheaded decrees – for example, the ban on dancing in hotels," which proved to be short-lived. The more permissive atmosphere in other European municipalities meant that foreigners were more likely to choose one of those places over Berlin as a vacation destination. But the official stance against fun was not the only force to blunt Germany's competitive edge. There was also the "tremendous [*ungeheuer*] pressure applied by taxes," which made it "all but impossible for the German hospitality industry to compete with destinations abroad."[44] The policies of the state and the municipal governments, more than geopolitical or other economic forces, were sinking the industry, the 1924/25 report suggested. Without some reversal, the industry would soon succumb. Yet the German economy, as well as the profits and the prospects of Berlin's hotel industry, were actually improving. The managing directors and chairman of the board were obscuring this fact in the annual report for 1924/25 – a fact that should have been apparent to each of them in the spring of 1925 when they sat down to write or edit.

The annual report for 1926/27, penned in the summer of 1927, downplayed improvements again by freighting the good news with words of caution and complaining of the myriad ways in which the government, both in its local and national forms, was undermining the hotel industry and commerce more generally. When the directors referred to increasing

---

[44] Annual report of the Hotel Management Corporation for 1924/25, in LAB A Rep. 225-01, Nr. 4.

revenues and profits, they were quick to deploy qualifying phrases that had the effect of dampening any sense of optimism – for example: "The results of this most recent fiscal year [1926/27] more or less met those of the previous fiscal year [1925/26], despite ... the higher expenditure on taxes."[45] The phrasing was slippery. A higher expenditure on taxes actually reflected, in this context, greater revenue, not a higher *rate* of taxation, but Meinhardt and his directors were comfortable leaving this fact buried in the summary of accounts that followed the introductory essay. They were still using the annual report as an opportunity to campaign against the present tax regime.

For the 1927/28 report, composed amid further improvement to business conditions, Lüpschütz, Pelzer, Voremberg, and Meinhardt, instead of acknowledging their good fortunes, attacked national, state, and local governments anew, this time for the failure to spur tourism. The city of Berlin had, their report conceded, made great efforts to increase traffic to the capital. "Large-scale events and the creation of new attractions" were supposed to have "revived tourism in Berlin." The hotel industry, too, had done its part, Meinhardt and the others contended, but all such efforts foundered on the rocks of local, state, and national tax policies. Success could only have been possible with a "reprieve" from taxes, which were still too high to allow any business, but particularly a hotel, to turn a profit and thus give back in some way to the national economy, or so the argument went.[46] Again, the annual report became a place for railing against tax policy and, by extension, making claims that were political in suggesting how the state should and should not collect and distribute revenue for the purpose of improving national and local economic conditions. The 1927/28 report, indeed all the reports of the later 1920s, took every opportunity to argue that lowering or even eliminating corporate taxes, however crucial the proceeds were to the social and economic goals of the government, would ultimately revive the German economy and, in turn, stabilize German social relations and politics.

The annual report for fiscal year 1928/29 – approved by Meinhardt and authored by Lüpschütz, Voremberg, and Kalveram, who had replaced Pelzer, now deceased – began to register the decline in tourism that accompanied a general slowdown in the German economy after the middle of 1928. Although the number of foreign guests had

---

[45] Annual report of the Hotel Management Corporation for 1926/27.
[46] Annual report of the Hotel Management Corporation for 1927/28.

increased slightly, there was not enough of a surplus to compensate for the shortfall in domestic custom.[47] For all their efforts to maintain a dark outlook on the future of the business, the managing directors and Meinhardt did not foresee, when they finalized this report in the spring of 1929, that the coming autumn would bring a global economic disturbance of unprecedented intensity in modern history. The pessimism of the reports does not indicate that Meinhardt and his managing directors were able to predict or were even trying to predict the future. Rather, the expression of pessimism served, first, as justification to shareholders of several consecutive years of low dividends, and second, as an intervention in public-political discussions on taxation, state expenditure, and local and national policies related to commerce and the hotel industry in particular.

Having collapsed the political and the financial in their reports, Meinhardt and the managing directors misrepresented the state of affairs for the Hotel Management Corporation between 1924 and 1929. An independent study of the corporation, published in *Der deutsche Volkswirt* in November 1929, did indeed confirm some of the reports' negative points – the decrease in German hotel guests and the failure of government programs to boost tourism, for example. But the study also established grounds for optimism, especially with respect to the gastronomy concessions. Moreover, overall revenues had increased dramatically: 4.5 percent from 1925/26 to 1926/27, another 55.6 percent by 1927/28, and then another 29.8 percent by the summer of 1929.[48] These figures had been present in the annual reports but buried under introductory essays that did all they could to divert attention from the good news that followed.

In fact, the Hotel Management Corporation as a whole, in light of the performance of all its branches, was doing quite well by 1928. Its principal source of revenue being rents from retailers and not room fees or restaurant bills, the Hotel Management Corporation reaped a bumper crop of cash as soon as the German economy stabilized in 1924. In 1928/29, the corporation pulled in 1.1 million reichsmarks in rents, a full quarter of which came from the Central-Hotel's retail units. Yet this profitable side of the hotel business – the renting of shop space on ground

[47] Annual report of the Hotel Management Corporation for 1930/31.
[48] "Hotelbetriebs-Aktiengesellschaft (Bristol, Kaiserhof, Bellevue, Baltic, Centralhotel)," *Der Deutsche Volkswirt: Zeitschrift für Politik und Wirtschaft* 3 (November 8, 1929), 92.

floors – like other positive points, escaped mention in the annual reports. The only sign of optimism, an oblique one, was the rise in dividends for the fiscal year 1928/29, the first such increase since the war, from 7 to 9 percent. If this development engendered optimism, however, it did not come to light. Meinhardt and his managing directors persisted throughout the 1920s in downplaying the various ways in which business had improved since the tumults of 1918–23.

Why did Meinhardt and his managing directors mislead in this way? Why did they bury good news under pessimistic introductions? A look at the business reports of other hotel corporations reveals an industry-wide tendency to downplay the positive. The tone of the Berlin Hotel Corporation's annual reports, for example, before its absorption into the Hotel Management Corporation, tended to be mixed, giving several examples of improvement only to dash readers' hopes with dramatic pronouncements of decline. The business reports of Aschinger's Incorporated were likewise mixed, if more extreme in the swings between optimism and pessimism. There were the same complaints about "suffering" under the burden of taxes both from the state and the municipality and about the failure of the authorities to do enough to increase tourism. The first half of 1926, Aschinger's managing directors reported, had indeed been bad, but then conditions improved so that, by the end of the year, an "encouraging picture" had emerged – a picture that stood in stark contrast to the one rendered by the Hotel Management Corporation, Aschinger's recent acquisition. Aschinger's tentative optimism persisted well into 1927, when the managing directors drafted a particularly rosy report for the preceding year.[49] But in 1928, the government's foreign policy came into Aschinger's crosshairs: "The monstrous burden of the Dawes Plan and the duty to pay 'reparations,' which rests on all levels of society, is impeding ... the recovery of the German economy," as the annual report has it.[50]

In this statement, Aschinger's managing directors made a series of political claims. First, the managing directors used scare quotes to express a rejection of the terms of the peace settlement. Then, they presented this protest under the guise of altruism: Their concern is not only for themselves but for *every* class of German. But Aschinger's managing directors were not heaping scorn on the Entente alone, which, after all, had not forced the hotel industry to pay up. In fact, the terms of the Dawes Plan

[49] Annual report of Aschinger's Incorporated for 1926, in LAB A Rep. 225, Nr. 636.
[50] Annual report of Aschinger's Incorporated for 1927, in LAB A Rep. 225, Nr. 636.

exempted hotels and related businesses.[51] But the Reich government, as a means of spreading the burden of reparations more evenly across the economy, chose to extract a portion of the payments from the hotel industry.[52] This line in Aschinger's annual report, then, worked similarly and in parallel to conservative and ultra-conservative revisionist claims that the Entente was not the only or even principal author of German suffering. It was the republic that must bear the guilt of having accepted and agreed to administer the unjust punishment.

The same report made further forays into politics with specious arguments about the effects of socialist labor policy: "The labor laws around the catering trades have become a special burden." In the same breath, however, the managing directors had to contradict themselves and admit that neither the catering nor the hotel business was going badly. "With respect to our hotels," in fact, there had been "an improvement" – "despite," of course, missing the mark of the "prewar period." Nostalgia for the old regime was a particular feature of Aschinger's reports. The managing directors instructed readers to discount any good news in the figures through comparison to the good old days:

If we find ourselves able to report a substantial expansion of the business, of openings and reopenings and also of the acquisition of two properties, then these facts are not to be taken as a sign that operations have returned to that prewar trajectory so favorable to the development of our enterprise. No, the necessary conditions for that, embedded in the way things used to be, no longer exist.[53]

This report was a model of anti-republicanism and echoed reports from the period of hyperinflation, inflation, unrest, and revolution. But the 1927 report did something different, too. It told readers – shareholders and interested parties in industry and government – exactly how to interpret the data: to interpret it against reason.

The data pointed to good news, not bad: rates of growth near 1913 levels and a hotel industry healthier than it had been in fifteen years. The problem from the perspective of the board, the managing directors, and the shareholders was not that the state was killing the business. It was not. The problem was that the state was taking too large a cut of

[51] On the Dawes Plan's exemptions, see Albrecht Ritschl, *Deutschlands Krise und Konjunktur, 1924–1934: Binnenkonjunktur, Auslandsverschuldung und Reparationsproblem zwischen Dawes-Plan und Transfersperre* (Berlin: Akademie, 2002), 196–98.
[52] Audit report by Price, Waterhouse & Co., February 5, 1926.
[53] Annual report of Aschinger's Incorporated for 1927.

the proceeds. And for that, Aschinger's managing directors peppered the annual reports with anti-republican arguments, firmly asserted yet patently unsupported.

By 1927, Aschinger's was taking a harder line against the republic than was the Hotel Management Corporation. The latter had Mein-hardt as its chairman, a left-liberal by affiliation. Fritz Aschinger, on the other hand, was drifting ever rightward. Nonetheless, the chairmen and managing directors of both corporations used their annual reports to protest government policy and at some points to malign the republic, its labor and fiscal policies in particular. In these cases, the tendency to see the darkest side of any development in the business – this chronic pessimism in the face of improving conditions – easily spilled over into anti-republicanism, even when, as in the case of the Hotel Manage-ment Corporation, the business was headed by a Jewish member of the German Democratic Party.

COPING WITH THE GREAT DEPRESSION

Despite their pessimism, the Great Depression took Berlin's grand hote-liers by surprise. In the aftermath of the collapse of stock prices in late October 1929, the profits of Aschinger's Incorporated dwindled. Margins fell almost to 1924 levels, and this after revenue from the first nine months of the year had appeared to guarantee an increase in annual profits. Indeed, "there is very little good to say about our hotel business," communicated the board in its annual report for 1929. It cited the *Jahresbericht der Berliner Handelskammer* (Annual Report of the Berlin Chamber of Commerce) in its declaration that "since 1923," under hyperinflationary conditions, there had been "no year as inaus-picious as this."[54]

The main problem, according to the board of Aschinger's Incor-porated in 1930, was the steady reduction of clientele, particularly business travelers. Compounding the effects of this development, the average duration of a guest's stay had begun to slide in the last quarter of 1929.[55] Data on 1931 showed the situation to be worsening. At "every impasse" in the course of this "crisis," there was an accompa-nying drop in the number of business travelers. Moreover, the aver-age nightly stay per guest continued to decrease. Tourism, especially

[54] Annual report of Aschinger's Incorporated for 1929, in LAB A Rep. 225, Nr. 637.
[55] Ibid.

international tourism, also suffered. To make matters worse, increasing
political violence in Berlin in 1932 caused foreigners to stay away. Of
the 2,200 steamer passengers who arrived at Bremerhaven in summer
of that year, only eighty listed Berlin as a destination. Americans, "deci-
sive" in hoteliers' efforts to turn a profit in summer, were now scarce on
the ground. By autumn 1932, foreign attendance at Berlin hotels was
in free fall.[56]

The figures portended disaster, said managing director Adolf Schick
to the board of the Hotel Management Corporation at a meeting on
July 19, 1932.[57] In the first half of 1929, the total number of foreigners
at Berlin hotels had been 790,000. For the same period in 1931, that
figure had dropped to 628,000. In 1932, it was 473,000. Under these
circumstances, revenues plunged. Between 1931 and 1932, the hotels
of Aschinger's Incorporated – the Fürstenhof, Palast-Hotel, and Grand
Hotel am Knie – brought in a full 20 percent less. For 1932, the Hotel
Management Corporation, the majority stake of which belonged to
Aschinger's, lost 561,824 reichsmarks.[58] These shortfalls were happening throughout the German economy, where between 1929 and 1933
the Depression erased the gains of the period 1924 to the end of October
1929.[59] It was in the course of this swift decline that hoteliers' longstanding pessimism turned to fatalism.

The "severe decline in consumers' purchasing power," as the board
of Aschinger's Incorporated observed in 1930, put extraordinary
downward pressure on prices. As Berliners and other Germans could
afford less and less, reported Director Schick in July 1932, the hotel
industry found itself offering more services for lower prices.[60] Nevertheless, the discounts failed to increase the demand. Despite a reduction
in ticket prices at the Wintergarten in 1932, performances still played
to small audiences. The Hotel Management Corporation concluded
that if by the end of 1932 attendance had not improved, and in particular if foreign tourists continued to stay away from Berlin and the
Wintergarten, the storied performance space would have to close. The
rest of the business, too, looked to be in danger of collapse as a result

---

[56] Minutes of a meeting of the board of directors of the Hotel Management Corporation,
July 19, 1932, in LAB A Rep. 225-01, Nr. 32.
[57] Ibid.
[58] Annual report of Aschinger's Incorporated for 1932, in LAB A Rep. 225, Nr. 407.
[59] Peukert, *Weimar Republic*, 12.
[60] Minutes of a meeting of the board of directors of the Hotel Management Corporation,
July 19, 1932.

of Germany's quickly deflating currency. Price cuts brought the fee for a room down 20 percent over the course of 1931. By summer 1932, the price of accommodation was now only 30 percent of what it had been at the end of 1929. (Food and drink prices dropped, too, but at a slightly slower rate.) The hoteliers recognized the hand of the state in these developments as the "deflationary measures" (*Preissenkungsaktion*) of the Reich government, a blunt instrument of attack on the working class and on the reputation of the republic.[61]

Prices fell, cutbacks ensued, standards slipped. Hoteliers now looked to entice less elite customers. In spring 1931, the Central-Hotel collaborated with the travel agency Kempinski-Reisen and the Mitteleuropäisches Reisebüro to offer package deals for a weekend trip to Berlin (Figure 5.1). One such product promised two nights' accommodation, meals at "first-class restaurants," guided tours of the city, a visit to the pleasure palace Haus Vaterland, a show at the Wintergarten, and an excursion to Potsdam.[62] Unlike earlier advertisements, this one emphasized price, 45.50 reichsmarks, low enough to attract the frugal traveler. With a heterogeneous clientele – tourists, business travelers, and families – the Central had always balanced its messaging between economy and luxury, but now the scale tipped in favor of cheapness.[63] Lüpschütz defended his decision by citing the difficulty in finding guests in summer, particularly on Sunday nights. Lüpschütz was careful to emphasize privately that these guests would get no more than what they deserved and likely even less than what they expected. "Accommodation will be as basic as possible, perhaps two or three to a room," he told Aschinger. "Should a guest have any special wishes," Lüpschütz continued, "he must of course pay extra."[64] This was not first-class treatment and reflected Lüpschütz's expectation of a high response rate among second-class travelers.[65]

---

[61] Larry Eugene Jones, "Franz von Papen, Catholic Conservatives, and the Establishment of the Third Reich, 1933–1934," *Journal of Modern History* 83 (2011), 273–74. Cf. Sidney Pollard, "German Trade Union Policy, 1929–1933, in the Light of the British Experience," in *Economic Crisis and Political Collapse: The Weimar Republic, 1924–1933*, ed. Jürgen von Kruedener (New York: Berg, 1990), 43–44; Knut Borchardt, "A Decade of Debate about Brüning's Economic Policy," in Kruedener, *Economic Crisis*, 99–151.

[62] Kurt Lüpschütz to Fritz Aschinger (with sample advertisement), June 6, 1931, in LAB A Rep. 225, Nr. 797.

[63] On heterogeneity in grand hotels, see Siegfried Kracauer, "Luxushotel von unten gesehen," *Frankfurter Zeitung*, December 28, 1930; "Grand Hotel … !" *Frankfurter Zeitung*, June 24, 1928.

[64] Lüpschütz to Aschinger, June 6, 1931.

[65] Cf. Baum, *Menschen im Hotel*, 17–20.

FIGURE 5.1 Advertisement by the Hotel Management Corporation
and partners, 1932
Image credit: Landesarchiv Berlin

Higher incidences of theft in hotels prompted further associations with a lower sort of customer. As in the early 1920s, the Kaiserhof had patrons in the early 1930s sign a document stating that the hotel bore no responsibility for guests' property. The document stood up in court when Hilde Eisenreich lost her case against the Kaiserhof in 1931. She and her husband had been guests in the hotel the previous year. In the middle of their stay, they reported to the manager that 590 reichsmarks' worth in goods – a watch, a bracelet, and a ring – had gone missing from their room. After a fruitless police investigation, Eisenreich brought civil suit against the hotel, but she lost because of the document the Kaiserhof had had her sign upon check-in.[66] In addition to such waivers of responsibility, hoteliers relied on the police to investigate thoroughly and, in their reports, absolve the management of any wrongdoing such as negligence or worse. Indeed, in 1932, the officials of the Hotel Management Corporation complained that the police were not doing enough and called on the Reich finance minister to ask that the hotel business be better and more extensively policed.[67] Hotel employees should also police each other, the heads of the Hotel Management Corporation urged. An October 1931 memo to the managers of the Bristol, Kaiserhof, Central, and Baltic requested that workers be reminded to report any suspicious behavior within the ranks and that maids, in particular, should follow proper protocol by never agreeing to work alone.[68]

Crime, grit, and intrigue did not necessarily repel all guests, as a new crop of visitors arrived to see firsthand the depravity of late Weimar Berlin. Some came out of concern. In March 1931, Charlie Chaplin told reporters at the Adlon that while in town he wanted to see a prison and "something of street life in the poorer quarters."[69] A *New York Times* article by George Bernhard of the previous year had encouraged tourists to venture beyond "the Hotel Adlon" and "the palaces of the President and the government buildings" by following Wilhelmstraße northwards; if on "the historic Unter den Linden, do not stop at the former Imperial

---

[66] Verdict (copy), Hilde Eisenreich v. Hotel Management Corporation, October 22, 1931, District Court (Amtsgericht) of Berlin-Mitte (Abteilung 44), October 22, 1931, in LAB A Rep. 225, Nr. 797.

[67] Hotel Management Corporation to the Reich finance minister, addendum, October 27, 1931, in LAB A Rep. 225, Nr. 757.

[68] Memorandum to hotel managers Bollbuck (Bristol), Schröder (Kaiserhof), Weidner (Central-Hotel), and Wessel (Baltic), October 27, 1931, in LAB A Rep. 225, Nr. 797.

[69] "Chaplin in Berlin," *The New York Times*, March 10, 1931.

castle but cross the Spree and wander along the eastern direction of the city." The first thing to observe, according to Bernhard, would be women, whose "silk or near-silk stockings and short skirts" barely concealed "the fact that these people belong to the working classes." In slumming, the tourist might find the real Berlin, now in an exciting "age of ferment."[70]

In his *Führer durch das "lasterhafte" Berlin* (Guide to "Depraved" Berlin), Curt Moreck presented the city in similar fashion as a unit of two opposed entities: the one official, historical, and apparent, the other peripheral, dynamic, and hidden. "Berlin is a city of opposites," Moreck declared, "and it is a pleasure to discover them." A "confusing metropolis of pleasure," Berlin would confound visitors, particularly those who visited its "underworld," a "labyrinth" that could only be accessed, maneuvered, and made intelligible by a knowledgeable guide or, barring that, the guidebook Moreck was shilling. Like Bernhard of *The New York Times*, Moreck urged readers to leave Unter den Linden and Wilhelmstraße, a "mummified yesteryear" lined with "milestones of ennui," and head for the outer-lying districts to access new "experiences …, adventures …, and sensations."[71] The guidebook and the *Times* article emphasized the proximity of Berlin's old center, the neighborhoods of Friedrichstadt and Dorotheenstadt, to the working-class districts to the east and north.

A liability for hotel corporations even before the war, this proximity became a major cause for concern after 1929, in light of high unemployment and civil unrest. At the same time, grand hoteliers of Friedrichstadt and nearby neighborhoods continued to note the westward drift of attractions and population that pitted the old center against a newer, glittering district on the other side of the Tiergarten. "The rivalry between the Center and the West has had a very real effect on our business," Kalveram reported in September 1931. More and more guests were going west for dinner, and almost as many now preferred to stay there overnight. This trend benefitted not only the Eden, the only grand hotel west of Potsdamer Platz, but also many of the smaller hotels and pensions there. Although the Hotel Management Corporation tried through its advertising materials to strike back by claiming theirs as "the *actual* center," some corporate officers sensed a looming defeat.

---

[70] George Bernhard, "An Age of Ferment in German Culture," *The New York Times*, August 31, 1930.
[71] Curt Moreck, *Führer durch das "lasterhafte" Berlin* (Leipzig: H. Haessel, 1931), 7–10.

Exhortations to go west crept up everywhere, it seemed. Even the *Hotel-Revue*, which the Hotel Management Corporation supplied for free in all its guest rooms, urged guests to seek refined entertainments in the west. The east and parts of the center were for slumming, the book suggested. A grand hotel manager complained that the publication's tips related to the city's eastern entertainments often sent guests to "seedy pubs [*Nepplokale*]—of a homosexual tone, even"; in taking one of these "pleasure tours, recommended *by the hotel itself*, guests came back understandably displeased."[72] The real and imagined decline of the old center compromised almost all of the city's grand hotels.

While the *Hotel-Revue* was responding to what some guests wanted to experience – the city's dens of iniquity – hoteliers worried that this disaster tourism contributed to the general dissipation of grand hotels' exclusive atmosphere. As prices fell, hoteliers looked for new sources of revenue among groups heretofore peripheral to its publicity efforts, such as middling businessmen and budget travelers. "Perhaps it was a mistake," wrote Paul Arpé, manager of the Fürstenhof, in his report on the New Year's celebrations for 1930/31, "to price the menu so cheaply. Some 50 percent of the night's attendees were 'first-timers.'" Not all of the guests behaved. Numbering only 105, they consumed 94 bottles of champagne that night, almost the same number of bottles drunk the previous year, when the guest list had been twice as long.[73]

At 9:30 p.m., hotel staff wheeled out a large radio so that everyone would be able to hear President Hindenburg's 1931 New Year's address. The speech, which admonished Germans to "walk hand in hand toward the future," could not be heard in its entirety on account of what Arpé described as "political troublemaking."[74] There is no more information about what happened, but the event portended the deleterious effects of political polarization on grand hotel operations.

HITLER'S KAISERHOF

From 1926, but with increasing focus after 1929, the Nazi party directed its energies toward Berlin. Within Berlin itself, Hitler and his top aides came ever closer to the centers of power, into Friedrichstadt, replete with grand hotels. In the 1920s, Hitler's accommodation of choice had

---

[72] Emphasis in the original: Heinz Kalveram to Hans Lohnert, September 17, 1931, in LAB A Rep. 225, Nr. 797.
[73] "Denkschrift Silvester 1931," in LAB A Rep. 225, Nr. 1156.
[74] Ibid.

been the Sanssouci, a mediocre hotel garni, 27 rooms, on a side street west of Potsdamer Platz, separate from the heart of Friedrichstadt.[75] The quarter still supported the city center's zone of intense commercial and political activity by harboring large railroad stations, streetcar and underground interchanges, lesser hotels, and unglamorous dining concessions and businesses. But in February 1931, fresh from a major electoral victory in September 1930, which gave the Nazi party 107 seats in the Reichstag, Hitler crossed Potsdamer Platz, swept into the Leipziger octagon, passed the Wertheim luxury department store, hung left at Wilhelmstraße, and rode into the portico of the Kaiserhof, adjacent to the chancellery.[76]

As Hitler prepared his party for power, the Kaiserhof proved to be both instrumental and problematic for him. In the winter and spring of 1932, the months leading up to the presidential election in which Hitler would try and fail to unseat Hindenburg, the Kaiserhof saw more visits from him than ever before. Between January 1, 1932, and January 30, 1933, Hitler stayed at the Kaiserhof more than 100 nights, spread across almost all thirteen months.[77]

Fame brought with it heightened scrutiny. On April 4, 1932, six days before the second round of the presidential election, with Hitler in the running, the liberal weekly *Die Welt am Montag* published a facsimile of one of the Nazis' recent Kaiserhof bills. The editors pointed out that the nightly cost of one of the twelve rooms that Hitler had rented was equal to "the maximum that two unemployed persons can claim for an entire week's support."[78] Hitler therefore had no right to represent a workers' party, as he claimed to do. Hitler sued the editors for libel and won. A sympathetic court called the bill a forgery after the Kaiserhof management denied its veracity and even reported to the police the theft of a ream of receipt forms.[79] The Kaiserhof bill affair,

---

[75] Friedrich, *Hitler's Berlin*, 28.

[76] Jelavich, *Berlin Alexanderplatz*, 157.

[77] Friedrich, *Hitler's Berlin*, 245.

[78] "So lebt Hitler!" *Die Welt am Montag*, April 4, 1932.

[79] Walter Raeke, on behalf of the NSDAP, to the Public Prosecutor's Office (Staatsanvaltschaft, Landgericht I) of Berlin, petition of May 31, 1932, in LAB A Rep. 358-01, Nr. 1092; *Die Welt am Montag* to the Berlin Police Presidium, August 10, 1932, in LAB A Rep. 358-01, Nr. 1092; Berlin Police Presidium to the Public Prosecutor's Office (Landgericht I) of Berlin, August 10, 1932, in LAB A Rep. 358-01, Nr. 1092; Public Prosecutor's Office to the District Court of Charlottenburg, August 18, 1932, in LAB A Rep. 358-01, Nr. 1092; statement by Fritz Schroeder, manager of the Kaiserhof, October 20, 1932, in LAB A Rep. 358-01, Nr. 1092.

FIGURE 5.2 Otto Dietrich with Adolf Hitler in his suite
at the Kaiserhof, January 30, 1933
Image credit: Scherl/Süddeutsche Zeitung

whether or not it was a setup, lobbed a serious and familiar criticism at Hitler: hypocritical disparity between what the man said and what he and his party did.

Hitler's chief press officer, Otto Dietrich, in 1934 was still trying to spin the story to the Führer's advantage (Figure 5.2). Hitler had not chosen the Kaiserhof to pamper himself, Dietrich explained, but for three "reasons of expediency." First, the luxury and formality of the property served the political purpose of encouraging the republic's conservative elites to take Hitler seriously. Second, the location lent itself to the progression of Hitler's seizure of power. There, he was in full view of the "old chancellery building," the establishment occupants of which "laid countermines" and made other "insidious and malicious" attempts to "prevent the onrushing movement from gaining power." Proximity would help Hitler stymie their schemes. Finally, Dietrich accentuated the historical significance of the Kaiserhof. "One of Bismarck's houses," it was a symbol of unification and empire, the hotel of choice for delegates to the most important conferences and congresses of the last quarter of the nineteenth century. It thus had to be the hotel of choice for Hitler; it was his "gateway" to the chancellery, "from which Bismarck had ruled the German Empire," of which Hitler would "take possession ... in turn."[80]

The move to the Kaiserhof in 1931 and from the Kaiserhof to the chancellery on January 31, 1933, could be read as a script for Hitler's relationship to the past, as he wanted Germans to understand it: History had taken him from the Hotel Sanssouci, named for the favorite of Frederick the Great's palaces; to the Kaiserhof, named for Emperor Wilhelm I, whom Bismarck propelled into position as ruler of a new Germany; to the old chancellery, which Hitler made his own. The lineage passed from Frederick the Great to Bismarck to the Nazi assumption of power – from the First to the Second to the Third Reich.

The problem, from the perspective of the Hotel Management Corporation in 1932, was that Hitler did not belong at the Kaiserhof. His low social status aside, the bad behavior of his hangers-on, gauchely dressed in paramilitary uniforms and ignorant of the conventions of good comportment in an elite commercial establishment, indicated the Nazis' unsuitability as guests. In scaring away much of the clientele, they were also bad for business. Meanwhile, the hotel industry overall continued to suffer.

IN THE CRISIS OF GERMAN DEMOCRACY

In despair, the managing directors of Aschinger's Incorporated wrote to the Reich Ministry of Finance, the Prussian Ministry of Finance, and the Executive Office of Berlin for help in November 1932. Their revenues, which "in normal years stood at 30 million [reichsmarks]," were unlikely to reach even 10 million by the end of 1932. This 20-million-mark retraction was the greatest since the beginning of the Depression and, indeed, in the history of the business. From 1930 to 1931, revenues had dropped 21 percent. By the autumn of 1932, the decline since 1930 had reached 44 percent. The firm, according to its leaders, needed some form of government assistance and indeed deserved it: "the fault lies not in the failure of the leadership [of Aschinger's], nor in organizational or financial shortcomings," the directors argued, "but in the severe economic difficulties under which Germany and the whole world suffer."[81] With

---

[80] Otto Dietrich, *Mit Hitler in die Macht: Persönliche Erlebnisse mit meinem Führer* (Munich: Eher, 1934), 149–50.

[81] Aschinger's Incorporated to the Reich Ministry of Finance, the Prussian Ministry of Finance, and the Executive Office of the City of Berlin (Hauptverwaltung der Stadt Berlin), petition of November 10, 1932, in LAB A Rep. 225, Nr. 757.

"monstrous losses mounting by the day," the letter asked, "why not just close shop?" The letter then answered its own question: because the company, not with its luxury hotels but through its low-cost café concessions, had spread "deep roots" in Berlin and proved itself "indispensable to the lower middle class [*kleinen Mittelstand*] and the workers." The directors went on to present themselves as models of altruism, never having "wanted ... to seek help ... from public sources." Instead, Aschinger's management had tried to find savings in cutbacks and rationalization and would continue to do so. The salaries of the firm's "leading figures," for example, had "been reduced considerably." But Aschinger's had reached its limits, the letter argued, and would now have to apply for a concession – the mitigation of an "unbearable" tax burden.

There was no more room for savings, the letter emphasized, and no point in further rationalization and economization without "a generous settlement" on the issue of those "taxes and duties" which, having cost the corporation 20 percent more in 1931 than in 1930, "threatened to overwhelm the business" and presently, with indications of a similar increase from 1931 to 1932, eliminated any chance of "survival." Aschinger's directors also beseeched the addressees to call off the mess of "agencies and authorities" now "robbing [us] of [our] time" and instead assign all activities related to taxation to "a central office." Both the level and the manner of taxation were bringing the business grief and needed correcting if Aschinger's was "to hold itself upright" any longer.[82]

The directors' assessment was accurate, in part. High taxes as a response to the Depression were having terrible effects in Germany as elsewhere, especially on consumers.[83] Still, hoteliers would have found a more pointed argument for why the state was to blame if they had also focused on Chancellor Heinrich Brüning's deflationary measures and the conservatives' efforts to dismantle the republic by further ruining the economy. Ferdinand von Lüninck (German National People's Party), a prominent anti-republican, described the strategy most succinctly: "Improvements in the existing system will never be possible through

[82] Ibid.
[83] Dietmar Rothermund, *The Global Impact of the Great Depression, 1929–1939* (London: Routledge, 2003), 16–17. On taxation and the Great Depression in Germany, see Dietmar Keese, "Die volkswirtschaftliche Gesamtgrößen für das Deutsche Reich, 1925–1936," in *Die Staats- und Wirtschaftskrise des Deutschen Reichs, 1929/1933*, eds. Werner Conze and Hans Raupach (Stuttgart: Ernst Klett, 1967), 35–37. See also Theo Balderston, "The Beginning of the Depression in Germany, 1927–1930: Investment and the Capital Market," *Economic History Review* 36 (1983), 396–97.

reform but only through the total elimination [of the system itself], and this is only possible by letting it collapse from the weight of its own incompetence."[84] It was an incompetence that Brüning would have to engineer with deliberately cruel policy.

As conditions worsened, hoteliers used increasingly hysterical language to describe the effects of taxation. Indeed, as in 1919–23, hotel firms blamed the state for their misfortune and seized on taxes as the means by which the fiscus was seeking to destroy free, profitable enterprise. "We have made every effort" to right the business and only failed to turn a profit on account of "our tax burden," the Hotel Management Corporation claimed in its annual report for 1931/32.[85] This emphasis on taxes as the principal cause of the emergency – an emphasis that tended to cast the government as rapacious, anti-business, and even anti-German – obscured the other sources of strain on Berlin's grand hotel industry. First, weaknesses within the business model itself had brought properties to their knees in the course of every crisis, large or small, in the years since 1914. Second, the government's policy of deflation, in the German case an attempt to damage the economy further and erode confidence in the republic, had helped shrink hotels' profits to nothing. Instead of calling on the state to end this practice, hoteliers chose almost never to acknowledge it. When they did speak up, it was only to ask for a "temporary" reprieve from the austerity, not for an end to deflation.[86] This move tended to cast the present difficulties as part of a longer history of over-taxation under coalitions of the center-left and not as a result of the newer conservative policies aimed at restricting the money supply and credit. For hotel corporations' annual reports to have targeted deflation as well as taxes would have been to cast the leadership as saboteurs – which they were – intent on pursuing a policy that would victimize Germans and thereby drive them to turn on the republic.

While hoteliers were trying to make sense of the deepening economic crisis, they witnessed the continued rightward drift of the German electorate. In April 1932, Hindenburg won reelection to the presidency, ensuring the continued presence of anti-republicans in the chancellery. Two weeks later, the National Socialist German Workers' Party (NSDAP, the

---

[84] Letter of February 4, 1930, quoted in Jones, "Franz von Papen," 276. See also Ritschl, *Deutschlands Krise*, 131–33, 220ff.

[85] Annual report of the Hotel Management Corporation for 1931/32, in LAB A Rep. 225-01, Nr. 189.

[86] "Ein Hilfsprogramm für die deutsche Hotelwirtschaft: Entschließung des Reichsverbandes der Deutschen Hotels E.V.," flyer, October 6, 1932, in LAB A Rep. 225, Nr. 798.

Nazis) prevailed in elections for the parliaments of Hamburg, Anhalt, Württemberg, Bavaria, and Prussia. Then, in July, Chancellor Papen, under the president's power to legislate by emergency decree, took over the government of Prussia and effectively abrogated parliamentary rule there. In the national elections eleven days later, the Nazi party won 37.3 percent of the vote and became the strongest faction in the Reichstag. Hermann Göring became its president in August. These were the political conditions under which the boards of the Hotel Management Corporation and Aschinger's Incorporated continued to labor.

The minutes of board meetings and correspondence among hoteliers in 1931 and 1932 show a high frequency of fatalist pronouncements. The reports' authors suggested that they were washing their hands of the industry and of any effort to salvage it. "Stagnation," "crisis," and "catastrophe" became the words used most frequently to describe the situation.[87] Although the reports paid scant attention to the international dimensions of the Depression, the board members of the Hotel Management Corporation were aware of conditions in hotel industries abroad. In the United States, for example, some 70 percent of hotels were out of business, bankrupt, or in receivership by the start of 1932.[88] The Depression discredited the American example, which Berlin's hoteliers had until very recently held up as the model of rational, responsible enterprise. Now there were no models, only the reality that a business as big and costly to operate as a grand hotel had finally and conclusively proved itself to be less viable than almost any other kind of business.[89] In public, Berlin's grand hoteliers implicated only the state's tax policies in the failures. In private, however, they attended to the full scope of the crisis, including the Nazi ascent.

SEPTEMBER 15, 1932

How do we begin to make sense of Meinhardt and the board's decision to let the Nazis use the Kaiserhof as their Berlin headquarters? In the absence of any further testimony from Meinhardt and the other board members, all we can do is reconstruct their perspective on events and

---

[87] Annual report of Aschinger's Incorporated for 1930, in LAB A Rep. 225, Nr. 636.

[88] Lisa Pfueller Davidson, "'A Service Machine': Hotel Guests and the Development of an Early-Twentieth-Century Building Type," *Perspectives in Vernacular Architecture* 10 (2005), 124–25.

[89] "Ein Hilfsprogramm für die deutsche Hotelwirtschaft: Entschließung des Reichsverbandes der Deutschen Hotels E.V.," flyer, October 6, 1932.

try to recover the context. The most important factor was the pervasive atmosphere of uncertainty, emergency, and fear in September 1932 that clouded board members' judgment to the extent that they, even the Jewish ones, invited into their own house the man who would ruin them.

On September 15, 1932, the board of the Hotel Management Corporation met at the Bristol to discuss the challenges facing the Kaiserhof and the rest of the corporation's properties. The minutes enumerate the banking crisis, the credit crisis, and the "almost total closing off of the borders" as national governments retrenched. Board members in attendance included Meinhardt as chair; Hans Lohnert; Fritz Aschinger; Wilhelm Kleemann, manager of Dresdner Bank; Eugen Landau, a diplomat and member of the boards of the Schultheiß-Patzenhofer brewing concern and two banks; and Walter Sobernheim, Landau's stepson, also a diplomat, and head of Schultheiß-Patzenhofer.[90] Managing directors Kalveram, Schick, and Voremberg were also there, as well as two employee representatives.

At the start of the meeting, Schick rose to deliver some bad news about the Kaiserhof. The hotel was experiencing the "greatest decline in sales" of all the Hotel Management Corporation's properties. The presence in the hotel of Hitler's SA (Sturmabteilung) and SS (Schutzstaffel), as well as the Stahlhelm, a right-radical paramilitary league, had led to "substantial losses." Given the Nazis' electoral successes, Schick counseled the board to expect a further influx of right-radicals, an additional resulting decline in patronage by the hotel's standard clientele, and a series of "substantial cutbacks" in service. Schick avoided mentioning specific behaviors and actions on the part of the Nazis that were causing the standard clientele to stay away. At any rate, with five of the seven board members in attendance being Jews, the disadvantages of the Nazi presence did not need elaboration.

The minutes show that a representative from the Kaiserhof's managerial staff spoke next; he is named only as Krasemann and described as a white-collar employee. Krasemann does not appear elsewhere in the corporate records and distinguishes himself here with an uncommonly accusatory tone. "Not enough is being done," he charged, despite it being common knowledge "that Hitler has been in residence in the house for

---

[90] Apologies came in from Hans Arnhold (banker), Karl August Harter (banker), and Heinrich von Stein (banker and diplomat). On bankers and the links between bank boards and corporate boards, see Philippe Marguerat, *Banques et grande industrie: France, Grande-Bretagne, Allemagne, 1880–1930* (Paris: Presses de Sciences Po, 2015), chapter 4.

FIGURE 5.3 At the Kaiserhof for a reception after the Reichstag elections
of July 1932, from left to right: Curt von Ulrich, Edmund Heines, Heinrich
Himmler, Franz Epp, Ernst Röhm, and Wolf-Heinrich von Helldorf
Image credit: Bundesarchiv, Bild 146-2000-005-23

some time, that the Stahlhelm have commandeered [*militärisch aufgezogen*] the Kaiserhof for use as a headquarters, that too much of the clientele has been lost ... that the whole Jewish clientele has stayed away." The Kaiserhof and its guests were being mistreated, he claimed. And "of course, this has played a role in the decline in sales and the layoffs that come with it."

Only at the end of the meeting, after all the Hotel Management Corporation's other businesses had been addressed, did Meinhardt finally face the issue and make his judgment. The Nazis could stay because, for the good of the company, "our houses must remain open to all." That included Nazis, though they were poorly behaved and bad for business. Meinhardt's response, again: "We cannot do anything about it." Kleemann, also Jewish, spoke next and brought Meinhardt back to reality: "I know for certain that Jewish guests no longer stay at the Kaiserhof and no longer visit the restaurant, either." It was then that Meinhardt noted "how hard it is for the house's restaurant director to exercise the requisite tact in face of these difficult questions."[91]

---

[91] Minutes of the meeting of the board of directors of the Hotel Management Corporation, September 15, 1932.

No one discussed it at the meeting, but some of the same board members and hoteliers had faced a similar, though lower-stakes, question back in August 1927 and came up with a similar solution at the time. For Constitution Day that year, the magistrate requested that businesses, especially prominent ones, fly the republic's black-red-gold tricolor. But when Constitution Day came around, most of the grand hotels left their flagpoles bare. The magistrate first took note and then took punitive action, calling a boycott of several grand hotels. The minister-president of Prussia followed suit and compelled state employees to join the boycott. In his decree, he rebuked the Adlon, especially, for having flown the US flag on July 4 to celebrate the American republic but not the national flag on August 11 to celebrate that of the Germans. The minister-president, the magistrate, and the mayor went about canceling their upcoming events, costing the Adlon, Esplanade, and Hotel Management Corporation valuable bookings.[92]

The national press reported on this official and concerted "*Hotelboykott*" in late August. The hoteliers' responses to reporters only made the situation worse. Representatives from the Hotel Management Corporation and the Association of Berlin Hoteliers told *Vorwärts*, always critical of the industry, that the hoteliers had nothing in particular against the republic. It was only out of "concern for the business" that they had come together and decided that no one was to fly the national flag on Constitution Day. In this way, the hotels would maintain their "neutral stance." Neutrality was important, the hoteliers explained, because Berlin's grand hotels accommodated "republicans and members of the right" alike. To avoid offending either side, "we decided to recommend to members of the [Association of Berlin Hoteliers] that the national flag not be flown" on Constitution Day.[93] The decision foreshadowed that of September 15, 1932: equivocation in face of political polarization, refusal to do anything to support the republic, and deployment of liberal arguments about openness to opposing viewpoints – and this to defend a decision rightly understood as acquiescence to the republic's enemies. The hoteliers had not supported the republic in 1927, nor would they do so in 1932. Much more serious than the 1927 decision, the 1932 decision gave Hitler free run of the house.

---

[92] Kurt Lüpschütz to Fritz Aschinger, August 30, 1927, in LAB A Rep. 225, Nr. 797; "Hotelkrieg gegen Schwarzrotgold: Preußische Maßnahmen gegen die Herabsetzung der Reichsflagge," *Vorwärts*, August 26, 1927.

[93] Quoted in "Berliner Hotels ohne Nationalflaggen: Der Magistrat besucht sie nicht mehr," *Vorwärts*, August 24, 1927.

Meinhardt's liberalism, and that of his party more generally, was of no help against the Nazis, who were adept at using the precepts of free speech, free political association, and equal access to gain entry to liberal institutions only for the purpose of destroying them.[94] Beyond the atmosphere of pessimism discussed above, several additional factors contributed to this failure. First, Meinhardt would have feared the negative consequences of ejecting the Nazis: the alienation of pro-Nazi customers and the risk of reprisals from a Nazi party that was growing in power and popularity. Second, there was the problem of Meinhardt's responsibility to shareholders and his duty to remain impartial. As chair of the board, he was not supposed to let his own politics or Jewishness guide his decisions. Third, there was the problem of Meinhardt's liberalism. To refuse service to someone on the basis of his or her political beliefs, however odious, would have looked like an illiberal thing to do, and Meinhardt was a committed liberal. Fourth, and finally, there was his position as a member of Germany's industrial elite, whose anti-republican stance might have made democratic solutions to Germany's problems less attractive to Meinhardt in the moment. Any of these factors could have caused Meinhardt to misjudge where his own interests and the interests of the corporation lay and decide to allow the Nazis to remain at the Kaiserhof after September 15, 1932.

The dangers that the Nazis posed to Jewish businesses in 1932, as well as the dangers associated with being Jewish – and a prominent Jewish businessman at that – were manifold and apparent. As early as October 13, 1930, a Nazi mob had descended on the area around Leipziger Platz to smash plate-glass windows and otherwise vandalize Jewish-owned retail establishments, the most prominent of which was the Wertheim department store.[95] If Wertheim was vulnerable, so too was the Kaiserhof and the other properties of the Hotel Management Corporation, all located a short walk from Wertheim. The following year brought another outburst of anti-Semitic violence when members of the NSDAP attacked Jews, and people suspected of being Jews, on Rosh Hashanah.[96] Occurring in broad daylight on Kurfürstendamm, this action increased the vulnerability of

[94] See Thomas Mergel, *Parlamentarische Kultur in der Weimarer Republik: Politische Kommunikation, symbolische Politik und Öffentlichkeit im Reichstag* (Düsseldorf: Droste, 2002).

[95] Jelavich, *Berlin Alexanderplatz*, 157.

[96] Sharon Gillerman, "German Jews in the Weimar Republic," in *The Oxford Handbook of the Weimar Republic*, eds. Nadine Rossol and Benjamin Ziemann (Oxford: Oxford University Press, 2020), 575.

FIGURE 5.4 William Meinhardt, chairman of the board of the
Hotel Management Corporation, 1931
Image credit: Bundesarchiv, Bild 183-2007-0307-506

even the capital's most vaunted commercial districts. The year 1932
brought still more violence into Berliners' daily lives and also into their
consciousness through the daily reports in newspapers. "Squads ... in
the provinces" were stopping cars and demanding to be taken to Berlin
on the eve of the national election on July 31, according to the *Berliner
Tageblatt*: "A great many sources lie before us that suggest that either the
central leadership of the SA or its regional subgroups have issued orders
that particular departments be put on alert and made ready to march [on
Berlin] in the days before and after the Reichstag elections."[97] These were
by all accounts frightening days. Fear may explain Meinhardt's decision
to give the Nazis the run of his house.[98] After all, the Kaiserhof had been
sacked once before by a roving paramilitary force, back in January 1919

[97] "S.-A.-Alarm," *Berliner Tageblatt*, July 29, 1932.
[98] Molly Loberg, *The Struggle for the Streets of Berlin: Politics, Consumption, and Urban
Space, 1914–1945* (Cambridge: Cambridge University Press, 2018), 160–71.

(see Chapter 4). Given the choice between physical damage and damage to the house's reputation, Meinhardt preferred the latter.

The dynamics of his firm's managerial hierarchy might have also played some role in his decision. Meinhardt's principal responsibility was to his shareholders, and it thus fell to him to ensure that the Kaiserhof would never be exposed to danger or damage. This responsibility to shareholders further entailed balancing their entitlement to dividends with the firm's need to make regular capital investments. (The latter, if managed properly, would ensure higher dividends in the future, or so the theory went.[99]) When he decided to allow the Nazis to remain at the Kaiserhof, Meinhardt would also have been considering his duty to shareholders: Which course was most likely to ensure the firm's assets and the possibility of dividends in the near future?

The amorality of other industrialists in their approach to the rise of Nazism might echo Meinhardt's. Overwhelming pessimism, which turned to fatalism during the Great Depression, eliminated any opportunity to see a way toward prosperity that did not involve a fundamental transformation of the German economy, German society, and even the German polity.[100] As Hitler consolidated his mass base in the years 1928–32, he appeared to be the most likely instrument of change. The fatalism that had emerged among the industrial elite caused them to prefer this change regardless of its quite apparent disadvantages.

MEINHARDT'S FALL

Some of the developments that brought Hitler to power took place inside the Kaiserhof.[101] Throughout 1932, Hitler took meetings there with present and future collaborators, including members of the government and their advisors who made the short trip from the chancellery across the square.[102] These visits increased in frequency after the September 15, 1932, board meeting in which the owners of the Kaiserhof decided that the Nazis could stay. From his headquarters in

---

[99] On dividends, see Franco Amatori and Andrea Colli, *Business History: Complexities and Comparisons* (New York: Routledge, 2011), 78–80.

[100] Theo Balderston, *The Origins and Course of the German Economic Crisis: November 1923 to May 1932* (Berlin: Haude & Spencer, 1993), 381–412.

[101] See Larry Eugene Jones, *Hitler versus Hindenburg: The 1932 Presidential Elections and the End of the Weimar Republic* (Cambridge: Cambridge University Press, 2016).

[102] Volker Ullrich, *Hitler*, vol. 1, *Ascent*, trans. Jefferson S. Chase (New York: Knopf, 2016), 263, 288, 339, 370.

the hotel, Hitler played master negotiator and statesman, even as he oversaw extralegal efforts to seize power.

To complement these backroom, backstairs negotiations, Hitler also unleashed wave after wave of violence across Germany.[103] As Berlin and other towns appeared to be descending into civil war in December 1932, Hindenburg dismissed Papen as chancellor and replaced him with Kurt von Schleicher. This last-ditch effort on Hindenburg's part to appease and defang the Nazis' mass base failed, as did Schleicher's efforts to maintain his authority over the cabinet and members of Hindenburg's entourage.

It is worth emphasizing the spatial dimension of Schleicher's difficulties – that is, the physical proximity of Hitler to power. "The choice of the Kaiserhof as my headquarters in Berlin, diagonally opposite the chancellery building," Hitler is supposed to have said, "has already left the men there profoundly shaken." Sitting up with their Führer in his salon "until the gray light of dawn," Joseph Goebbels reported sometime later, "plans are hatched as if we are already in power."[104]

In the first weeks of 1933, intermediaries rushed between the chancellery and the Kaiserhof to set up meetings between Nazi leaders and the government.[105] After several such meetings at secret locations in and around Berlin, Hitler departed the area on January 23, 1933, for Frankfurt an der Oder and then traveled onward to Munich. Three days later, he was back at the Kaiserhof to consider the last stages of his party's ascent to power.[106] When Schleicher finally stepped down on January 28, the wheels began to turn: Papen made the successful case to Hindenburg that Hitler should be chancellor and that he, Papen, should be vice-chancellor. Two days later, shortly after 11 a.m. on January 30, Hitler made his way from the Kaiserhof to the chancellery to accept his prize.

---

[103] On violence in Berlin and the Nazi assumption of power, see Loberg, *Struggle for the Streets*, 186–94. See also Richard Bessel, "Political Violence and the Nazi Seizure of Power," in *Life in the Third Reich*, ed. Richard Bessel (Oxford: Oxford University Press, 1987), 1–16; McElligott, *Rethinking the Weimar Republic*, chapter 8; Robert Gellately, *Backing Hitler: Consent and Coercion in Nazi Germany* (Oxford: Oxford University Press, 2001).

[104] Quoted in Friedrich, *Hitler's Berlin*, 219, 256.

[105] On meetings between the nationalists (German National People's Party) and NSDAP leaders, see Hermann Beck, *The Fateful Alliance: German Conservatives and Nazis in 1933 – The Machtergreifung in a New Light* (New York: Berghahn, 2008), 70–88. On meetings between industrialists and NSDAP leaders, see Gerard Braunthal, *The Federation of German Industry in Politics* (Ithaca, NY: Cornell University Press, 1965), 15ff. Cf. Henry Ashby Turner Jr., *German Big Business and the Rise of Hitler* (New York: Oxford University Press, 1985).

[106] Friedrich, *Hitler's Berlin*, 310.

Once in power, the Nazis unleashed further waves of terror and repression over the capital, worrying the city's grand hoteliers. On February 1, not even forty-eight hours into Hitler's chancellorship, Hindenburg agreed to dissolve the Reichstag, and the hunt for Nazism's enemies began immediately. The press, too, found itself muzzled in those early days: On February 4, an emergency decree limited freedom of speech as well as the right to free assembly. The end of the month brought further attacks on what remained of Weimar's democratic institutions. On February 27, the Reichstag building sustained heavy damage by fire; the next day, the Reichstag Fire Decree (*Reichstagsbrandverordnung*) removed many of the civil liberties guaranteed by the Weimar constitution and mandated the ruthless pursuit of leaders and members of the KPD (Communist Party of Germany), leading to the destruction of the party along with other sources of opposition. On March 8, an emergency decree ejected all KPD delegates from the national parliament.[107] And every day, the assaults on certain Berliners, Communists in particular, intensified.[108] The insurance industry even sought to capitalize on the fear evoked by this unrestrained violence, as a letter of March 1, 1933, from one insurer to the Hotel Management Corporation attests: "Current events give us cause to bring your attention to the possibility that riot insurance ... will allay your anxiety over the protection of all your tangible assets – an anxiety made worse by the fact that no one knows what tomorrow will bring."[109] The letter addressed pervasive unease among hoteliers, whose businesses sat at the center of the consolidation of Nazi power and terror. Of all the grand hotels, only the Eden was more than a fifteen-minute walk from the chancellery and Prinz-Albrechtstraße, headquarters of the Gestapo from May 1933.

The reach of Nazi persecution soon made its way into the hotels themselves. In May 1933, this persecution began in the form of an institution set up for the express purpose of *Gleichschaltung*, a multifaceted program of forced synchronization with the new regime. On May 18, a circular arrived at the offices of the Hotel Management Corporation

---

[107] Manfred Görtemaker, ed. *Weimar in Berlin: Porträt einer Epoche* (Berlin: BeBra, 2002), 211.

[108] See Richard J. Evans, *The Coming of the Third Reich* (London: Penguin, 2003), 450–56.

[109] Königstadt Corporation for Real Estate and Industry (Königstadt Aktien-Gesellschaft für Grundstücke und Industrie) to the Hotel Management Corporation, March 1, 1933, in LAB A Rep. 225, Nr. 975.

saddling the managing directors with a new task in the service of *Gleich-schaltung*: to gather information on the political and racial background of employees.[110] This meant the identification and promotion of Nazis and pro-Nazis, on the one hand, and the identification and elimination of Jews, on the other.[111]

Two Nazis external to the corporation would join Kalveram, one of the managing directors who was neither a Nazi nor a sympathizer.[112] Together, they would have to distribute a survey aimed at collecting information on the political and racial makeup of the firm's employees and owners. In addition to requesting the names of anyone with a position in the NSDAP or Stahlhelm, the survey also demanded the following: the number of white-collar employees, male and female; the number of workers, male and female; the number of apprentices, male and female; and the "*absolute* total count of *Jewish* members of the firm (white-collar employees, workers, and apprentices)."[113] Kalveram and the two Nazi overlords who shared with him the authority to carry out this survey had one week to supply this "absolutely essential" information, which, according to the circular, must be delivered "without delay."[114] The survey results are lost, but another document, as curious as it is damning, about the Aryanization of the business does appear in the records of Aschinger's Incorporated, parent company to the Hotel Management Corporation since 1927. This typewritten page, which immediately followed the blank survey form for employees of the Hotel Management Corporation, lists various board members and managing directors of the Hotel Management Corporation and Aschinger's (Figure 5.5).[115] There is no explanation for why some names appear on this list while others do not. In the list itself, however, certain patterns emerge.

---

[110] On Gleichschaltung and German business, see Adam Tooze, *The Wages of Destruction: The Making and Breaking of the Nazi Economy* (London: Penguin, 2008), chapter 4.

[111] Association for the Protection of Large Retail and Related Concerns (Schutzgemeinschaft der Großbetriebe des Einzelhandels und verwandter Gruppen) to the Hotel Management Corporation, circular, May 18, 1933, in LAB A Rep. 225-01, Nr. 36.

[112] Notes on a meeting between Fritz Aschinger and Heinz Kalveram, May 30, 1933, in LAB A Rep. 225-01, Nr. 43; memorandum of May 26, 1933, in LAB A Rep. 225-01, Nr. 36; Max Kersten to Hans Lohnert, May 27, 1933, in LAB A Rep. 225-01, Nr. 36.

[113] Emphasis in the original: Association for the Protection of Large Retail and Related Concerns to the Hotel Management Corporation, circular, May 18, 1933.

[114] Ibid.

[115] List of names, n.d., in LAB A Rep. 225-01, Nr. 36. In the file, the list comes between letters dated May 26, 1933, and May 27, 1933. Both letters concern the Aryanization of the boards of Aschinger's Incorporated and the Hotel Management Corporation.

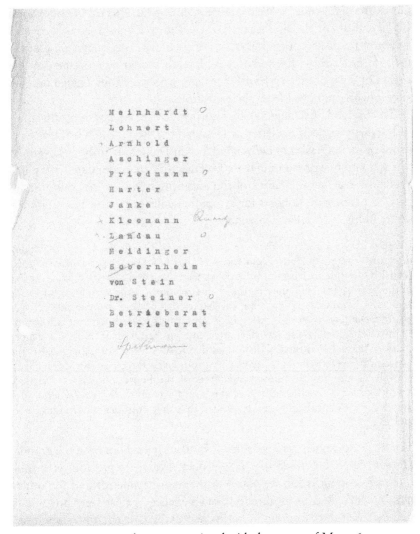

FIGURE 5.5 List of names associated with the survey of May 26, 1933
Image credit: Landesarchiv Berlin

The list features the names of all Jewish board members as well as board members whose backgrounds or names might suggest Jewish heritage. (As a successful entrepreneur from the provinces, Aschinger – who was not Jewish – fits the bill.) An unlikely candidate was added later, in pencil: Reinhold Georg Quaatz, an industrialist, conservative politician, and anti-Semite who had worked closely with Hitler's important

ally Alfred Hugenberg. With one Jewish parent, Quaatz likely escaped
the first draft of the list because of the indirect assistance he provided
to Hitler in his ascent to power.[116] Although the precise meaning of the
list's slashes, circles, Xs, and dots are lost, these markings attend only the
names of Jews or men of Jewish heritage, who were thus singled out and
subsequently removed from their positions.

To that end, Aschinger's chief corporate officer, Lohnert, did much
of the dirty work, if his letter of October 10, 1938, to the NSDAP local
group leader (*Ortsgruppenleiter*) of Berlin-Dahlem is to be believed. By
1938, a kindly worded note from Lohnert to Voremberg dated 1933 had
somehow reached the hands of the authorities, who in response threatened to investigate Lohnert for sympathetic dealings with Jews. Lohnert
wrote in his own defense in 1938:

I would like to point out that the correspondence with the Jewish managing
director Voremberg dates from the year 1933, from a period in which the
Jewish Question had begun but by no means reached a crisis point as it has
in the year 1938. This must be taken into account at the very first, for in the
year 1933, right about the time the letter [in question, to Voremberg] was
written, the Jews were still riding high, and it was exceedingly difficult for me
to throw them out, these Jewish gentlemen, who had been at the firm for more
than 25 years. My difficulty dismissing the Jewish Herr Voremberg aside, the
board was overwhelmingly against me, too, since the chairman [Meinhardt]
as well as four [sic] additional members of the board were Jews. Even so,
I wrote to two Jewish members of the board – namely, Consul-General Landau and Dr. Sobernheim – and requested that they consider the circumstances
and resign.[117]

The letter misremembered events. Aryanization had not been the gradual
affair Lohnert described in 1938. In fact, five years previously, it took
only a few months for the Nazis to threaten Meinhardt and the others
with murder. Bad press abroad about violence against Germany's Jews
had incensed the top brass in Berlin, especially Göring, who summoned
the leaders of the city's more assimilationist Jewish organizations to

---

[116] Hermann Weiß and Paul Hoser, eds. *Die Deutschnationalen und die Zerstörung der
Weimarer Republik: Aus dem Tagebuch von Reinhold Quaatz, 1928–1933* (Munich:
Oldenbourg, 1989), 17–21ff.; Dieter Ziegler, "'Aryanization' and the Role of the
German Great Banks," in *Networks of Nazi Persecution: Bureaucracy, Business,
and the Organization of the Holocaust*, eds. Gerald D. Feldman and Wolfgang Seibel
(New York: Berghahn, 2006), 48–50; Beck, *Fateful Alliance*, 24–25, 90–92.

[117] Emphasis in the original: Hans Lohnert to the local group leader of Berlin-Dahlem,
October 10, 1938. In early 1933, the board contained, in addition to Meinhardt, six
members of Jewish ancestry, not four.

demand that elite Jews use their influence and halt the avalanche of negative reports about the new regime in foreign newspapers.[118] The message
to transmit to the international press was not that German Jews were
being mishandled – "barefaced lies," according to one of Hitler's spokes-
men – but that the German government was tired of being flogged in the
public sphere for acts that Nazi officials refused to confirm. "Unless you
put a stop to these libelous accusations immediately, I shall no longer be
able to vouch for the safety of German Jews."[119] Meinhardt lost little
time and fled to London. Eventually, he would help coordinate relief
efforts under the auspices of the Association of Jewish Refugees.[120]

CONCLUSION

Meinhardt left no record of his impressions and preoccupations in 1932.
Nonetheless, the context has provided clues. He and his fellow board
members found themselves in a complicated, perilous situation, which
they approached first with pessimism and then with fatalism, a result of
years of difficulties, the worst of which had been the hyperinflation of
1923. Many of them blamed the republic for their woes and decided, in
the end, not to defend it.

Under the conditions of 1932 – mounting anti-Semitic violence, a collapse in demand, mass unemployment – a defense of liberalism might
have seemed out of reach, even to committed liberals such as Meinhardt. That commitment was weak among his colleagues, after all. It
had wavered after 1914 and then broken under the hyperinflationary
conditions of 1923. The period of relative stability (1924–29) did little to
make amends. Instead, stabilization indicated the likely endurance of the
republic, its social programs, and, especially, the taxes that paid for those
programs. In their annual reports and trade publications, more and more
hoteliers turned anti-republican and anti-liberal. They railed against the

---

[118] For example, see Dorothy Thompson's famous interview with Hitler at the Kaiserhof,
published in the March 1932 issue of *Cosmopolitan* under the title "I Saw Hitler!" See
also Deborah Cohen, *Last Call at the Hotel Imperial: The Reporters Who Took on a
World at War* (New York: Random House, 2022), 139–42.

[119] Quoted in Will Wainewright, *Reporting on Hitler: Rothay Reynolds and the British
Press in Nazi Germany* (London: Biteback, 2017), 75.

[120] Tobies, *Iris Runge*, 342; Meinhardt, Wilhelm [*sic*], biographical entry, *Deutsche Biographie*, www.deutsche-biographie.de/pnd127299904.html, accessed July 13, 2022. On
the personal ruin of progressive, liberal, and conservative elites like Meinhardt, see
Noah Benezra Strote, *Lions and Lambs: Conflict in Weimar and the Creation of Post-
Nazi Germany* (New Haven: Yale University Press, 2017), 12.

government and its tax regime with such zeal that when the republic needed them, even the liberal hoteliers lacked the words and the nerve to come to democracy's defense. Instead, Meinhardt equivocated over the issue of whether to favor Jews or Nazis and then chose the latter. By September 15, 1932, there was no space left in the boardroom for a full-throated condemnation of liberalism's antithesis, Nazism, or of Hitler, who should have been the Kaiserhof's least welcome guest.

Epilogue

The Hotel Kaiserhof in 1932 stood at the center of the fight for control of Germany and its capital. On the one side of this contest was
a liberal vision of commercial hospitality and urbanism that prized,
and profited from, access for all – even its enemies – and on the other
side was an anti-liberal vision that seized the opportunity to expunge,
publicly and with impunity, an enemy-minority from the very house
that had decided to keep its doors open to Hitler.[1] In the fateful days
and nights before his assumption of power on January 30, 1933, Hitler
used rooms at the Kaiserhof as his Berlin base and home. But by the
mid-1930s, his propagandists were using the Kaiserhof for another
purpose, as a site of mythmaking about the origins of the regime.[2] In
1935, the Central Press of the Nazi Party published Joseph Goebbels's
alleged diary entries for the period January 1, 1932, to May 1, 1933,
and titled it *Vom Kaiserhof zur Reichskanzlei* (From the Kaiserhof to
the Chancellery).

The Kaiserhof was the first elite, cosmopolitan institution to fall
to the Nazis and exclude Jewish guests. In 1932, Hitler and his SA
henchmen had accomplished this in an informal way, for they had yet
to attain power. The approach reflected the Nazis' wider practices of
threat-making and incitements to violence. These practices had already
turned several of Berlin's neighborhoods into battlegrounds and marked

---

[1] Claudia Koonz, *The Nazi Conscience* (Cambridge, MA: Harvard University Press,
2003), 2–7.
[2] On mythmaking, see Clark, *Iron Kingdom*, 662; Ian Kershaw, *The "Hitler Myth": Image
and Reality in the Third Reich* (Oxford: Clarendon, 1987), 11–12.

the experience of the city center for many Berliners by September 1932. The expulsion of Jews from the Kaiserhof, which did not come to violence but depended on the context of widespread violence elsewhere and the threat of violence to come, began a process whereby the Nazis, once they were in power at the end of January 1933, took control of the city center. First, they installed the Gestapo in Friedrichstadt and tortured victims there. The cries permeated the district and were audible to passersby and neighbors.[3] Second, they used violence and the threat of violence to clear Friedrichstadt of undesirable elements: Jews, homosexuals, Socialists, Communists, and bohemians and other types of nonconformists.[4]

But once the movement became a regime, neither violence nor the threat of violence fit with its deepening commitment, popular among Germans, to the restoration and preservation of order.[5] In other words, by late 1933, running amok in the city center no longer served Nazi priorities. Hence, the city center was transformed from a battleground to an arena for the realization of an ethnic-fundamentalist vision. Friedrichstadt would need to be remade to reflect and support the greatness of the ethnic collective, the *Volksgemeinschaft* or community of the folk. That meant promising Berliners a restoration of dignity, prosperity, and peace – in a word, normalcy.[6] Yet, as Berlin's grand hoteliers learned the hard way in the 1930s and '40s, this was an empty promise.[7]

It took a few years for the disappointments to pile up. After the first year of Nazi rule, and for the first time in a generation, the business reports of Aschinger's Incorporated found reason to praise the state. "The strong [*kraftvoll*] initiatives of the National Socialist government ... have finally halted the years-long, enfeebling [*zermürbend*] decline in all sectors of the economy."[8] With words like "strong" for the Nazi regime and "enfeebling" for the Weimar period, the report's writers set up a familiar opposition, associating Weimar with weakness

---

[3] See Helmut Bräutigam and Oliver C. Gleich, "Nationalsozialistische Zwangslager in Berlin I: Die 'wilden' Konzentrationslager und Folterkeller, 1933/34," in *Berlin-Forschungen*, ed. Wolfgang Ribbe (Berlin: Colloquium, 1987), 2:141–78.

[4] See David Clay Large, *Berlin* (New York: Basic, 2000), 300–301.

[5] On the Nazis' efforts to seem like a party of law and order, see Bessel, "Political Violence," 11–15; Loberg, *Struggle for the Streets*, 201.

[6] Large, *Berlin*, 300; Kristin Semmens, *Seeing Hitler's Germany: Tourism to the Third Reich* (New York: Palgrave, 2005), 95.

[7] Loberg, *Struggle for the Streets*, 193–201.

[8] Annual report of Aschinger's Incorporated for 1933, in LAB A Rep. 225, Nr. 406.

and even femininity, the Nazi regime with progress and potency.[9] The following year's report, drafted in 1935, went so far as to announce that the economy, "revivified," had taken a "flying leap" (*Wirtschaftsschwung*).[10] That report and the report of the following year, 1935 (drafted in 1936), used the term "purposeful" (*zielbewußt*) to describe the new leadership.[11] The drop in unemployment did indeed improve business at the corporation's fast food concessions, if only modestly. The hotels, however, tell a different story, the sad facts of which the board was at pains to minimize.

Berlin's grand hotels continued to suffer shortfalls of custom and revenue well into the Nazi period. In 1934, the board of Aschinger's admitted in its annual report that conditions were still "unfavorable" to the business, though the report's drafters were now careful not to name any of those conditions or, of course, lay blame with a regime that did not endear itself to prospective tourists, who continued to read articles about Nazi terror in Berlin.[12] Unable or unwilling to blame the present regime, the board of Aschinger's referred shareholders to the mistakes of the previous one.[13] Yet by 1936, this explanation made less and less sense. A republic dormant for almost three and a half years could not be held responsible for present difficulties. The Nazis were failing to draw visitors to Berlin in numbers that might sustain the city's luxury hospitality industry.[14]

Tourism to Berlin improved in the mid-1930s, after the chaos of the late Weimar era, but the hospitality industry under the Nazis never saw the levels of demand it had enjoyed in the period of Weimar's relative stability. The Hotel Management Corporation registered the shortfall in its 1934/35 annual report, which nonetheless began with the customary offering of thanks for the "improvement [with respect to] tourism to Berlin." Such improvement fell far short of what the Nazis had promised: the reinvigoration of all sectors of the German economy. In fiscal year

---

[9] See Eleanor Hancock, "'Only the Real, the True, the Masculine Held Its Value': Ernst Röhm, Masculinity, and Male Homosexuality," *Journal of the History of Sexuality* 8 (1998), 617.

[10] Annual report of Aschinger's Incorporated for 1934, in LAB A Rep. 225, Nr. 405.

[11] Annual report of Aschinger's Incorporated for 1935, in LAB A Rep. 225, Nr. 404.

[12] Annual report of Aschinger's Incorporated for 1933.

[13] On blaming the Weimar Republic in the Nazi period, see Detlev J. K. Peukert, *Inside Nazi Germany: Conformity, Opposition, and Racism in Everyday Life*, trans. Richard Deveson (New Haven: Yale University Press, 1987), 57.

[14] On tourism in the Third Reich and the regime's failures, see Semmens, *Seeing Hitler's Germany*, 95.

1934/35, Berlin's hoteliers saw four-fifths the number of visitors they had seen in 1930/31, near the height of the Great Depression. The problem in 1935 was threefold. First, the length of stay, a key indicator of profits for hoteliers, was as short as it had ever been. Second, the number of registrations by German nationals was too low, at a value far below what it had been in 1930/31. Third, and most worrying, the number of registrations by foreign nationals at Berlin hotels was abysmally low, just a little over half the figure in 1929/30.[15] Foreigners were staying away from Hitler's capital.

The result was that revenues missed the mark right down to the start of World War II. Although sales and rents at Aschinger's Incorporated went up 13 percent in 1933, 17 percent in 1934, 8 percent in 1935, and 11 percent in 1936, those figures belied the situation at the company's hotels and the hotels of the Hotel Management Corporation, of which Aschinger's still held the controlling shares.[16] In July 1933, the *Berliner Börsen-Courier* ran the headline "Hotel Business Without Dividends Again," a familiar refrain for the Hotel Management Corporation, the subject of the article.[17] Board members of the parent company struck an apologetic tone in the annual report for 1933, drafted in October 1934. "The unfavorable situation for the hotels of the Hotel Management Corporation," as well as the "poor condition of our own hotels" caused the parent corporation a net loss for 1933. The 17 percent increase in revenues from other parts of the business did not even produce enough to cover the shortfall. An additional 1.95 million reichsmarks had to come out of the fund for renovations and new equipment.[18] In August 1935, Aschinger's sold the second largest of its three hotels, the Palast-Hotel, and the following year, offloaded its shares in the Hotel Management Corporation, removing from its portfolio all but one grand hotel, the Fürstenhof.[19]

As municipal and Reich authorities prepared for the 1936 Olympics in Berlin, the city's grand hoteliers hoped to offset some of the year's losses with full occupancy for a few weeks; they were disappointed when they received orders from Goebbels himself a little less than a year before the games. A price decree (*Preisdiktat*) delivered to the Trade Association of

[15] Annual report of the Hotel Management Corporation for 1934/35.
[16] Annual reports of Aschinger's Incorporated for 1933, 1934, and 1935; annual report of Aschinger's Incorporated for 1936, in LAB A Rep. 225, Nr. 403.
[17] "Hotelbetrieb wieder dividendlos," *Berliner Börsen-Courier*, July 18, 1933.
[18] Annual report of Aschinger's Incorporated for 1933.
[19] Annual report of Aschinger's Incorporated for 1935.

the Restaurant and Hospitality Industry (Wirtschaftsgruppe Gaststätten-
und Beherbergungsgewerbe Gau Berlin) compelled the leadership of that
organization to communicate to hoteliers that they would have four room
rates from which guests could choose: 4, 6, 9, and 15 reichsmarks.[20] Yet
the normal rate for the finest rooms, where profit margins were highest,
was actually 30 reichsmarks. Goebbels was forcing Berlin's grand hoteliers to operate at a loss during the Olympics. Although a city official
promised to forward the hoteliers' protest, the price decree came into
force on August 1, 1936, and would not lift until the end of the games.[21]

As with the Olympics, Berlin's grand hoteliers also missed out on
the benefits of the proposed redevelopment of the capital. Six months
after the games, Albert Speer became the General Building Inspector (Generalbauinspektor) of Berlin and started in earnest on a new
city plan. Out of this draft would eventually come the architectural
model of the renamed city, Germania, the so-called "world capital"
(*Welthauptstadt*), which so fascinated the Führer.[22] Yet Speer executed
little of the plan. Before the outbreak of war on September 1, 1939,
only a few changes, some of them in fact a function of earlier plans,
were realized. In 1938, the Victory Column moved from in front of
the Reichstag to the Tiergarten's Großer Stern traffic circle, its radial
roads now much wider. In the same year, the new Reichsbank building
opened across from the Friedrichswerder Church. A few other projects
began, too, and early in 1939, Hitler and members of the diplomatic
corps were able to celebrate the opening of his new chancellery building. The last large prewar infrastructure project in Berlin, the subterra-
nean S-Bahn line, opened two of its stations and a tiny stretch of track
between Anhalt Station and Potsdamer Platz roughly five weeks after
the invasion of Poland. Speer hoped to marshal this new north–south
S-Bahn line for service along the so-called Prachtallee (Avenue of Splendor), which was projected to extend south from an intersection with the
even grander East–West Axis near the Adlon.[23] That hotel would have

---

[20] Managing directors of the Hotel Management Corporation to Hans Lohnert, May 17,
1935, in LAB A Rep. 225-01, Nr. 82.

[21] David Clay Large has shown that managers of some of the smaller hotels ignored the
price controls. In the case of Berlin's grand hotels, however, I found no evidence of
subversion. See Large, *Nazi Games: The Olympics of 1936* (New York: W. W. Norton,
2007), 115–16.

[22] See Frederic Spotts, *Hitler and the Power of Aesthetics* (Woodstock, NY: Overlook,
2009), 311–29.

[23] Martin Kitchen, *Speer: Hitler's Architect* (New Haven: Yale University Press, 2015),
65–71.

to be torn down, anyway, to make room for public buildings of cruel proportions in heavy granite.

In summer 1941, plans materialized for a gargantuan hotel project, and Fritz Aschinger was hoping to build it. Although Aschinger's had mostly withdrawn from the hotel scene in Berlin, the hotel scene in Germania, "world capital," presented an altogether different opportunity. The cost of construction would come in at 70 million reichsmarks. The scale would be commensurate with the other "monumental structures on the North South Axis," the initial permit application read.[24] There would be an enormous garden, café, and department store. The complex would be composed of two or three ten-story buildings, behind which would rise two towers of thirty floors each. One tower would house a restaurant for 1,000 diners on its twenty-eighth floor, the other would have a roof garden. In addition to a theater, there would be multiple dance halls, restaurants, cafés, and shops in the cavernous cellars. Farther below would be an air-raid shelter for 4,000 (not even half the hotel's projected occupancy).[25] Neither the air-raid shelter nor the hotel complex materialized.

Early in the morning of September 1, 1939, Berliners listening to the radio learned of the outbreak of war with Poland. By all accounts, there was little public reaction and perhaps less public discussion.[26] In fact, the word "war" appears only a few times in the corporate records of Aschinger's Incorporated and the Hotel Management Corporation before the massive death tolls of 1942 and 1943.[27] Nevertheless, state intervention into the supply of food, clothes, and certain raw materials intensified immediately after the outbreak of World War II. On October 12, 1939, Fritz Aschinger himself admonished Paul Arpé, manager of the Fürstenhof, to make certain that prices on the menus did not exceed 1936 levels. When in doubt, Aschinger wrote, lower the price: "Even careless errors, no matter how small, can bring the gravest of consequences."[28] In this way, the regime's terroristic threats filtered down through the corporate chain of command.[29] By December 1939, Arpé was sending

[24] Initial application for a permit to build a hotel on the North–South Axis, May 7, 1941, in LAB A Pr. Br. Rep. 030-07, Nr. 1056.

[25] Ibid.

[26] Peukert, *Inside Nazi Germany*, 62.

[27] Annual report of Aschinger's Incorporated for 1940, written in November 1941, in LAB A Rep. 225, Nr. 399.

[28] Fritz Aschinger to Paul Arpé, October 12, 1939, in LAB A Rep. 225, Nr. 369.

[29] On terror, conformity, privacy, and institutions, see Peukert, *Inside Nazi Germany*, 236–42.

weekly price reports to the managing directors. He concluded each with
the declaration, "I hereby confirm that I have checked the prices on the
menus and find everything to be in order."[30]

Again, as in World War I and its aftermath, mounting shortages
placed extraordinary upward pressure on prices, which the regime tried
to counteract with price controls and rationing.[31] But even as early as
November 1939, what variety there was on the shelves of Aschinger's
fast-food counters began to disappear. If we must serve "crispy
Maultaschen" every day for a week, then at least change the side dish
or the description, Aschinger instructed.[32] Even at the Fürstenhof, standards slipped considerably.[33] The hotel restaurant had been loading its
menus with organ meat as early as January 1940, when three gentlemen
sat down and ordered calf's liver. Two of them produced the ration
coupons required for 100 g of meat, while the third produced only half
the coupons but requested the same portion as the others. The headwaiter refused. Regulations were taken very seriously at the Fürstenhof, he said, and one of the three might be an undercover agent. "The
gentlemen were very amused by this," the headwaiter reported, "and
explained to me that I was actually dealing with gentlemen from the
Price Commissariat. They proved it by producing a document and told
me, 'You got lucky.'"[34]

Germany's fortunes changed on the Eastern Front in early 1942. In
January alone there were somewhere near 44,200 soldiers killed and an
additional 10,100 missing.[35] Annual reports of Aschinger's Incorporated
began to list the dead: "We remember with deep gratitude our coworkers-
in-arms who died on the field of honor for the Führer and the Reich."[36]
Hoteliers had already established relief funds and benefit societies for
workers and employees, "especially [their] widows and orphaned children."[37] Hitler had made a particularly spirited call for donations to the

---

[30] Correspondence of Paul Arpé, 1939–1945, in LAB A Rep. 225, Nr. 369.

[31] On price-setting to combat inflation in Nazi Germany, see Tooze, *Wages of Destruction*,
108, 142, 231, 260, 494–95, and 642–44.

[32] Fritz Aschinger, "Gestaltung der Speisekarte," memo of November 24, 1939, in LAB A
Rep. 225, Nr. 369.

[33] Fritz Aschinger to Paul Spethmann, March 25, 1941, in LAB A Rep. 225, Nr. 369.

[34] Headwaiter to the management of the Fürstenhof and its parent company (letter and
report), February 4, 1940, in LAB A Rep. 225, Nr. 369.

[35] Statistisches Bundesamt, ed. *Statistisches Jahrbuch für die Bundesrepublik Deutschland
1960* (Stuttgart: W. Kohlhammer, 1960), 78.

[36] Annual report of Aschinger's Incorporated for 1940, written in November 1941.

[37] Louis Adlon to the District Court of Berlin-Charlottenburg (Amtsgericht Berlin-
Charlottenburg), October 20, 1941, in LAB B Rep. 042, Nr. 28200.

regime's own charity, the Winter Relief Campaign (Winterhilfswerk), on September 12, 1941, as the Royal Air Force began to refine its ability to bomb Berlin by night.[38]

Air raids did not arrive in full strength until early 1943. More planes carrying more and heavier bombs arrived at shorter intervals than ever before. On January 17, 1943, more than 250 British bombers dropped 700 tons of ordnance. In February, Goebbels rallied a rattled public around the cause of total war. Children as young as fifteen had already been enlisted as air force assistants (*Luftwaffenhelfer*) to operate searchlights and acoustic locators while the bombs rained down. Attacks continued, increasing in intensity. On March 2, 1943, blockbusters and firebombs destroyed or badly damaged several landmarks in Friedrichstadt, rendered 35,000 people homeless, and killed 711. Amid renewed bombing campaigns in August, the authorities began a partial evacuation of Berlin.[39]

The city's grand hotels were still largely intact in autumn 1943, when the building authority began its precautionary inspections for faulty ventilation systems. That initiative appears to have been suspended as, bit by bit, aerial bombardment destroyed Friedrichstadt.[40] Between November 18 and December 3, 1943, the Royal Air Force carried out five extensive attacks.[41] The Fürstenhof took direct hits on two consecutive nights in November but remained in business with a small fraction of its rooms available for use; the Kaiserhof took several direct hits and burned down for the second time in its history (Figure E.1).[42]

The Bristol was lost to fire, too. A married couple already bombed out of their home in the Tiergarten district took the opportunity to steal some of the hotel's blankets and sheets.[43] (By the end of 1943, some 400,000 Berliners had lost their homes.[44]) The raids worsened

---

[38] Laurenz Demps, ed. *Luftangriffe auf Berlin: Die Berichte der Hauptluftschutzstelle, 1940–1945* (Berlin: Ch. Links, 2012), 36.

[39] Ibid., 15, 25, 27, 35–39, 56–58, 73, 85, 98, 103, 108, 126–27, 138, 142, 153–55, 164, 235, 289.

[40] Office of the City President (Stadtpräsident) to the Executive Office of the Building Police (Baupolizei-Hauptabteilung), September 27, 1943, in LAB A Pr. Br. Rep. 030-07, Nr. 420, f. 4.

[41] Demps, *Luftangriffe*, 37–39, 87, 289 (Table 4).

[42] Damage report of February 24, 1945, in LAB A Rep. 225, Nr. 1257.

[43] Statement by the witness Adelheid Steglich, March 9, 1944, in LAB A Rep. 358-02, Nr. 13401, f. 2.

[44] Demps, *Luftangriffe*, 287–89.

FIGURE E.1 The Kaiserhof in ruins, 1946
Image credit: Landesarchiv Berlin

in the new year, with massive bombings happening throughout January 1944.[45] On the night of January 2, even more of the Fürstenhof was knocked out of commission, along with parts of other hotels in the vicinity.[46] In March 1944, American bombers joined the melee in full force.

It is difficult to find details on conditions in Berlin's grand hotels after spring 1944. Little survives beyond a few postcards sent by bombed out Berliners, a few reports by the authorities, one police investigation of looting, and dozens of photographs taken shortly after the end of the war. It is clear, nonetheless, that by autumn of 1944, nothing resembling grand hotel life survived anywhere in Berlin. Guests who chose to stay at a grand hotel were opting to rough it in partial ruins that could not even be used after nightfall and now, quite often, not even during the day, since daytime attacks were happening with increasing frequency. But because Berlin's grand hotels were destroyed by degrees, through several raids over the course of several months, sometimes years, hoteliers managed to accommodate guests until the end.

[45] Ibid.
[46] Damage report of February 24, 1945.

The end came for the Fürstenhof on February 3, 1945, in the largest attack yet by the US Army Air Force, which killed at least 2,600
people.[47] To assess the damage, a representative from the Building Council (Stadt- und Oberbaurat) roamed the site and took notes. The facades,
he later reported, had been disfigured by shrapnel and other projectiles.
The marble stair with its bronze trim had been smashed to pieces. The elevator shafts had collapsed. Blast forces had dislodged most of the walls.
Only thirty percent of the doors could be salvaged. All the windows were
ripped out by the frame. The roof would soon collapse.[48]

* * *

A century earlier, investors, hoteliers, designers, and architects saw great
opportunity in Berlin's grand hotel scene, yet the enterprises, in the end,
succumbed to tensions both internal and external to the industry. Some
of the internal tensions were visible on the surface, such as that between
cosmopolitan and nationalist cultural imperatives. The other, more
pressing internal tensions of the imperial period resided within liberalism itself. Liberalism, the creed of freedom, relegated workers to dismal
cellars and fetid attics where class animosities seethed and eventually
exploded after World War I. Like other liberals, Berlin's grand hoteliers
prized mobility and free trade, while at the same time impeding workers'
advancement and locking them in place.

The external tensions, primarily with the state, developed in the Weimar period, when successive republican governments took actions against
free enterprise, as Berlin's grand hoteliers saw it. Price and wage controls,
however limited and temporary, as well as high taxes, offended hoteliers'
liberal sensibilities. Even as controls eased and business improved, complaints persisted. The hyperinflation of 1923 had convinced hoteliers that
the republic was bad for business. Their complaints then intensified after
1929, as Germany's problems appeared to defy liberal solutions. In face of
the Great Depression, right-radical nationalism, and the ever-expanding
role of the state in the economy, hoteliers leaned toward what they thought
would be best for business: the anti-republican right. Businessmen, even
the Jewish ones, scarcely knew what was good for them until it was too
late. They let Hitler stay. Twelve years later, the grand hotels lay in ruins.
They had fallen in the fiery consequences of a plot hatched in and around
the Kaiserhof during the Weimar Republic's very last autumn.

---

[47] Demps, *Luftangriffe*, 40, 96–98, 137, 331.
[48] Damage report of February 24, 1945.

Bibliography

PRIMARY SOURCES

Landesarchiv Berlin

LAB A Pr. Br. Rep. 030	Polizeipräsidium Berlin
LAB A Pr. Br. Rep. 030-03	Polizeipräsidium Berlin, Zentralkartei für Mordsachen und Lehrmittelsammlung
LAB A Pr. Br. Rep. 030-07	Polizeipräsidium Berlin, Baupolizei
LAB A Rep. 001-02	Magistrat der Stadt Berlin, Generalbüro
LAB A Rep. 010-02	Magistrat der Stadt Berlin, Städtische Baupolizei
LAB A Rep. 013-01-08	Magistrat der Stadt Berlin, Lebensmittelversorgungsstellen, Kartoffelversorgung
LAB A Rep. 225	Aschinger's Aktien-Gesellschaft
LAB A Rep. 225-01	Hotelbetriebs-Aktiengesellschaft
LAB A Rep. 358-01	Generalstaatsanwaltschaft beim Landgericht Berlin, Strafverfahren, 1919–1933
LAB A Rep. 358-02	Generalstaatsanwaltschaft beim Landgericht Berlin, Strafverfahren, 1933–1945
LAB B Rep. 042	Amtsgericht Charlottenburg
LAB F Rep. 290	Allgemeine Fotosammlung

Other Archives

Bundesarchiv (Berlin-Lichterfelde)
Historisches Archiv für Tourismus (Berlin)
Schweizerisches Wirtschaftsarchiv (Basel)
Staatsbibliothek zu Berlin – Stiftung Preußischer Kulturbesitz

Periodicals

Allgemeine Illustrirte Zeitung (Stuttgart)
Atlas zur Zeitschrift für Bauwesen

Berliner Börsen-Courier
Berliner Börsen-Zeitung
Berliner Illustrirte Zeitung
Berliner Lokal-Anzeiger
Berliner Tageblatt
Berliner Wirtschaftsberichte
Berliner Zeitung
B.Z. am Mittag
Bibliothèque universelle et Revue Suisse
Blätter für literarische Unterhaltung
Brandenburgia: Monatsblatt der Gesellschaft für Heimatkunde der Provinz Brandenburg
Chicago Tribune (Paris edition)
Das Hotel
Der Deutsche Volkswirt: Zeitschrift für Politik und Wirtschaft
Deutsche Bauzeitung
Deutsche Versicherungs-Zeitung: Organ für das gesamte Versicherungswesen
Die Frauenbewegung: Revue für die Interessen der Frauen
Die Gegenwart: Wochenschrift für Litteratur, Kunst und öffentliches Leben
Die Welt am Montag
Die Zukunft
Economist
Frankfurter Zeitung
Illustrirte Zeitung (Leipzig)
Innen-Dekoration
Kritische Betrachtungen über Staats- und Gemeindehaushalt
Le Matin (Paris)
Licht und Lampe: Zeitschrift für die Beleuchtungsindustrie
Mitteilungen des Vereins Deutscher Reklamefachleute
Neues Wiener Journal
Neuer Social-Demokrat: Organ der Socialistischen Arbeiter-Partei Deutschlands
Technik im Hotel
The New York Times
Vorwärts (Berlin)
Zeitschrift für Bauwesen
Zentralblatt der Bauverwaltung

Published Books and Serials

Adlon, Hedda. *Das Hotel Adlon: Das Berliner Hotel, in dem die große Welt zu Gast war.* Munich: Deutsch, 1998.

Architekten-Verein zu Berlin and Verband Deutscher Architekten- und Ingenieur-Vereine, eds. *Berlin und seine Bauten.* 2 vols. Berlin: Architekten- und Ingenieur-Verein, 1877.

Architekten-Verein zu Berlin and Vereinigung Berliner Architekten, eds. *Berlin und seine Bauten.* 3 vols. Berlin: Wilhelm Ernst, 1896.

Baedeker, Karl, ed. *Baedeker's Berlin, Potsdam und Umgebung.* Leipzig: Karl Baedeker, 1878.

Baedeker's Berlin and Its Environs. Leipzig: Baedeker's, 1912.

Baedeker's Berlin und Umgebung. Leipzig: Baedeker's, 1904.

Baum, Vicki. *Menschen im Hotel.* Cologne: Kiepenheuer & Witsch, 2002. First published in 1929.

Die Berliner Emissionshäuser und ihre Emissionen in den Jahren 1871 und 1872: Ein Commentar zu dem Berliner Courszettel. Berlin: Fr. Lobeck's Verlag, 1873.

Bloch, Iwan. *Das Sexualleben unserer Zeit in seinen Beziehungen zur modernen Kultur.* Berlin: Louis Marcus, 1907.

Buchner, Eberhard, ed. *Kriegsdokumente.* Vol. 1, *Der Weltkrieg 1914 in der Darstellung der zeitgenössischen Presse.* Munich: Albert Langen, 1914.

Commenge, Oscar. *La prostitution clandestine à Paris.* Paris: Schleicher, 1897.

Damm-Etienne, Paul. *Das Hotelwesen.* Leipzig: B. G. Teubner, 1910.

Dietrich, Otto. *Mit Hitler in die Macht: Persönliche Erlebnisse mit meinem Führer.* Munich: Eher, 1934.

Dönhoff, Marion. *Before the Storm: Memories of My Youth in Old Prussia.* Translated by Jean Steinberg. New York: Knopf, 1990.

Eloesser, Arthur. *Die Straße meiner Jugend: Berliner Skizzen.* Berlin: Arsenal, 1987. First published in 1919.

Gaulke, Johannes. *Führer durch Berlins Kunstschätze: Museen, Denkmäler, Bauwerke.* Berlin: Globus, 1908.

Geddes, Patrick. *Cities in Evolution.* New York: Oxford University Press, 1950. First published in 1915.

Glücksmann, Richard. "Die Betriebswirtschaft des Hotels." In *Fremdenverkehr,* edited by Industrie- und Handelskammer zu Berlin, 360–98. Berlin: Georg Stilke, 1929.

Guyer, Eduard. *Das Hotelwesen der Gegenwart.* Zurich: Orell Füssli, 1874.

Haake, Heinz. *Das Ehrenbuch des Führers: Der Weg zur Volksgemeinschaft.* Düsseldorf: Floeder, 1933.

Henne-am-Rhyn, Otto. *Kulturgeschichte der jüngsten Zeit: Von der Errichtung des Deutschen Reiches bis auf die Gegenwart.* Leipzig: Otto Wigand, 1897.

Hirschfeld, Magnus. *Die Homosexualität des Mannes und Weibes.* Berlin: Louis Marcus, 1912.

Industrie- und Handelskammer zu Berlin, ed. *Fremdenverkehr.* Berlin: Georg Stilke, 1929.

Kessler, Harry. *Das Tagebuch, 1880–1937.* 9 vols. Stuttgart: Cotta, 2004–2019.

Liefmann, Robert. *Beteiligungs- und Finanzierungsgesellschaften: Eine Studie über den modernen Effektenkapitalismus in Deutschland, den Vereinigten Staaten, der Schweiz, England, Frankreich und Belgien.* 3rd ed. Jena: Gustav Fischer, 1921.

Loyal National League. *The Great Questions of the Times.* New York: C. S. Westcott & Co., 1863.

Lüpschütz, Kurt. "Organisation der Hotels." In *Fremdenverkehr*, edited by Industrie- und Handelskammer zu Berlin, 399–446. Berlin: Georg Stilke, 1929.

Mitra, Siddha Mohana. *Anglo-Indian Studies*. London: Longmans, 1913.

Meinhardt, William. *Kartellfragen: Gesammelte Reden und Aufsätze*. Berlin: OSRAM, 1929.

Meinhardt, William. *Entwicklung und Aufbau der Glühlampenindustrie*. Berlin: Heymann, 1932.

Moreck, Curt. *Führer durch das "lasterhafte" Berlin*. Leipzig: H. Haessel, 1931.

Murray, John. *A Hand-Book for Travellers on the Continent: Being a Guide through Holland, Belgium, Prussia, and Northern Germany, and along the Rhine from Holland to Switzerland*. 5th ed. London: A. & W. Galignani, 1845.

Nitsch, Harry. *Das Hotel- und Gastgewerbe: Moderne Propaganda-Methoden*. Düsseldorf: Floeder, 1927.

Ostwald, Hans. *Männliche Prostitution im kaiserlichen Berlin*. Berlin: Janssen, 1991. First published in 1906.

Siddons, J. H. *Norton's Handbook to Europe, or, How to Travel in the Old World*. New York: Charles B. Norton, 1860.

Simmel, Georg. "The Metropolis and Mental Life." Translated by Kurt Wolff. In *Georg Simmel: On Individuality and Social Forms – Selected Writings*, edited by Donald N. Levine, 324–39. Chicago: University of Chicago Press, 1971. First published in 1903.

Simmel, Georg. "The Sociology of Sociability." Translated by Everett Hughes. *American Journal of Sociology* 55 (1949): 254–61. First published in 1911.

State of New York. *Laws of the State of New York, Passed at the Eighty-Fourth Session of the Legislature, Begun January First, and Ended April Sixteenth, 1861, in the City of Albany*. Albany: Munsell & Rowland, 1861.

State of New York. *Ninth Annual Report of the Superintendent of the Insurance Department: Life Insurance*. Albany: Charles van Benthuysen & Sons, 1868.

Statistisches Bundesamt, ed. *Statistisches Jahrbuch für die Bundesrepublik Deutschland 1960*. Stuttgart: W. Kohlhammer, 1960.

Swope, Herbert. *Inside the German Empire in the Third Year of the War*. New York: Century, 1917.

Twain, Mark. "The Chicago of Europe." In *The Complete Essays of Mark Twain*, 87–89. Garden City, NY: Doubleday, 1963. First published in 1892.

United States Centennial Commission. *International Exhibition, 1876: Reports and Rewards*. Vol. 7, *Groups XXI–XXVII*. Washington, DC: Government Printing Office, 1880.

Wilhelm II. "Die wahre Kunst." In *Die Berliner Moderne, 1885–1914*, edited by Jürgen Schutte and Peter Sprengel, 571–74. Stuttgart: Reclam, 1987. First published in 1901.

Wöhler, Max. *Gasthäuser und Hotels: Die Bestandteile und die Einrichtung des Gasthauses*. 2 vols. Leipzig: J. G. Göschen, 1911.

SECONDARY SOURCES

Abrams, Lynn. "Prostitutes in Imperial Germany, 1870–1918: Working Girls or Social Outcasts?" In *The German Underworld: Deviants and Outcasts in German History*, edited by Richard J. Evans, 190–205. London: Routledge, 1988.

Adam, Thomas, ed. *Philanthropy, Civil Society, and the State in German History, 1815–1989*. Rochester, NY: Camden House, 2016.

Alborn, Timothy. *Regulated Lives: Life Insurance and British Society, 1800–1914*. Toronto: University of Toronto Press, 2009.

Aldcroft, Derek H. *The European Economy, 1914–2000*. 4th ed. London: Routledge, 2001.

Aldrich, Robert. *The Seduction of the Mediterranean: Writing, Art and Homosexual Fantasy*. London: Routledge, 1993.

Amatori, Franco, and Andrea Colli. *Business History: Complexities and Comparisons*. New York: Routledge, 2011.

Anderson, Margaret Lavinia. *Practicing Democracy: Elections and Political Culture in Imperial Germany*. Princeton: Princeton University Press, 2000.

Arsenschek, Robert. *Der Kampf um die Wahlfreiheit im Kaiserreich: Zur parlamentarischen Wahlprüfung und politischen Realität der Reichstagswahlen, 1871–1914*. Düsseldorf: Droste, 2003.

Asprey, Robert. *The German High Command at War: Hindenburg and Ludendorff Conduct World War I*. New York: W. Morrow, 1991.

Augustine, Dolores L. "Arriving in the Upper Class: The Wealthy Business Elite of Wilhelmine Germany." In Blackbourn and Evans, *German Bourgeoisie*, 46–75.

Balderston, Theo. "The Beginning of the Depression in Germany, 1927–1930: Investment and the Capital Market." *Economic History Review* 36 (1983): 395–415.

Balderston, Theo. *The Origins and Course of the German Economic Crisis: November 1923 to May 1932*. Berlin: Haude & Spencer, 1993.

Bailey, Peter. "White Collars, Gray Lives? The Lower Middle Class Revisited." *Journal of British Studies* 38 (1999): 273–90.

Barth, Boris. *Dolchstoßlegenden und politische Desintegration: Das Trauma der deutschen Niederlage im Ersten Weltkrieg, 1914–1933*. Düsseldorf: Droste, 2003.

Beachy, Robert. *Gay Berlin: Birthplace of a Modern Identity*. New York: Knopf, 2014.

Beck, Hermann. *The Fateful Alliance: German Conservatives and Nazis in 1933 – The Machtergreifung in a New Light*. New York: Berghahn, 2008.

Becker, Felix. *Allgemeines Lexikon der bildenden Künstler von der Antike bis zur Gegenwart*. Vol. 20. Leipzig: Seemann, 1927.

Becker, Tobias. "Unterhaltungstheater." In Morat, Becker, Lange, Niedbalski, Gnausch, and Nolte, *Weltstadtvergnügen*, 28–73.

Beiser, Frederick C. *Enlightenment, Revolution, Romanticism: The Genesis of Modern German Political Thought, 1790–1800*. Cambridge, MA: Harvard University Press, 1992.

Berens, Carol. *Hotel Bars and Lobbies*. New York: McGraw Hill, 1997.

Berger, Molly W. *Hotel Dreams: Luxury, Technology, and Urban Ambition in America, 1829–1929.* Baltimore: Johns Hopkins University Press, 2011.

Bergers, Hendrik. *Der Fall Krupp: Ein Skandal der Homosexualität?* Munich: GRIN, 2014.

Berghahn, Volker R. *Modern Germany: Society, Economy and Politics in the Twentieth Century.* 2nd ed. Cambridge: Cambridge University Press, 1987.

Bernet, Claus. "The 'Hobrecht Plan' (1862) and Berlin's Urban Structure." *Urban History* 31 (2004): 400–19.

Bessel, Richard. *Germany after the First World War.* Oxford: Clarendon, 1993.

Bessel, Richard. "Political Violence and the Nazi Seizure of Power." In *Life in the Third Reich*, edited by Richard Bessel, 1–16. Oxford: Oxford University Press, 1987.

Beyrer, Klaus. "The Mail-Coach Revolution: Landmarks in Travel in Germany between the Seventeenth and Nineteenth Centuries." *German History* 24 (2006): 375–86.

Blackbourn, David. *The Long Nineteenth Century: A History of Germany, 1780–1918.* Oxford: Oxford University Press, 1997.

Blackbourn, David, and Richard J. Evans, eds. *The German Bourgeoisie: Essays on the Social History of the German Middle Class from the Late Eighteenth to the Early Twentieth Century.* London: Routledge, 1993.

Blanning, Tim. *The Pursuit of Glory: Europe, 1648–1789.* London: Allen Lane, 2007.

Blum, Matthias. "War, Food, Rationing, and Socioeconomic Equality in Germany during the First World War." *Economic History Review* 66 (2013): 1063–83.

Bolz, Cedric. "From 'Garden City Precursors' to 'Cemeteries for the Living': Contemporary Discourse on Krupp Housing and *Besucherpolitik* in Wilhelmine Germany." *Urban History* 37 (2010): 90–116.

Bonzon, Thierry, and Belinda J. Davis. "Feeding the Cities." In Winter and Robert, *Capital Cities at War*, 1:305–41.

Borchardt, Knut. "A Decade of Debate about Brüning's Economic Policy." In Kruedener, *Economic Crisis*, 99–151.

Börsch-Supan, Eva. *Berliner Baukunst nach Schinkel, 1840–1870.* Munich: Prestel, 1977.

Braunthal, Gerard. *The Federation of German Industry in Politics.* Ithaca, NY: Cornell University Press, 1965.

Braunthal, Gerard. *Socialist Labor and Politics in Weimar Germany: The General Federation of German Trade Unions.* Hamden, CT: Archon, 1978.

Bräutigam, Helmut, and Oliver C. Gleich. "Nationalsozialistische Zwangslager in Berlin I: Die 'wilden' Konzentrationslager und Folterkeller, 1933/34." In *Berlin-Forschungen*, edited by Wolfgang Ribbe, 2:141–78. Berlin: Colloquium, 1987.

Breckman, Warren G. "Disciplining Consumption: The Debate about Luxury in Wilhelmine Germany." *Journal of Social History* 24 (1991): 485–505.

Briggs, Asa. "The Language of 'Class' in Early Nineteenth-Century England." In *Literature and Western Civilisation: The Modern World.* Vol. 2, *Realities*, edited by David Daiches and Anthony Thorlby, 43–61. London: Aldus, 1972.

Brock, Peter. *Pacifism in the United States: From the Colonial Era to the First World War*. Princeton: Princeton University Press, 1968.

Burn, W. L. *The Age of Equipoise: A Study of the Mid-Victorian Generation*. New York: W. W. Norton, 1964.

Canning, Kathleen. "Social Policy, Body Politics: Recasting the Social Question in Germany." In *Gender and Class in Modern Europe*, edited by Sonya Rose and Laura Frader, 211–37. Ithaca, NY: Cornell University Press, 1996.

Carrington, Tyler. *Love at Last Sight: Dating, Intimacy, and Risk in Turn-of-the-Century Berlin*. New York: Oxford, 2019.

Certeau, Michel de. *The Practice of Everyday Life*. Translated by Steven Rendall. Berkeley: University of California Press, 1984.

Chickering, Roger. *The Great War and Urban Life in Germany: Freiburg, 1914–1918*. Cambridge: Cambridge University Press, 2007.

Childers, Thomas. "The Social Language of Politics in Germany: The Sociology of Political Discourse in the Weimar Republic." *American Historical Review* 95 (1990): 331–58.

Clark, Christopher. *Iron Kingdom: The Rise and Downfall of Prussia, 1600–1947*. Cambridge, MA: Belknap Press of Harvard University Press, 2006.

Clark, Vincent. "A Struggle for Existence: The Professionalization of German Architects." In *German Professions, 1800–1950*, edited by Geoffrey Cocks and Konrad H. Jarausch, 143–62. New York: Oxford University Press, 1990.

Cohen, Deborah. *Last Call at the Hotel Imperial: The Reporters Who Took on a World at War*. New York: Random House, 2022.

Conrad, Sebastian. *Globalisation and the Nation in Imperial Germany*. Translated by Sorcha O'Hagan. Cambridge: Cambridge University Press, 2010.

Cooper, Sandi E. *Patriotic Pacifism: Waging War on War in Europe, 1815–1914*. New York: Oxford University Press, 1991.

Costigliola, Frank. "The United States and the Reconstruction of Germany in the 1920s." *Business History Review* 50 (1976): 477–502.

Crozier, Michel, and Eberhard Friedberg. *L'acteur et le système: Les contraintes de l'action collective*. Paris: Seuil, 1977.

Davidson, Lisa Pfueller. "'A Service Machine': Hotel Guests and the Development of an Early-Twentieth-Century Building Type." *Perspectives in Vernacular Architecture* 10 (2005): 113–29.

Davis, Belinda J. "Food Scarcity and the Female Consumer." In *The Sex of Things: Gender and Consumption in Historical Perspective*, edited by Victoria de Grazia with Ellen Furlough, 287–310. Berkeley: University of California Press, 1996.

Davis, Belinda J. *Home Fires Burning: Food, Politics, and Everyday Life in World War I Berlin*. Chapel Hill: University of North Carolina Press, 2000.

Demps, Laurenz. *Berlin-Wilhelmstraße: Eine Topographie preußisch-deutscher Macht*. Berlin: Ch. Links, 2000.

Demps, Laurenz. *Geschichte Berlins von den Anfängen bis 1945*. Berlin: Dietz, 1987.

Demps, Laurenz, ed. *Luftangriffe auf Berlin: Die Berichte der Hauptluftschutzstelle, 1940–1945*. Berlin: Ch. Links, 2012.

Denby, Elaine. *Grand Hotels: Reality and Illusion – An Architectural and Social History.* London: Reaktion, 1998.

Dobson, Sean. *Authority and Upheaval in Leipzig, 1910–1920: The Story of a Relationship.* New York: Columbia University Press, 2001.

Eeckhout, Patricia Van den. "Waiters, Waitresses, and their Tips in Western Europe before World War I." *International Review of Social History* 60 (2015): 349–78.

Elder, Sace. *Murder Scenes: Normality, Deviance, and Criminal Violence in Weimar Berlin.* Ann Arbor: University of Michigan Press, 2010.

Eley, Geoff. *From Unification to Nazism: Reinterpreting the German Past.* London: Allen & Unwin, 1986.

Elias, Norbert. *The Court Society.* Translated by Edmund Jephcott. Oxford: Blackwell, 1983.

Ettinger, Elżbieta. *Rosa Luxemburg: A Life.* Boston: Beacon, 1986.

Evans, Richard J. *The Coming of the Third Reich.* London: Penguin, 2003.

Evans, Richard J. "Liberalism and Society: The Feminist Movement and Social Change." In *Society and Politics in Wilhelmine Germany*, edited by Richard J. Evans, 186–214. London: Routledge, 1976.

Fear, Jeffrey R. *Organizing Control: August Thyssen and the Construction of German Corporate Management.* Cambridge, MA: Harvard University Press, 2005.

Feinstein, Charles H., ed. *Banking, Currency, and Finance in Europe between the Wars.* Oxford: Clarendon, 1995.

Feinstein, Charles H., Peter Temin, and Gianni Toniolo. "International Economic Organization: Banking, Finance, and Trade in Europe." In Feinstein, *Banking, Currency, and Finance*, 131–50.

Feldman, Gerald D. *The Great Disorder: Politics, Economics, and Society in the German Inflation, 1914–1924.* New York: Oxford University Press, 1993.

Fischer, Conan. *The Ruhr Crisis: 1923–1924.* Oxford: Oxford University Press, 2003.

Fohlin, Caroline. *Finance Capitalism and Germany's Rise to Power.* Cambridge: Cambridge University Press, 2006.

Föllmer, Moritz, ed. *Sehnsucht nach Nähe: Interpersonale Kommunikation in Deutschland seit dem 19. Jahrhundert.* Stuttgart: Franz Steiner, 2004.

Forty, Adrian. *Words and Buildings: A Vocabulary of Modern Architecture.* London: Thames & Hudson, 2004.

Foucault, Michel. "Governmentality." In *The Foucault Effect: Studies in Governmentality*, edited by Graham Burchell, Colin Gordon, and Peter Miller, 87–104. London: Harvester, 1991.

Foucault, Michel. *The History of Sexuality.* Vol. 1, *An Introduction.* Translated by Robert Hurley. New York: Pantheon, 1978.

Fowkes, Ben, trans. and ed. *The German Left and the Weimar Republic: A Selection of Documents.* Leiden: Brill, 2014.

Freydank, Ruth, ed. *Theater als Geschäft: Berlin und seine Privattheater um die Jahrhundertwende.* Berlin: Hentrich, 1995.

Friedrich, Thomas. *Hitler's Berlin: Abused City.* Translated by Stewart Spencer. New Haven: Yale University Press, 2012.

Fritzsche, Peter. *Reading Berlin 1900*. Cambridge, MA: Harvard University Press, 1996.

Fritzsche, Peter. "Vagabond in the Fugitive City: Hans Ostwald, Imperial Berlin, and the Grossstadt-Dokumente." *Journal of Contemporary History* 29 (1994): 385–402.

Fröhlich, Paul. *Rosa Luxemburg: Ideas in Action*. Translated by Joanna Hoornweg. London: Pluto/Bookmarks, 1994.

Gall, Lothar. *Walther Rathenau: Porträt einer Epoche*. Munich: C. H. Beck, 2009.

Gall, Lothar, Gerald D. Feldman, Harold James, Carl-Ludwig Holtfrerich, and Hans E. Büschgen. *Die Deutsche Bank, 1870–1995*. Munich: C. H. Beck, 1995.

Gary, Bruce. *Through the Lion Gate: A History of the Berlin Zoo*. New York: Oxford University Press, 2017.

Geist, Johann Friedrich. *Die Kaisergalerie: Biographie der Berliner Passage*. Munich: Prestel, 1997.

Gellately, Robert. *Backing Hitler: Consent and Coercion in Nazi Germany*. Oxford: Oxford University Press, 2001.

Gerwarth, Robert. *The Vanquished: Why the First World War Failed to End*. New York: Farrar, Straus and Giroux, 2016.

Gerwarth, Robert, and John Horne. "Vectors of Violence: Paramilitarism in Europe after the Great War, 1917–1923." *Journal of Modern History* 83 (2011): 489–512.

Gillerman, Sharon. "German Jews in the Weimar Republic." In *The Oxford Handbook of the Weimar Republic*, edited by Nadine Rossol and Benjamin Ziemann, 563–86. Oxford: Oxford University Press, 2020.

Giloi, Eva. *Monarchy, Myth, and Material Culture in Germany, 1750–1950*. Cambridge: Cambridge University Press, 2011.

Görtemaker, Manfred, ed. *Weimar in Berlin: Porträt einer Epoche*. Berlin: Be.Bra, 2002.

Graf, Rüdiger. *Die Zukunft der Weimarer Republik: Krisen und Zukunftsaneignungen in Deutschland, 1918–1933*. Munich: R. Oldenbourg, 2008.

Grazia, Victoria de. *Irresistible Empire: America's Advance through Twentieth-Century Europe*. Cambridge, MA: Belknap Press of Harvard University Press, 2005.

Green, Abigail. *Fatherlands: State-Building and Nationhood in Nineteenth-Century Germany*. Cambridge: Cambridge University Press, 2001.

Gross, Michael B. *The War against Catholicism: Liberalism and the Anti-Catholic Imagination in Nineteenth-Century Germany*. Ann Arbor: University of Michigan Press, 2004.

Groth, Paul. *Living Downtown: The History of Residential Hotels in the United States*. 2nd ed. Berkeley: University of California Press, 1999.

Guagnini, Anna. "Technology." In *A History of the University in Europe*. Vol. 3, *Universities in the Nineteenth and Early Twentieth Centuries, 1800–1945*, edited by Walter Rüegg, 593–636. Cambridge: Cambridge University Press, 2004.

Hacke, Jens. *Existenzkrise der Demokratie: Zur politischen Theorie des Liberalismus in der Zwischenkriegszeit*. Berlin: Suhrkamp, 2018.

Hacke, Jens. *Liberale Demokratie in schwierigen Zeiten: Weimar und die Gegenwart*. Hamburg: Europäische Verlagsanstalt, 2021.

Hadley, Elaine. *Living Liberalism: Practical Citizenship in Mid-Victorian Britain*. Chicago: University of Chicago Press, 2010.

Hagemann, Karen, and Stefanie Schüler-Springorum, eds. *Home/Front: The Military, War, and Gender in Twentieth-Century Germany*. New York: Berg, 2002.

Hamilton, John Maxwell. *Journalism's Roving Eye: A History of American Foreign Reporting*. Baton Rouge: Louisiana State University Press, 2009.

Hancock, Eleanor. "'Only the Real, the True, the Masculine Held Its Value': Ernst Röhm, Masculinity, and Male Homosexuality." *Journal of the History of Sexuality* 8 (1998): 616–41.

Hannover-Drück, Elisabeth, and Heinrich Hannover, eds. *Der Mord an Rosa Luxemburg und Karl Liebknecht: Dokumentation eines politischen Verbrechens*. Frankfurt am Main: Suhrkamp, 1967.

Hardach, Gerd. "Banking in Germany, 1918–1939." In Feinstein, *Banking, Currency, and Finance*, 269–95.

Hartmann, Heinrich. *Organisation und Geschäft: Unternehmensorganisation in Frankreich und Deutschland, 1890–1914*. Göttingen: Vandenhoeck & Ruprecht, 2010.

Hausen, Karin. "Family and Role-Division: The Polarisation of Sexual Stereotypes in the Nineteenth Century – An Aspect of the Dissociation of Work and Family Life." In *The German Family: Essays on the Social History of the Family in Nineteenth- and Twentieth-Century Germany*, edited by Richard J. Evans and W. Robert Lee, 51–83. London: Routledge, 1981.

Healy, Maureen. *Vienna and the Fall of the Habsburg Empire: Total War and Everyday Life in World War I*. Cambridge: Cambridge University Press, 2004.

Heerding, Andries. *The History of N. V. Philips' Gloeilampenfabrieken*. Vol. 2, *A Company of Many Parts*. Translated by Derek S. Jordan. Cambridge: Cambridge University Press, 1989.

Heidenhain, Brigitte. *Juden in Schwedt: Ihr Leben in der Stadt von 1672 bis 1942 und ihr Friedhof*. Potsdam: Universitätsverlag Potsdam, 2010.

Henderson, William O. *The Industrial Revolution on the Continent: Germany, France, Russia, 1800–1914*. London: F. Cass, 1961.

Hewitt, Martin, ed. *An Age of Equipoise? Reassessing Mid-Victorian Britain*. London: Routledge, 2000.

Hindmarch-Watson, Katie. *Serving a Wired World: London's Telecommunications Workers and the Making of an Information Capital*. Berkeley: University of California Press, 2020.

Hochman, Erin R. "Ein Volk, ein Reich, eine Republik: Großdeutsch Nationalism and Democratic Politics in the Weimar and First Austrian Republics." *German History* 32 (2014): 29–52.

Hoelger, Angelika. "The History of Popular Culture in Berlin, 1830–1918." PhD dissertation, Johns Hopkins University, 2011.

Hoffmann, Moritz. *Geschichte des deutschen Hotels: Vom Mittelalter bis zur Gegenwart*. Heidelberg: A. Hüttig, 1961.

Holtfrerich, Carl-Ludwig. *The German Inflation, 1914–1923: Causes and Effects in International Perspective*. Translated by Theo Balderston. Berlin: Walter de Gruyter, 1986.

Hughes, Michael L. *Paying for the German Inflation*. Chapel Hill: University of North Carolina Press, 1988.

Jacob, Margaret C. *Strangers Nowhere in the World: The Rise of Cosmopolitanism in Early Modern Europe*. Philadelphia: University of Pennsylvania Press, 2006.

James, Kathleen. "From Messel to Mendelsohn: German Department Store Architecture in Defence of Urban and Economic Change." In *Cathedrals of Consumption: The European Department Store, 1850–1939*, edited by Geoffrey Crossick and Serge Jaumain, 252–78. Aldershot: Ashgate, 1999.

Jelavich, Peter. *Berlin Alexanderplatz: Radio, Film, and the Death of Weimar Culture*. Berkeley: University of California Press, 2006.

Jelavich, Peter. *Berlin Cabaret*. Cambridge, MA: Harvard University Press, 1993.

Jerram, Leif. "Bureaucratic Passions and the Colonies of Modernity: An Urban Elite, City Frontiers, and the Rural Other in Germany, 1890–1920." *Urban History* 34 (2007): 390–406.

Jones, Larry Eugene. "Franz von Papen, Catholic Conservatives, and the Establishment of the Third Reich, 1933–1934." *Journal of Modern History* 83 (2011): 272–318.

Jones, Larry Eugene. *Hitler versus Hindenburg: The 1932 Presidential Elections and the End of the Weimar Republic*. Cambridge: Cambridge University Press, 2016.

Jones, Mark. *Founding Weimar: Violence and the German Revolution of 1918–1919*. Cambridge: Cambridge University Press, 2016.

Jones, Robert, and Oliver Marriott. *Anatomy of a Merger: A History of G.E.C., A.E.I. and English Electric*. London: Cape, 1970.

Joyce, Patrick. *The Rule of Freedom: Liberalism and the Modern City*. London: Verso, 2003.

Kaplan, Justin. *When the Astors Owned New York: Blue Bloods and Grand Hotels in a Gilded Age*. New York: Viking, 2006.

Kaschuba, Wolfgang. *Die Überwindung der Distanz: Zeit und Raum in der europäischen Moderne*. Frankfurt am Main: Fischer, 2004.

Keese, Dietmar. "Die volkswirtschaftliche Gesamtgrößen für das Deutsche Reich, 1925–1926." In *Die Staats- und Wirtschaftskrise des Deutschen Reichs, 1929/1933*, edited by Werner Conze and Hans Raupach, 35–81. Stuttgart: Ernst Klett, 1967.

Keller, Peter. *"Die Wehrmacht der Deutschen Republik ist die Reichswehr": Die deutsche Armee, 1918–1921*. Paderborn: Ferdinand Schöningh, 2014.

Kershaw, Ian. *The "Hitler Myth": Image and Reality in the Third Reich*. Oxford: Clarendon, 1987.

Kiecol, Daniel. *Selbstbild und Image zweier europäischer Metropolen: Paris und Berlin zwischen 1900 und 1930*. Frankfurt am Main: Peter Land, 2001.

Kitchen, Martin. *Speer: Hitler's Architect*. New Haven: Yale University Press, 2015.

Knoch, Habbo. "Geselligkeitsräume und Societyträume: Grandhotels im wilhelminischen Berlin." In Reif, *Berliner Villenleben*, 327–350.

Knoch, Habbo. "Das Grandhotel." In *Orte der Moderne: Erfahrungswelten des 19. und 20. Jahrhunderts*, edited by Habbo Knoch and Alexa Geisthövel, 131–40. Frankfurt am Main: Campus, 2005.

Knoch, Habbo. *Grandhotels: Luxusräume und Gesellschaftswandel in New York, London und Berlin um 1900*. Göttingen: Wallstein, 2016.

Knoch, Habbo. "Simmels Hotel: Kommunikation im Zwischenraum der modernen Gesellschaft." In Föllmer, *Sehnsucht nach Nähe*, 87–108.

Kocka, Jürgen. *Arbeitsverhältnisse und Arbeiterexistenzen: Grundlagen der Klassenbildung im 19. Jahrhundert*. Bonn: J. H. W. Dietz, 1990.

Kocka, Jürgen. "The Entrepreneur, the Family and Capitalism: Some Examples from the Early Phase of Industrialisation in Germany." In *German Yearbook on Business History 1981*, edited by Wolfram Engels, Hans Pohl, and the German Society for Business History, 53–82. Berlin: Springer, 1981.

Kocka, Jürgen. "The European Pattern and the German Case." In *Bourgeois Society in Nineteenth-Century Europe*, edited by Jürgen Kocka and Allan Mitchell, 3–39. Oxford: Berg, 1993.

Kocka, Jürgen. *Facing Total War: German Society, 1914–1918*. Translated by Barbara Weinberger. Cambridge, MA: Harvard University Press, 1984.

Koinzer, Thomas. *Wohnen nach dem Krieg: Wohnungsfrage, Wohnungspolitik, und der Erste Weltkrieg in Deutschland und Großbritannien, 1914–1932*. Berlin: Duncker & Humblot, 2001.

Koning, Niek. *The Failure of Agrarian Capitalism: Agrarian Politics in the United Kingdom, Germany, the Netherlands and the USA, 1846–1919*. London: Routledge, 1994.

Koonz, Claudia. *The Nazi Conscience*. Cambridge, MA: Harvard University Press, 2003.

Kornher, Svenja. "Hairdressing around 1900 in Germany: Traditional Male versus Illicit Female Work?" In *Shadow Economies and Irregular Work in Urban Europe: 16th to Early 20th Centuries*, edited by Thomas Buchner and Philip R. Hoffmann-Rehnitz, 183–96. Berlin: Lit, 2011.

Koshar, Rudy. *German Travel Cultures*. Oxford: Berg, 2000.

Koszyk, Kurt. *Geschichte der deutschen Presse*. Vol. 2, *Deutsche Presse im 19. Jahrhundert*. West Berlin: Colloquium, 1966.

Kovac, Matthew. "'Red Amazons'? Gendering Violence and Revolution in the Long First World War, 1914–23." *Journal of International Women's Studies* 20 (2019): 69–82.

Kremer, Arndt. *Deutsche Juden – deutsche Sprache: Jüdische und judenfeindliche Sprachkonzepte und -konflikte, 1893–1933*. Berlin: De Gruyter, 2012.

Kreutzmüller, Christoph. "An den Bruchlinien der Volkswirtschaft: Jüdische Gewerbebetriebe in Berlin, 1918 bis 1933." In *Was war deutsches Judentum, 1870–1933*, edited by Christina von Braun, 237–47. Berlin: De Gruyter Oldenbourg, 2015.

Kruedener, Jürgen von, ed. *Economic Crisis and Political Collapse: The Weimar Republic, 1924–1933*. New York: Berg, 1990.

Krueger, Rita. *Czech, German, and Noble: Status and National Identity in Habsburg Bohemia.* Oxford: Oxford University Press, 2009.

Kühnel, Anita, ed. *Julius Klinger: Plakatkünstler und Zeichner.* Berlin: Gebr. Mann, 1997.

Kundrus, Birthe. "Gender Wars: The First World War and the Construction of Gender Relations in the Weimar Republic." In Hagemann and Schüler-Springorum, *Home/Front,* 159–79.

Lachmayer, Herbert, Christian Gargerle, and Géza Hajós. "The Grand Hotel." *AA Files* 22 (1991): 33–41.

Ladd, Brian. *Urban Planning and Civic Order in Germany, 1860–1914.* Cambridge, MA: Harvard University Press, 1990.

Lange, Kerstin. "Tanzvergnügen." In Morat, Becker, Lange, Niedbalski, Gnausch, and Nolte, *Weltstadtvergnügen,* 74–108.

Lapp, Benjamin. *Revolution from the Right: Politics, Class, and the Rise of Nazism in Saxony, 1919–1933.* Boston: Humanities Press, 1997.

Large, David Clay. *Berlin.* New York: Basic, 2000.

Large, David Clay. *Nazi Games: The Olympics of 1936.* New York: W. W. Norton, 2007.

Lässig, Simone. "Bürgerlichkeit, Patronage, and Communal Liberalism in Germany, 1871–1914." In *Philanthropy, Patronage, and Civil Society: Experiences from Germany, Great Britain, and North America,* edited by Thomas Adam, 198–218. Bloomington, IN: Indiana University Press, 2004.

Lawrence, Jon. "The Transition to War in 1914." In Winter and Robert, *Capital Cities at War,* 1:135–63.

Lees, Andrew. "Between Anxiety and Admiration: Views of British Cities in Germany, 1835–1914." *Urban History* 36 (2009): 42–66.

Lees, Andrew. *Cities, Sin, and Social Reform in Imperial Germany.* Ann Arbor: University of Michigan Press, 2002.

Lees, Andrew, and Lynn Hollen Lees. *Cities and the Making of Modern Europe, 1750–1914.* Cambridge: Cambridge University Press, 2007.

Levy, Hermann. *Industrial Germany: A Study of Its Monopoly Organisations and Their Control by the State.* Cambridge: Cambridge University Press, 1935.

Lefebvre, Henri. *The Production of Space.* Translated by Donald Nicholson-Smith. Oxford: Blackwell, 1992.

Lenger, Friedrich. "Bürgertum, Stadt und Gemeinde zwischen Frühneuzeit und Moderne." *Neue Politische Literatur* 40 (1995): 14–29.

Lerner, Paul. "Consuming Pathologies: Kleptomania, Magazinitis, and the Problem of Female Consumption in Wilhelmine and Weimar Germany." *WerkstattGeschichte* 42 (2006): 45–56.

Lerner, Paul. *The Consuming Temple: Jews, Department Stores, and the Consumer Revolution in Germany, 1880–1940.* Ithaca, NY: Cornell University Press, 2015.

Lipmann, Anthony. *Divinely Elegant: The World of Ernst Dryden.* New York: Penguin, 1989.

Loberg, Molly. *The Struggle for the Streets of Berlin: Politics, Consumption, and Urban Space, 1914–1945.* Cambridge: Cambridge University Press, 2018.

Lüdtke, Alf. *Eigen-Sinn: Fabrikalltag, Arbeitererfahrung und Politik vom Kaiserreich bis in den Faschismus.* Münster: Westfälisches Dampfboot, 2015.

Lüdtke, Alf. "Organizational Order or Eigensinn? Workers' Privacy and Workers' Politics in Imperial Germany." In *Rites of Power: Symbolism, Ritual, and Politics since the Middle Ages,* edited by Sean Wilentz, 303–34. Philadelphia: Temple University Press, 1985.

Maier, Charles S. "Between Taylorism and Technocracy: European Ideologies and the Vision of Industrial Productivity." *Journal of Contemporary History* 5 (1970): 27–61.

Manchester, William. *The Arms of Krupp, 1857–1968.* Boston: Little, Brown, 1968.

Manning, Jonathan. "Wages and Purchasing Power." In Winter and Robert, *Capital Cities at War,* 1:255–85.

Marcus, Sharon. *Apartment Stories: City and Home in Nineteenth-Century Paris and London.* Berkeley: University of California Press, 1999.

Marguerat, Philippe. *Banques et grande industrie: France, Grande-Bretagne, Allemagne, 1880–1930.* Paris: Presses de Sciences Po, 2015.

Marks, Sally. "Mistakes and Myths: The Allies, Germany, and the Versailles Treaty, 1918–1921." *Journal of Modern History* 85 (2013): 632–59.

Matthias, Bettina. *The Hotel as Setting in Early Twentieth-Century German and Austrian Literature.* Rochester, NY: Camden House, 2006.

McElligott, Anthony. *Rethinking the Weimar Republic: Authority and Authoritarianism, 1916–1936.* London: Bloomsbury, 2014.

McKitrick, Frederick L. *From Craftsmen to Capitalists: German Artisans from the Third Reich to the Federal Republic, 1939–1953.* New York: Berghahn, 2016.

Mergel, Thomas. *Parlamentarische Kultur in der Weimarer Republik: Politische Kommunikation, symbolische Politik und Öffentlichkeit im Reichstag.* Düsseldorf: Droste, 2002.

Miller, Michael B. *The Bon Marché: Bourgeois Culture and the Department Store, 1869–1920.* Princeton: Princeton University Press, 1981.

Morat, Daniel, Tobias Becker, Kerstin Lange, Johanna Niedbalski, Anne Gnausch, and Paul Nolte, eds. *Weltstadtvergnügen: Berlin, 1880–1930.* Göttingen: Vandenhoeck & Ruprecht, 2016.

Morgan, Simon. "Between Public and Private: Gender, Domesticity, and Authority in the Long Nineteenth Century," *Historical Journal* 54 (2011): 1197–1210.

Müller, Frank Lorenz. *Our Fritz: Emperor Frederick III and the Political Culture of Imperial Germany.* Cambridge, MA: Harvard University Press, 2011.

Nava, Mica. *Visceral Cosmopolitanism: Gender, Culture and the Normalisation of Difference.* Oxford: Berg, 2007.

Nolan, Mary. "Economic Crisis, State Policy, and Working-Class Formation in Germany, 1870–1900." In *Working-Class Formation: Nineteenth-Century Patterns in Western Europe and the United States,* edited by Ira Katznelson and Aristide R. Zolberg, 352–93. Princeton: Princeton University Press, 1986.

Nolan, Mary. *Visions of Modernity: American Business and the Modernization of Germany.* New York: Oxford University Press, 1994.

Ogborn, Miles. *Spaces of Modernity: London's Geographies, 1680–1780.* New York: Guilford, 1998.

Oltmer, Jochen. *Migration und Politik in der Weimarer Republik.* Göttingen: Vandenhoeck & Ruprecht, 2005.

Otter, Chris. "Making Liberalism Durable: Vision and Civility in the Late Victorian City," *Social History* 27 (2002): 1–15.

Owzar, Armin. "'Schweigen ist Gold': Kommunikationsverhalten in der wilhelminischen Gesellschaft." In Föllmer, *Sehnsucht nach Nähe*, 65–86.

Palmowski, Jan. *Urban Liberalism in Imperial Germany: Frankfurt am Main, 1866–1914.* Oxford: Oxford University Press, 1999.

Patch, William L., Jr. *Christian Trade Unions in the Weimar Republic, 1918–1933.* New Haven: Yale University Press, 1985.

Peukert, Detlev J. K. *Inside Nazi Germany: Conformity, Opposition, and Racism in Everyday Life.* Translated by Richard Deveson. New Haven: Yale University Press, 1987.

Peukert, Detlev J. K. *The Weimar Republic: The Crisis of Classical Modernity.* Translated by Richard Deveson. New York: Hill and Wang, 1992.

Plumpe, Werner. "Carl Duisberg, the End of World War I, and the Birth of Social Partnership from the Spirit of Defeat." In *Business in the Age of Extremes: Essays in Modern German and Austrian Economic History*, edited by Hartmut Berghoff, Jürgen Kocka, and Dieter Ziegler, 40–58. New York: Cambridge University Press, 2013.

Pollard, Sidney. "German Trade Union Policy, 1929–1933, in the Light of the British Experience." In Kruedener, *Economic Crisis and Political Collapse*, 21–44.

Poovey, Mary. *Making a Social Body: British Cultural Formation, 1830–1864.* Cambridge, MA: Harvard University Press, 1991.

Proctor, Robert. "Constructing the Retail Monument: The Parisian Department Store and Its Property, 1855–1914." *Urban History* 33 (2006): 393–410.

Puschner, Uwe. *Die völkische Bewegung im wilhelminischen Kaiserreich: Sprache, Rasse, Religion.* Darmstadt: Wissenschaftliche Buchgesellschaft, 2001.

Radicke, Dieter. "Verkehrsentwicklung und Suburbanisierung durch Villenvororte: Berlin, 1871–1914." In Reif, *Berliner Villenleben*, 49–60.

Rappaport, Erika Diane. *Shopping for Pleasure: Women in the Making of London's West End.* Princeton: Princeton University Press, 2000.

Reif, Heinz, ed. *Berliner Villenleben: Die Inszenierung bürgerlicher Wohnwelten am grünen Rand der Stadt um 1900.* Berlin: Gebr. Mann, 2008.

Retallack, James. *The German Right, 1860–1920: Political Limits of the Authoritarian Imagination.* Toronto: University of Toronto Press, 2006.

Ritschl, Albrecht. *Deutschlands Krise und Konjunktur, 1924–1934: Binnenkonjunktur, Auslandsverschuldung und Reparationsproblem zwischen Dawes-Plan und Transfersperre.* Berlin: Akademie, 2002.

Röhl, John C. G. *Kaiser Wilhelm II: A Concise Life.* Cambridge: Cambridge University Press, 2014.

Röhl, John C. G. *Wilhelm II.: Der Weg in den Abgrund, 1900–1941.* Munich: C. H. Beck, 2008.

Rose-Redwood, Reuben and Anton Tantner, "Introduction: Governmentality, House Numbering, and the Spatial History of the Modern City." *Urban History* 39 (2012): 607–13.

Ross, Corey. "Mass Politics and Techniques of Leadership: The Promise and Perils of Propaganda in Weimar Germany." *German History* 24 (2006): 184–211.

Rothermund, Dietmar. *The Global Impact of the Great Depression, 1929–1939.* London: Routledge, 2003.

Rowe, Dorothy. *Representing Berlin: Sexuality and the City in Imperial and Weimar Germany.* Aldershot: Ashgate, 2003.

Rykwert, Joseph. *The Dancing Column: On Order in Architecture.* Cambridge, MA: MIT Press, 1998.

Sandoval-Strausz, A. K. *Hotel: An American History.* New Haven: Yale University Press, 2007.

Scheck, Raffael. *Mothers of the Nation: Right-Wing Women in Weimar Germany.* Oxford: Berg, 2004.

Schick, Afra. *Möbel für den Märchenkönig: Ludwig II. und die Münchener Hofschreinerei Anton Pössenbacher.* Stuttgart: Arnold, 2003.

Schivelbusch, Wolfgang. *The Railway Journey: The Industrialization of Time and Space in the Nineteenth Century.* Berkeley: University of California Press, 1986.

Schlör, Joachim. *Nights in the Big City: Paris, London, Berlin, 1840–1930.* Translated by Pierre Gottfried Imhof and Dafydd Rees Roberts. Chicago: University of Chicago Press, 1998.

Schmitt, Michael. *Palast-Hotels: Architektur und Anspruch eines Bautyps, 1870–1920.* Berlin: Gebr. Mann, 1982.

Schraut, Sylvia. "Burghers and other Townspeople: Social Inequality, Civic Welfare and Municipal Tasks during Nineteenth-Century Urbanism." In *Towards an Urban Nation: Germany since 1780*, edited by Friedrich Lenger, 69–85. Oxford: Berg, 2002.

Schwenk, Herbert. *Lexikon der Berliner Stadtentwicklung.* Berlin: Haude & Spener, 2002.

Semmens, Kristin. *Seeing Hitler's Germany: Tourism to the Third Reich.* New York: Palgrave, 2005.

Sheehan, James J. *German Liberalism in the Nineteenth Century.* Chicago: University of Chicago Press, 1978.

Short, Emma. *Mobility and the Hotel in Modern Literature: Passing Through.* Cham, Switzerland: Palgrave Macmillan, 2019.

Simmons, Sherwin. "Ernst Kirchner's Streetwalkers: Art, Luxury, and Immorality in Berlin, 1913–16." *Art Bulletin* 82 (2000): 117–48.

Smith, Barbara Peters. "From White City to Green Acres: Bertha Palmer and the Gendering of Space in the Gilded Age." MA thesis, University of South Florida, 2015.

Smith, Helmut Walser. *The Continuities of German History: Nation, Religion, and Race across the Long Nineteenth Century.* Cambridge: Cambridge University Press, 2008.

Smith, Jill Suzanne. *Berlin Coquette: Prostitution and the New German Woman, 1890–1933.* Ithaca, NY: Cornell University Press, 2013.

Spenkuch, Hartwin. *Das Preußische Herrenhaus: Adel und Bürgertum in der Ersten Kammer des Landtages, 1854–1918*. Düsseldorf: Droste, 1998.

Spotts, Frederic. *Hitler and the Power of Aesthetics*. Woodstock, NY: Overlook, 2009.

Steedman, Carolyn. *Labours Lost: Domestic Service and the Making of Modern England*. Cambridge: Cambridge University Press, 2009.

Stoetzler, Marcel. *The State, the Nation, and the Jews: Liberalism and the Antisemitism Dispute in Bismarck's Germany*. Lincoln: University of Nebraska Press, 2008.

Strandmann, Hartmut Pogge von. "The Liberal Power Monopoly in the Cities of Imperial Germany." In *Elections, Mass Politics, and Social Change in Modern Germany: New Perspectives*, edited by Larry Eugene Jones and James Retallack, 93–118. Cambridge: Cambridge University Press, 1993.

Stratigakos, Despina. *A Women's Berlin: Building the Modern City*. Minneapolis: University of Minnesota Press, 2008.

Strohmeyer, Klaus, and Marianne Strohmeyer, eds. *Berlin in Bewegung: Literarischer Spaziergang*. 2 vols. Reinbek bei Hamburg: Rowohlt, 1987.

Strote, Noah Benezra. *Lions and Lambs: Conflict in Weimar and the Creation of Post-Nazi Germany*. New Haven: Yale University Press. 2017.

Swett, Pamela E., S. Jonathan Wiesen, and Jonathan R. Zatlin, eds. *Selling Modernity: Advertising in Twentieth-Century Germany*. Durham, NC: Duke University Press, 2007.

Thies, Ralf. *Ethnograph des dunklen Berlin: Hans Ostwald und die "Großstadt-Dokumente," 1904–1908*. Cologne: Böhlau, 2006.

Tobies, Renate. *Iris Runge: A Life at the Crossroads of Mathematics, Science, and Industry*. Basel: Springer, 2012.

Tooze, Adam. *The Wages of Destruction: The Making and Breaking of the Nazi Economy*. London: Penguin, 2008.

Triebel, Armin. "Coal and the Metropolis." In Winter and Robert, *Capital Cities at War*, 1:342–73.

Turner, Henry Ashby, Jr. *German Big Business and the Rise of Hitler*. New York: Oxford University Press, 1985.

Ullrich, Volker. *Hitler*. Vol. 1, *Ascent*. Translated by Jefferson S. Chase. New York: Knopf, 2016.

Ullrich, Volker. *Die Revolution von 1918/19*. Munich: C. H. Beck, 2009.

Umbach, Maiken. *German Cities and Bourgeois Modernism, 1890–1924*. Oxford: Oxford University Press, 2009.

Vascik, George S., and Mark R. Sadler, eds. *The Stab-in-the-Back Myth and the Fall of the Weimar Republic: A History in Documents and Visual Sources*. London: Bloomsbury, 2016.

Veblen, Thorstein. *The Theory of the Leisure Class*. New York: Macmillan, 1899.

Verhey, Jeffrey. *The Spirit of 1914: Militarism, Myth and Mobilization in Germany*. Cambridge: Cambridge University Press, 2000.

Wainewright, Will. *Reporting on Hitler: Rothay Reynolds and the British Press in Nazi Germany*. London: Biteback, 2017.

Walkowitz, Judith R. *Nights Out: Life in Cosmopolitan London*. New Haven: Yale University Press, 2012.

Walkowitz, Judith R. "The 'Vision of Salome': Cosmopolitanism and Erotic Dancing in Central London, 1908–1918." *American Historical Review* 108 (2003): 337–76.

Wealleans, Anne. *Designing Liners: A History of Interior Design Afloat*. New York: Routledge, 2006.

Weber, Petra. *Gescheiterte Sozialpartnerschaft – Gefährdete Republik? Industrielle Beziehungen, Arbeitskämpfe und der Sozialstaat: Deutschland und Frankreich im Vergleich, 1918–1933/39*. Munich: Oldenbourg, 2010.

Weichlein, Siegfried. "Regionalism, Federalism and Nationalism in the German Empire." In *Region and State in Nineteenth-Century Europe: Nation-Building, Regional Identities, and Separatism*, edited by Joost Augusteijn and Eric Storm, 93–110. Basingstoke: Palgrave Macmillan, 2012.

Weir, Todd H. *Secularism and Religion in Nineteenth-Century Germany: The Rise of the Fourth Confession*. Cambridge: Cambridge University Press, 2014.

Weiß, Hermann, and Paul Hoser, eds. *Die Deutschnationalen und die Zerstörung der Weimarer Republik: Aus dem Tagebuch von Reinhold Quaatz, 1928–1933*. Munich: Oldenbourg, 1989.

Weitz, Eric D. *Weimar Germany: Promise and Tragedy*. Princeton: Princeton University Press, 2007.

Welskopp, Thomas. *Unternehmen Praxisgeschichte: Historische Perspektiven auf Kapitalismus, Arbeit und Klassengesellschaft*. Tübingen: Mohr Siebeck, 2014.

Wenzel, Maria. *Palasthotels in Deutschland: Untersuchungen zu einer Bauaufgabe im 19. und frühen 20. Jahrhundert*. Hildesheim: Olms, 1991.

Williams, Andrew. *Liberalism and War: The Victors and the Vanquished*. New York: Routledge, 2006.

Winter, Jay M. *The Experience of World War I*. Oxford: Equinox, 1988.

Winter, Jay M., and Jean-Louis Robert, eds. *Capital Cities at War: Paris, London, Berlin, 1914–1919*. Vol. 1. Cambridge: Cambridge University Press, 1997.

Wrobel, Kurt. *Der Sieg der Arbeiter und Matrosen: Berliner Arbeiterveteranen berichten über ihren Kampf in der Novemberrevolution*. East Berlin: Bezirksleitung der SED Groß-Berlin, 1958.

Zabel, Hans-Henning, "Gottlieb Adelbert Delbrück." In *Neue Deutsche Biographie*, edited by Historische Kommission bei der Bayerischen Akademie der Wissenschaften, 3:576–77. Berlin: Duncker & Humblot, 1956.

Ziegler, Dieter, "'Aryanization' and the Role of the German Great Banks." In *Networks of Nazi Persecution: Bureaucracy, Business, and the Organization of the Holocaust*, edited by Gerald D. Feldman and Wolfgang Seibel, 44–68. New York: Berghahn, 2006.

Index

Printed in the USA
CPSIA information can be obtained
at www.ICGtesting.com
LVHW051307261023
761848LV00013B/62